T0330539

Union Organizing

After many years of decline, trade union members and organizations are now being reorganized and revitalized. Strategies, commonly known as "union organizing," are being used to recruit members and re-energize unions around the globe. This book considers how trade unions are working to achieve this, providing a much-needed evaluation of these rebuilding strategies.

By using historical and contemporary evidence, often through case studies, to assess the impact of various organizing campaigns, *Union Organizing* assesses the progress of unions across Europe and America. It raises key issues about the "organizing culture" and considers the impact of recent union recognition laws on employment relations and how the UK Government's *Fairness at Work* policy is faring.

A topical and in-depth study into the experiences of trade unions across Europe and America, it is a comprehensive and thought-provoking book which is essential reading for all those in the field of employment and industrial relations.

Dr. Gregor Gall is a Reader in Industrial Relations in the Department of Management and Organization at the University of Stirling, UK.

Routledge Studies in Employment Relations
Series editors: Rick Delbridge and Edmund Heery
Cardiff Business School

Aspects of the employment relationship are central to numerous courses at both undergraduate and postgraduate level.

Drawing insights from industrial relations, human resource management and industrial sociology, this series provides an alternative source of research-based materials and texts, reviewing key developments in employment research.

Books published in this series are works of high academic merit, drawn from a wide range of academic studies in the social sciences.

Union Organizing
Campaigning for trade union recognition
Edited by Gregor Gall

Also available from Routledge Research in Employment Relations:

Union Organizing
Campaigning for trade union recognition

Edited by Gregor Gall

With a foreword by Sheldon Friedman, AFL–CIO

Routledge
Taylor & Francis Group
LONDON AND NEW YORK

First published 2003
by Routledge
11 New Fetter Lane, London EC4P 4EE

Simultaneously published in the USA and Canada
by Routledge
29 West 35th Street, New York, NY 10001

Routledge is an imprint of the Taylor & Francis Group

© 2003 editorial matter and selection by Gregor Gall;
individual chapters, the contributors

Typeset in Baskerville by Exe Valley Dataset Ltd, Exeter
Printed and bound in Great Britain by
Antony Rowe Ltd, Chippenham, Wiltshire

British Library Cataloguing in Publication Data
A catalogue record for this book is available
from the British Library

Library of Congress Cataloging in Publication Data
A catalog record for this book has been requested

ISBN 0–415–26782–X

Dedicated to all those workers who have struggled for union recognition. May those who won their struggle inspire others.

Contents

Illustrations

Contributors

Peter Bain, Lecturer in HRM, University of Strathclyde.

Rick Delbridge, Professor of Organisational Analysis, Cardiff University.

Patricia Findlay, Senior Lecturer in Organisation Studies, University of Edinburgh.

Jack Fiorito, Professor of Labour Relations, Florida State University.

Sheldon Friedman, Senior Economist, Department of Public Policy, AFL-CIO, Past President, Industrial Relations Research Association.

Gregor Gall, Reader in Industrial Relations, University of Stirling.

Ed Heery, Professor of HRM, Cardiff University.

Otto Jacobi, Head of the Frankfurt-based independent research centre Laboratorium Europa. Member of Advisory Board of the European Trade Union Institute.

Bill Knox, Senior Lecturer in History, University of St Andrews.

Alan McKinlay, Professor of Management, University of St Andrews.

John Salmon, Lecturer in HRM, Cardiff University.

Melanie Simms, Lecturer in Industrial Relations and HRM, Canterbury Business School, University of Kent.

Dave Simpson, Lecturer in HRM, Cardiff University.

Phil Taylor, Senior Lecturer in Industrial Relations, University of Stirling.

Brian Towers, Associate Fellow, Warwick Business School, University of Warwick.

Jane Wills, Reader in Geography, Queen Mary and Westfield College, University of London.

Abbreviations of trade unions and trade union bodies in Britain

ACM	Association of College Management
AEEU	Amalgamated Engineering and Electrical Union
AEP	Association of Educational Psychologists
AEU	Amalgamated Engineering Union
AFA	Association of Flight Attendants
ALGUS	Alliance and Leicester Group Union of Staff
AMO	Association of Magisterial Officers
ANSA	Abbey National Staff Association
ASLEF	Associated Society of Locomotive Engineers and Firemen
ASTMS	Association of Scientific, Technical and Managerial Staffs
ATL	Association of Teachers and Lecturers
AUEW	Amalgamated Union of Engineering Workers
AUT	Association of University Teachers
BACM-TEAM	British Association of Colliery Management – Technical, Energy and Administrative Management
BALPA	British Air-Line Pilots Association
BDA	British Dental Association
BECTU	Broadcasting, Entertainment, Cinematograph and Theatre Union
BFAWU	Bakers, Food and Allied Workers Union
BSU	Britannia Staff Union
CATU	Ceramic and Allied Trades Union
Connect	The union for professionals in communications
CSEU	Confederation of Shipbuilding and Engineering Unions
CSP	Chartered Society of Physiotherapy
CWU	Communication Workers' Union
EEPTU	Electrical, Electronic Telecommunications and Plumbers' Union
EIS	Educational Institute of Scotland
EMA	Engineers and Managers' Association
Equity	British Actors' Equity Association
GMB	General, Municipal, Boilermakers and Allied Trade Union: Britain's general union

GPMU	Graphical, Paper and Media Union
GSA	Guinness Staff Association
HCSA	Hospital Consultants and Specialists Association
IPMS	Institution of Professionals, Managers and Specialists
ISTC	Iron and Steel Trades Confederation
IUHS	Independent Union of Halifax Staff
IUOOC	Inter Union Offshore Oil Committee
KFAT	National Union of Knitwear, Footwear and Apparel Trades
MSF	Manufacturing, Science, Finance Union
MU	Musicians' Union
NACO	National Association of Co-operative Officials
NAHT	National Association of Head Teachers
NATFHE	The University and College Lecturers' Union
NGSU	Nationwide Group Staff Union
NUJ	National Union of Journalists
NULMW	National Union of Lock and Metal Workers
NUMAST	National Union of Marine, Aviation and Shipping Transport Officers
NUS	National Union of Seamen
OILC	Offshore Industry Liaison Committee
PAT	Professional Association of Teachers
POA	Prison Officers' Association
RBA	Retail Book Association
RCM	Royal College of Midwives
RMT	National Union of Rail, Maritime and Transport Workers
SHA	Secondary Heads' Association
SocAuth	Society of Authors
SSTA	Scottish Secondary Teachers' Association
STUC	Scottish Trades Union Congress
T&G	Transport and General: Britain's biggest general union
TASS	Technical, Administrative and Supervisory Section (of AUEW)
TGWU	Transport and General Workers' Union
TSSA	Transport Salaried Staffs' Association
TUC	Trades Union Congress
UCAC	Undeb Cenedlaethol Athrawon Cymru
UCATT	Union of Construction, Allied Trades and Technicians
UFS	Union of Finance Staff
UNIFI	The union for staff in financial services
UNISON	Britain's public sector union
USDAW	Union of Shop, Distributive and Allied Workers
WGGB	Writers' Guild of Great Britain

Foreword

For workers, the difference between having a strong union in their work-place and no union is enormous. Without a union, employers unilaterally set the terms and conditions of employment. With a strong union, terms and conditions are determined jointly, through collective bargaining between employers on the one hand and workers' democratically-chosen union representatives on the other. With a strong union in the workplace, autocracy gives way to democracy.

Absent a strong union, the employer's word is law in most workplaces. The employer hires and fires, and apart from government regulations which are relatively minimal in Britain and even more so in the United States, the employer makes all the important decisions. Workers who are sufficiently unhappy are free to quit their job, but often this imposes a heavy cost on them and their families. There may be a lengthy spell of unemployment, after which there is no guarantee that the situation will be better at the new place of employment. Without the strength that comes from collective action, most workers are pawns on a chessboard controlled by employers.

While the most tangible gain for workers from strong unions and collec-tive bargaining may be economic, arguably the most important is the enhancement of human dignity. Human beings are morally and ethically entitled to participate in making decisions about matters as important as the terms and conditions of their employment. As institutions that provide workers with the means to influence and participate in these decisions, unions and collective bargaining therefore advance and enhance human dignity.

It is for this reason that workers' freedom to form unions and bargain collectively have achieved well-deserved standing as fundamental human rights, as the 1948 Universal Declaration of Human Rights, the 1998 ILO Declaration on Fundamental Principles and Rights at Work, and much else, make clear. As a fundamental human right, workers' freedom to form unions and bargain collectively has the same status as freedom of religion or the right to be free from discrimination based on race, gender or sexual orientation. As a fundamental human right, workers' freedom to form unions and bargain collectively "is a moral right that prevails over considerations of convenience or efficiency . . . it trumps mere economic interests of employers or the public."[1] Workers' freedom to form unions and bargain collectively is a right that "all governments have a responsibility to uphold and promote, and which all individuals and employers have a responsibility to respect."[2]

The impact of aggregating worker power into strong unions, moreover, extends far beyond the workplace. Unions have had large and beneficial impacts on economic equality, the strength and coverage of society's safety net, and civic and political participation by working people. Strong and democratic unions are a vital counter-weight to unchallenged corporate power in a modern industrial society.

In the United States and doubtless also in Britain, unions raise wages the most, in relative terms, for workers whose position in the labor market is weakest, including women and minorities. Workers in low-wage jobs such janitors, hotel workers, farm workers and cashiers often find that unionization is the surest way out of poverty for themselves and their families. Unions thus help to narrow inequality in the distribution of income, a serious and growing economic and social problem on both sides of the Atlantic.

The strength of society's safety net for all workers depends on strong unions. In the United States, for example, vital programs such as unemployment insurance and compensation for workers who are injured as a result of their job are better for all workers, union and non-union alike, in states where unions are stronger. Indeed, a wide range of social and economic indicators are more favorable in states where unions are stronger. Wages and incomes are higher for all workers, not just union members, in states where unions are stronger. The incidence of poverty is lower in states where unions are stronger. Public health and education is better, and crime is lower, in states where unions are stronger. Of particular importance given widespread concern in the United States about the long-term decline in voter participation to the lowest level of any major industrialized democracy, voter participation is higher in states where unions are stronger.

For these and other reasons, the topics addressed in this volume could not be more important or timely. Although workers' freedom to form unions and bargain collectively is a fundamental human right that employers are have a moral duty to respect, the harsh reality is that few employers in fact do so voluntarily. The legal framework, though less of an obstacle than in the United States, stops far short of assuring that employers must respect workers' rights in Britain.

Workers and unions on both sides of the Atlantic increasingly face similar challenges and have much to learn from each other's experiences. The experiences documented in this volume are sobering. While their tactics generally are less aggressive than those of U.S. employers, most of the employers depicted in this volume had no hesitation in communicating the preference that their employees refrain from joining unions, or in making life difficult for those who did so nevertheless. The volume plays a valuable role in documenting the chilling impact of this sort of employer behavior.

While workers can still succeed in forming unions despite employer opposition, this volume shows that the road they must travel is rocky and British unions have yet to develop a reliable playbook to guide them successfully. Nor, if the contributors to this volume are correct, have they yet taken the difficult decisions to commit resources adequate to the enormity of the task at hand. In these respects the situation of British workers and their unions has much in common with the United States, even though union density is far higher in Britain.

With the stakes so high, not only for workers but for all of society, if this volume stimulates thought and action that helps workers who want unions to form them more readily, then it will have made an important contribution.

Sheldon Friedman, AFL-CIO[3]

Notes

1 Hoyt Wheeler, "Viewpoint: Collective Bargaining Is a Fundamental Human Right," *Industrial Relations*, Vol. 39, no. 3, July 2000.
2 Roy Adams and Sheldon Friedman, "The Emerging International Consensus on Human Rights in Employment," *Perspectives on Work*, Vol. 2, no. 2, 1998.
3 Organization listed for identification purposes only. The AFL-CIO does not necessarily agree with the following analysis or conclusions.

1 Introduction

Gregor Gall

There are two points of departure for this volume. The first is that since the late 1980s, various union leaders and commentators on union affairs, in response to declining union membership and union influence, have called on unions in Britain to revitalize themselves. A plethora of "r" words has emanated from these calls; in order to counter the "retreat," "retrenchment," and "ruin," another set of "r" words – "renewal," "reinvigoration," "reconstitution," "revival," "relaunching," and "reorganization" – were suggested and demanded. The response to these calls has been generally constructive, positive, and meaningful, albeit partial, slow, and uneven amongst unions in Britain. In the responses to decline, another "r" word has been central, that of recognition and specifically campaigns for union recognition. The extent to which unions are recognized by employers, for the purposes of representing their members and negotiating over their members' terms and conditions of employment, has fallen markedly in recent years. If unions can significantly increase the number of workplaces where they have union recognition, the prospect exists not only that more workers can collectively determine the conditions they work under, thus heightening the degree of democracy in the workplace, but also that unions can again become important players in the employment relationship and society at large.

The second point of departure is that the issue of workers' employment rights has now been put firmly back on the political agenda within Britain since the election of the Labour Party to government in 1997. A part of Labour's agenda, as a result of much union lobbying, has been the implementation of its policy on "fairness at work" to reverse some of the iniquities established under, and by, the previous Conservative governments (1979–97). Central to this plan has been the Employment Relations Act (ERA) 1999 and its provisions to establish two mechanisms for gaining statutory union recognition where a majority of the workforce wish it. These came into force on 6 June 2000. However, their widely heralded arrival (since it became clear Labour would probably win the forthcoming election in mid-1995) has meant that the impact of the law on union activity to secure union recognition predates the year 2000. In tandem with the anticipation and then presence of the ERA has been the recent move on the part of many unions to embody an "organizing culture" of devoting more attention and resources to recruiting, organizing, and representing in order to stave off further membership, organizational, and political decline. Largely as a result of these efforts membership levels have now stabilized and are showing some signs of growth. Thus, the legal, political, and industrial environments for gaining union recognition are more favorable than at any time since 1980.

The relaunching of the Trades Union Congress (TUC) under the banner of 1990s "New Unionism" and the spread of the "organizing culture" amongst affiliates (Heery 1998, Heery *et al.* 2000a, b, c) are indications of the measures taken by unionism in Britain to reconstitute and revive itself. The book considers arguably the key manifestation of this, namely campaigns for recognition from employers where previously recognition had not existed or was ended. This edited volume thus concerns campaigns by unions to secure rights of representation and negotiation for their members over terms and conditions of employment by campaigning for recognition from employers. It examines the central issues behind the trajectory workers and unions have created to gain recognition. Consideration is also given to the end point of recognition, that is the process by which workers seek to improve their terms and conditions of work through collective bargaining. The significance of the book revolves around the examination of how unions themselves are attempting to use a more favorable environment to rebuild their influence at work and in society. Although intimately connected with issues of union recruitment and union organization, the specific focus is on attempts to gain organizational rights with employers, not union recruitment and union organization *per se*. However given the scale of the current levels of activity on the recognition front, the book will directly and by implication have much to say about the latter.

At the first level or order of analysis are what we can term, macro-issues. One is an assessment of how unions are attempting to use more conducive conditions to recreate their influence at work and in society. In so doing, the traditional prerogatives of management and employers are being challenged and recast within an era dominated by employer policies of non- and anti-unionism. As Bain and Price (1983) recognized, recognition is also in large part dependent upon membership density and strength so that the campaigns to gain recognition are closely intertwined with those to maintain and increase membership levels. Another issue concerns models of union organization, union culture, and union structure. The "organizing model" (see Blyton and Turnbull 1998: 138, Heery 2002), conceptually at least, suggests a move towards a more decentralized, self-determined, and self-activity based form of unionism. It, therefore, implies more "participative unionism" (see Fairbrother 1989, 2000) and a lessening of the influence of central union bodies (i.e. headquarters) and bureaucratism. Consequently, debate exists as to whether this type of move is entirely desirable or feasible given the challenges facing unions (e.g. employer hostility), where the possibilities of ensuing continuing fragmentation, disorganization, and membership passivity loom. But variants of the "organizing model," in practice, range from the national union providing resources under its control and direction to fund recruitment and organizing to situations where resources are provided from regional and central funds but autonomy is given or gained over where and how these are best used.

The research presented examines the practice of the "organizing model" – its efficacy, required resources, and context set against the "benchmarks" of the "old" "servicing model" and the "new" "partnership approach." It considers whether within the "organizing model," in practice, significant components of "managerial" and "professional" unionism co-exist with "participative" unionism (see Heery and Kelly 1994). Following from this is an engagement with the "union revitalization" debate in terms of examining the implications for the "renewal" thesis propounded by Fairbrother (1989, 2000) and its critical engagement by, amongst others, Gall (1998, 2001), Heery (2003), and Kelly (1996, 2001). "Renewal" concerns the role and inter-relationship of the state, full-time union officials (FTOs), activists, and members in union activity. This volume highlights the importance of officials and activists, suggesting that union structure, membership spontaneity, and workplace internalism are relatively less important in developing union presence in the current context. Finally, the research deploys and engages with mobilization theory, as championed by Kelly (1998). Kelly has brought to our attention in a forceful and persuasive manner the need to consider power and power relations in studying industrial relations and employment relations, particularly in terms of the context and environments under which the process of individuals joining together to become collective actors may take place and how they may construct and exercise power. Although sympathetic, a constructive but critical position is adopted in deploying this "tool" and framework to understand the relative success and failures of organizing drives and recognition campaigns.

The second level of analysis concerns the meso-issues of the more immediate and instrumental components of campaigns for recognition. These fall within the larger concerns above and include the development of workers' senses of grievance, articulation and organization of discontent, opposition from employers, and the various influences of the new recognition legislation on these processes. Investigating these issues allows some light to be shed on why campaigns for recognition start in some locations and not others. Concerns here also include employer responses to unionization, union presence, and recognition and how these may be categorized with regard to management styles. In particular, the considerations of the ideological, organizational, and financial resources of employers to mount resistance to recognition campaigns are of significance. In turn, these necessitate an assessment of how they may shape union behavior and actions.

The third level of analysis involves a consideration of micro-issues such as what types of approaches, styles, tactics, and techniques are most effective for unions to use in seeking to carry out these tasks, and the resources required for these. Whether, and under what circumstances, the "partnership" approach to relationships with employers (varying from agnostic to reluctant to intransigent) can offer an effective route to recognition is part of this evaluation. Lying "opposite" these is the examination of the particular means by which employers seek to thwart recognition campaigns and how the employer actions may be ameliorated, marginalized, or overcome. Thus, this level of analysis is about examining the conditions for the success and failure of recognition campaigns as well as assessing the effectiveness and success of different campaigns and drawing lessons from these. In doing so some assessment of the ERA's impact on union behavior and the environment for gaining recognition in will be made. Thus, in terms of current policy agenda, the book will help illuminate whether the ERA should be seen as the "final settlement" in employment law in this area by the Labour governments (1997–2001, 2001–). Some consideration is given to the situation where winning recognition may be said to be "only half the battle," and maintaining recognition and delivering benefits for members the other half.

The subject matter of the book needs to be situated in broader developments and wider debates. The first concerns Europe and the European Union Directives on workers' rights. Directives, and their consequent Regulations and embodiment in national laws, have had considerable impact on member countries in general and Britain in particular with regard to workers' rights on information and consultation. Rights have been granted to make available certain data, some of which is disseminated through the creation of permanent and *ad hoc* workplace fora. Information and consultation covers issues of redundancies, acquisitions, mergers, and business plans. The salient issues revolve around whether, and in what circumstances, these rights given to workers, regardless of union membership, can provide hindrances and obstacles to recruiting union members and preventing successful campaigns for recognition. Put simply, do they provide disincentives to join and campaign because these rights are available regardless of union membership and recognition? Are they a substitute for some of the reasons that workers join unions and can employers thus successfully convince employees that their needs are already well served? Alternatively, may unions benefit from these developments because they are the only worker bodies that are capable of effectively utilizing them to advance worker interests? This line of reasoning suggest that it may take unions, with their organizational presence, resources, knowledge, and expertize, to make these new rights of practical benefit. Put another way, the rights may remain "on the shelf" unless unions are there to implement them on behalf of workers i.e. their members. Consequently, union membership is still required.

The chapters that follow are divided into thematic sections. The first of these provides some historical context to the consideration of the contemporaneous developments outlined later in the book. Thus, the chapters by McKinlay/Knox and Gall examine campaigns for recognition in pre-ERA periods and amongst employers who mounted fierce and successful resistance. Although legal redress was available in some of the periods under consideration, well-resourced employer intransigence was predominant. The second section, comprising two chapters by Heery *et al.* and Gall, provides overviews of two of the three central actors in the equation of recognition, namely the unions themselves and employers (the other being the government/state as legislator and ring-master). The first examines the unions' efforts to engage in organizing while the latter considers employer opposition to campaigns for recognition. With these first two sections providing background, context, and overview, the following section comprizes four studies of campaigns for recognition which examine different types of outcomes and activity. Simms examines a large national charity where recognition may be gained but not in the short term. Findlay/McKinlay provide a comparison between three different electronics companies, where employer opposition has taken the form of resisting recognition, conceding recognition but then trying to negate it, and signing a "sweetheart" agreement. Wills examines a transport company that first sought to resist recognition through granting recognition to another union but then conceded it. Taylor/Bain consider a call center operation where a campaign to gain recognition peaked, fell off after the dismissal of leading activists and the change of ownership to a less aggressive company before a "partnership" union recognition agreement was signed. These chapters therefore consider recognition campaigns in terms of different features, presenting a mix of evidence across the manufacturing/service, male/female, well-unionized industry/poorly unionized industry, younger/older worker axes. Also of import is the analysis of varying degrees of union "success" and "failure."

The final section contains three chapters examining recognition in the comparative contexts of the United States, Canada, and Germany. In order to appreciate more fully the contours and dynamics of the situation in Britain, three countries were chosen as comparators. Broadly speaking, the US provides a contrast as a country with a long-standing but for unions unhelpful statutory recognition mechanism in a context of widespread employer and government anti-unionism. Consequently, union density and recognition coverage are extremely low by the standards of developed economies. Contrastingly, Canada affords an example of a more favorable legal and industrial-political environment which appears to have helped create a much more influential union movement. Recognition procedures, in particular, stand in marked contrast to those in the US. Germany, on the other hand, offers a case of a highly juridified and institutionalized industrial relations system where it may be assumed there are no serious problems of recognition for unions. While this is largely true, the fraying of the core system of industrial relations around the edges has provided a number of difficulties. This may indicate the limits of support for recognition and unionism both in terms of statute book legal provision and the practical impact of this provision. The conclusion brings the various but related threads in the book together to consider the evidence and arguments for the unions' campaigning activity having the potential to revitalize and renew the union movement back to something of its former standing, i.e. whether a "phoenix can rise out of the ashes."

The book's origin lies not in a collection of papers from an academic conference but in an initiative to bring together the work a number of researchers who have examined unions, union organizing, and recognition. It is therefore hoped that the book is not so much a collection of papers with a loose thread running through them but a book where the invited authors use their data to examine a number of key and common issues in the manner of a fairly tightly defined project. This should give book greater cohesiveness and coherence, leading in turn to greater usefulness, to both academic and practitioner audiences.

The rest of this chapter sets out the key blocks for the following sections and chapters. The first examines the importance of recognition to workers and their unions. The next considers the downward trends in both union membership and recognition. This leads to an examination from a union perspective of ERA's recognition provisions and those of the previous two statutory mechanisms. Finally, the basic tenets of mobilization theory are considered. Mobilization theory is deployed as the most useful conceptual framework available by which to understand the issues behind, and concerned with, recognition campaigns. This is because it helps in the dissection of recognition campaigns, in terms of their genesis and progress, success and failure by examining an array of salient areas as a result of the key questions it poses.

What is union recognition?

Recognition is arguably both the key institutional mechanism and set of organizational rights by which unions establish their presence and value to workers. To Metcalf (1991: 25) union "recognition is the fulcrum on which membership moves" (cf. Wood 2000: 124). Put another way, recognition is both a weathervane for the health of the union movement in terms of its standing and credibility with employers and government, and at the same time, the basis on which unions operate. Recognition, defined as a set of information, representation, consultative, and, critically, negotiating or collective bargaining rights over all matters of employment between workers and employers is essential so that unions can deliver the fullest benefits of union membership to their members. Thus, recognition covers issues of the wage-effort bargain, that is remuneration, and managerial authority. Concretely this concerns pay, working hours, working arrangements, and so on. In effect, recognition is being defined here as "full" recognition as opposed to "partial" recognition which comprises all the same rights as full recognition except those of negotiation or restricts the scope of negotiation to exclude pay. However, while the particular form of recognition is important, so too are the factors which help determine whether the procedural agreement is matched by not only the existence of attendant institutions and process but also their meaningfulness and associated outcomes. The upholding of the "letter" and "spirit" of the procedural agreement would see information passed from employer to union, consultation and negotiating take place, and access available to management, all of which would be carried out fully and frankly. For example, information would not be selective or disingenuous, union opinion in consultation would be taken seriously, and bargaining would be entered into with a spirit of "give and take."

Following from this, the substantive outcomes must also be tangible and meaningful. The factors that influence these outcomes in an immediate way are broadly employer and union philosophies and employer and union resources. For the union side, their philosophies, ranging from "business" unionism to "militancy" and their strength based on membership density, membership cohesion, and leadership will be ranged against employer strength and management practice in the union's pursuit to enforce the recognition agreement and secure certain outcomes. The outcomes of recognition, and particularly collective bargaining, are thus heavily dependent upon the construction and exercise of union power. The same is true of campaigns to gain recognition which in turn are closely intertwined with those to increase membership levels.

To summarize, the value of formal recognition agreements with employers to unions and workers for the purposes of representation, consultation, and negotiations is potentially considerable. The nature of the procedural agreement and its substantive outcomes are heavily influenced by power relationships. At one extreme, *de jure* recognition may mean *de facto* non-recognition and employer unilateralism. At the other, *de jure* recognition may be *de facto* worker or union unilateralism. Of course, neither non-recognition nor derecognition prevent unions from providing limited forms of representation and advice for their members as well as possibly engaging in informal and implicit collective bargaining, particularly at the lower levels in an organization. The various possible outcomes of formal position and actual practice attest to the fluid nature of industrial relations.

Nonetheless, what recognition tends to create is a setting where the members and officers of the union have some legitimacy within the organization and in relation to the organization's management as well as affording them "organizational rights" for the protection and advancement of their members' interests, whether individually or collectively. This not only gives union membership a potentially much higher value than that in non-recognized or derecognized workplaces because the union can negotiate over pay and conditions, but it also gives some measure of stability and security to union workplace lay officers and union organization. This may be by virtue of the organization providing some resources for the operation of the union (union room, meeting rooms, telephone, e-mail, photocopying, internal mail distribution, and noticeboards), of the union being supplied with organizational information and being granted seats on various internal bodies, of the right to have meetings with management at the union's request or by the allowance of the officers of the union to proceed unhindered in the carrying out of their duties subject to reasonable claims on their work time.

Furthermore, recognition in Britain carries with it three specific connotations. The first is that under section 168 of the Trade Union and Labour Relations (Consolidation) Act 1992 time-off for union duties and training for officers of recognized unions must not be unreasonably refused. Second, under section 181 of the same Act employers have a duty to disclose information for collective bargaining and good industrial relations practice and a recognized union can apply to the Central Arbitration Council (CAC) for an order to secure company information that has not been forthcoming from the company. Third, under the Health and Safety at Work etc. Act 1974 an employer is bound to consult and inform the safety reps appointed by a recognized union on matters of health and safety. Such a setting of recognition is thus more likely to provide a more favorable basis for a union to maintain and increase its membership than one of non-recognition/derecognition where the union is regarded by the employer as an illegitimate and unwanted body.

Union decline and decline in recognition

Overall union membership and influence in Britain, in common with many other industrialized economies, have fallen markedly in the last twenty years. A key indication and component of this has been the fall in the extent and coverage of recognition and collective bargaining. Membership is a key power resource for unions within collective bargaining, relations with government, and wider society. Table 1.1 shows the overall decline in membership in Britain by a number of different measures with aggregate membership falls being halted in the late 1990s/early 2000s. While it is not possible to say whether this constitutes a permanent, albeit slight, reversal, it is nonetheless salient to ask whether this marginal improvement is wholly or partly attributable to the reorientation on recruitment and winning new recognition agreements. It would seem plausible to suggest that it is, in large part, given the continuing retrenchment of employment in "unionized sectors" and the growth in employment within "non-unionized sectors" as well as the continuing "PR problem" unions have, of being seen as "good

Table 1.1 Union membership and density in Britain 1979–2000

Year	Certification office	Labour force survey	LFS density	TUC membership
1979	13.289m	n/a	n/a	n/a
1983	11.236m	n/a	n/a	n/a
1987	10.475m	n/a	n/a	n/a
1991	9.585m	8.602m	37.5%	6.898m
1995	8.089m	7.309m	32.1%	6.756m
1997	7.795m	7.154m	30.2%	6.754m
1998	7.807m	7.152m	29.6%	6.764m
1999	7.898m	7.257m	29.5%	6.816m
2000	n/a	7.321m	29.5%	6.721m

Sources: Certification Office annual reports, *Labour Market Trends/Employment Gazette* and TUC annual Directories (various).

Notes: Certification Office 1999 figure is for 1999–2000. LFS density is for employees not those in employment (which excludes the armed forces). n/a=not available.

things" but relatively ineffectual. Put another way, new members are not falling into the arms of unions: they are, in the main, being fought for, albeit under more favorable public policy.

Whether membership gains continue will revolve around the "Catch 22" situation of the dependent relationship between recognition and recruitment. Recognition is unlikely without recruitment, particularly where there is any employer reluctance, but large-scale recruitment is unlikely without recognition (cf. Dickens and Bain 1986, Bain and Price 1983). With recognition is more likely to come both union legitimacy in the eyes of the employer, and thus workers, and tangible gains from union presence and collective bargaining. The conundrum for unions is how to make the two run together and be mutually reinforcing in a virtuous upward spiral. However, and looking further ahead, until recognition again becomes as widespread and as accepted in society as it was in the 1960s and 1970s, it is difficult to see how union membership and influence will easily return to their former levels: again a "Catch 22" situation, which can also be seen in the following formulation. In the absence of (or even alongside) statutory mechanisms for recognition, unions have two main methods of gaining it. The first is where the union seeks to impose costs on the employer for not granting recognition: loss of business through strikes and other forms of disruption or through loss of contracts through pressure on suppliers and buyers. The second concerns "adding value" to the business through the "business case" for unionism: not merely orderly and stable industrial relations but also legitimizing management decisions and effective implementation of these through co-determination. Both require high union density; the former to make the disruption effective and latter to be able to deliver on the promises.

Turning to the contours of recognition in Britain, Millward *et al.* (2000: 96) record recognition by establishment as falling from 66 percent in 1984 to 53 percent in 1990 to 42 percent in 1998 (see Table 1.2). This is largely attributed to the low level of recognition amongst new and growing workplaces because of low union membership densities rather than from derecognition in existing and older workplaces (ibid.: 228) Furthermore, Millward *et al.* (ibid.: 103) report from the panel survey that from 1990–8 derecognition affected 6 percent of establishments and new recognition 4 percent of establishments. But this amounted to 56 percent of these establishments recognizing unions in 1990 and 55 percent in 1998. In the British Social Attitudes (BSA) survey (Bryson and McKay 1997: 35), the percentages of people in workplaces with recognition has fallen from 66 percent in 1983 to 63 percent in 1987 to 58 percent in 1990 and to 56 percent in 1993 and finally to 46 percent in 1996.

Data from the Labour Force Survey on recognition coverage thus exhibits a similar trend to that of union membership – an overall fall in the 1990s, with evidence towards the end of that period of some small recovery in union fortunes. Another source of data on recognition comes from Gall and McKay (2002) (see Table 1.4).

Table 1.2 Coverage of recognition and collective bargaining, Britain

Year	% of establishments covered by union recognition	% of workforce covered by recognition	% of establishments covered by collective bargaining	% of workforce covered by collective bargaining
1980	64	n/a	n/a	n/a
1984	66	n/a	n/a	70
1990	53	54	n/a	54
1998	42	62	n/a	41

Sources: Column B – Millward *et al.* (2000: 96), Column C – Millward *et al.* (1992: 107), Column C – Cully *et al.* (1999: 92), Column E – Cully *et al.* (1999: 242).
Note: n/a=not available.

Table 1.3 Recognition coverage from the Labour Force Survey, Britain

Year	No of workers covered by recognition (m)	% change from previous year	% of workers covered by recognition
1993	10.420	n/a	48.9
1994	10.374	−0.4	48.2
1995	10.226	−1.8	46.8
1996	10.141	−0.8	45.8
1997	10.032	−1.1	44.3
1998	10.081	0.5	43.5

Source: *Labour Market Trends* (various).

Note: "n/a"=not applicable as LFS started in 1993. After 1998 the LFS questions were changed so continuing data on these three indices is not available. Data on union presence and coverage of collective bargaining is unavailable after 1998. Of the measures now available, the number of employees whose pay is affected by collective agreements is the nearest proxy to those covered by recognition. It shows a slight increase (0.4 percent) from 1999–2000.

Table 1.4 Reported new recognition agreements and cases of derecognition 1989–2001

Year	Recognition			Derecognition		
	No. of cases	Known no's covered (from no. of cases)	Known type of recognition	No. of cases	Known no's covered (from no. of cases)	Known type of derecognition
1989	58	6,550 (31)	16 full, 7 partial	52		
1990	49	5,120 (33)	17 full, 7 partial	47		
1991	76	4,050 (31)	17 full, 16 partial	62	73,000[a]	n/a
1992	56	9,050 (45)	15 full, 6 partial	75		
1993	57	5,270 (18)	n/a, n/a	46		
1994	27	9,520 (14)	6 full	15	3,800 (6)	13 full, 1 partial
1995	88	27,404 (64)	74 full, 11 partial	66	15,931 (42)	28 full, 33 partial
1996	85	26,377 (64)	61 full, 13 partial	54	16,851 (46)	25 full, 23 partial
1997	108	24,509 (75)	70 full, 10 partial	31	4,362 (17)	15 full, 4 partial
1998	119	39,820 (68)	79 full, 6 partial	7	432 (4)	3 full
1999	358	130,386 (263)	283 full, 18 partial	11	1,210 (9)	6 full, 3 partial
2000	525	156,665 (451)	469 full, 6 partial	4	1,700 (3)	1 full
2001	668	118,304 (405)	518 full, 7 partial	5	108 (1)	1 full
Totals	2274	563,035 (1562)	1625 full, 107 partial	475	117,394 (121)	92 full, 64 partial

Source: Gall and McKay 2002.
Note: [a]Estimated total for 1989–93; n/a=not available.

The data from Table 1.4 indicates that not only has the earlier pheno-menon of derecognition been eclipsed but that significant progress has been made by unions since 1999 in gaining new recognition agreements. Over 1,500 have been signed since then, covering (using a simple average multiplier for unknown cases based on known cases) around 560,000 workers. Of course, those workers experiencing derecognition over the longer period constitute a counter-balance to this advance for the unions, in that workers coming under recognition again or for the first time are paralleled by some losing recognition.

Nonetheless, there is an apparent incompatibility between the data sets. This can be explained by two factors. First, what is being measured is different, in that Workplace Industrial Relations Survey (WIRS) and BSA measure existing and overall recognition levels while Gall and McKay measure new cases of recognition (and derecognition). Thus, the popula-tions and the method of data collection are different: WIRS and BSA use a sample while Gall and McKay's cases are "self-selecting." Second, different time periods are used. In particular data collection for WIRS ended in July 1998 (Millward *et al.* 2000: xv). Therefore, the two pictures are not necessarily incompatible, for within the larger aggregate picture, shorter-term trends are evident. Indeed, the LFS data may reflect the tranche of new deals detected by Gall and McKay. To summarize, the coverage of recognition (and collective bargaining) by number of establishments and workers has fallen substantially over the last two decades but some signs of small improvement for unions are evident. As with union membership, it is again not yet possible to say whether this constitutes a permanent, albeit slight, reversal. But it is more than plausible to suggest the improvement is attributable to the reorientation to renewed campaigning for recognition and the move towards "organizing" within the context of the imminence, presence and use of the ERA and a generally more favorable legal and public policy climate towards (cooperative) unionism (see Gall and McKay 1999: 610–11).

While the preceding discussion has examined the "quantitative" aspects of recognition in Britain, the "qualitative" aspects are also important. The breadth and depth of recognition have changed in some significant ways in the last two decades (Cully *et al.* 1999, Wright 1998, 2000, Wright and Dunn 1994): both have generally narrowed whereby the range of issues subject to collective bargaining has lessened, and in those that remain subject to collective bargaining, unions exert less influence. The example of pay highlights both. In a considerable number of companies, annual so-called "automatic," "cost-of-living," and "across-the-board" pay rises deter-mined through bargaining have been replaced by management-controlled performance-related pay (PRP) schemes (on individual or team bases, centred on various criteria). This signifies a reduction in the range of terms and conditions subject to recognition. Alternatively, such PRP schemes may also signify the lessening of the depth of collective bargaining (see Heery

2000a). In some PRP schemes, the unions are able to bargain over the size of the "pot" of money available for distribution and the criteria by which the money is distributed but not the decision-making process by which awards are made. These types of retrenchment take both *de jure* and *de facto* forms. A slight counter-balance to this narrowing is the rise of new bargaining agendas on "family-friendly," equality, training, career/personal development, and human rights (information, privacy). The explanation for this movement in bargaining scope largely concerns the diminution of union influence and the ascendancy of management power, existing as they do in a zero-sum manner. On the one side, the general weakening of workplace and national union organization over the period has opened up, on the other, the space for management to move into and take control. The reasons for this weakening are many and varied (neo-liberal governments, economic restructuring, defeats in industrial conflicts, the decline of the left in Britain) but it is commonly agreed that amongst them the (pro-active) initiatives of employers to regain their managerial prerogative through such means as human resource management and so on have been important in this redrawing of the frontier of control in work and employment.

The Employment Relations Act 1999

The recognition provisions contained in the ERA set out the circumstances by which a recognition agreement may be achieved. These are, first, through a voluntary agreement between the parties. Second, where it has not been possible to achieve a voluntary agreement but where the union has already recruited a majority into membership and where the CAC does not order a ballot. Third, where the parties do not negotiate a voluntary agreement and the CAC determines that the criteria are met for a ballot, in which the union wins a majority of votes, which equates to at least 40 percent of all those entitled to vote in the bargaining unit. The latter two are known as "statutory awards."

Whilst the legislation is assisting unions to gain recognition, the ERA has several major weaknesses when viewed from a union perspective. First, it excludes all employers of twenty or fewer workers. This has been estimated to exclude around 5m workers. Second, in recognition ballots, not only must a simple majority be gained but this must also represent 40 percent of all those entitled to vote. Thus those who do not vote are counted as "No" votes. Third, bargaining units must be deemed to be "compatible with effective management." Fourth, the CAC cannot accept an application where recognition already exists, thus giving an incentive to employers to thwart recognition of one union by awarding it to another, on a voluntary basis. Fifth, statutory recognition agreements only cover pay, hours, and holidays. Sixth, single unionism is encouraged throughout the Act. Seventh, the complexity of the Act is unhelpful. With 172 paragraphs in Schedule 1, the ERA represents one of the longest single provisions on employment law ever passed. It is no wonder that the government's Explanatory Notes contain a set of exception-ally detailed flow-charts in an attempt to give guidance on how the law should operate. Finally, there is the length of time that the full statutory procedure will take. For most statutory claims, a period of some three months at least will pass from the date of submission of the request by the union to the date of the ballot. In workplaces with high turnovers of staff, this could make it difficult for unions to sustain campaigns.

The ERA encourages unions and employers to voluntarily agree recogni-tion procedures. The Explanatory Notes stress that the statutory procedures apply "when unions and employers are unable to reach agreement volun-tarily." This is why the Act places so much emphasis on encouraging negotiation between the parties, even after a formal application has been made to the CAC. Indeed, the voluntary approach is still encouraged once the adjudication process is underway: the parties can conclude voluntary agreements at almost every stage of the procedure and are indeed encour-aged to do so at specific stages within the procedure. The encouragement to negotiate voluntarily extends to the definition of the bargaining unit, which may be assisted by the Advisory, Conciliation, and Arbitration Service (ACAS). Where agreement between the parties is not forthcoming but may be solicited, the CAC can extend the relevant time periods for further negotiation. However, the CAC has significant new powers under the Act. It can determine the bargaining unit over which recognition may be claimed and can substitute an alternative bargaining unit to that proposed by the union. It can also require a ballot for recognition, even in those situations where the union has declared that it already has a majority in membership. In the event of a failure to agree a voluntary procedure following a declar-ation of recognition, it can impose a method for collective bargaining, which legally binds both employer and union.

Table 1.4 indicates that the ERA is working in the manner the govern-ment intended. With only 151 applications made between June 2000 and December 2001, of which twenty-eight cases resulted in statutory awards, over 94 percent of new agreements in this period were voluntary agree-ments signed without recourse to the CAC. Furthermore, the impact of the ERA can be detected prior to its provisions becoming enacted. Table 1.4 also shows the marked increase in agreements between 1998 and 1999, i.e. prior to June 2000. Simply put, not only has the imminence and presence of the ERA been deployed by the unions to add extra weight to their campaigns for recognition but it has stimulated campaigns for recognition (see Gall and McKay 2002 for more detailed explanation). Thus, between 1997 and 2001 the *Trade Union Trends* surveys (LRD/TUC 1997–2002) reported on 639 campaigns for recognition, covering nearly 440,000 workers. But contrary to the government's intention, less than 20 percent of the new deals are partnership agreements (Gall and McKay 2002). The vast majority are traditional recognition and collective bargaining agreements.

Previous statutory recognition mechanisms in Britain

British industrial relations have a well-known tradition of "voluntarism" or "collective *laissez-faire*." It was within this culture and practice that the previous two examples of statutory recognition mechanisms were inserted. The first was the Commission on Industrial Relations (CIR), the second the Advisory, Conciliation, and Arbitration Service (ACAS). The CIR, established in 1969 as a Royal Commission, was charged from 1969–71 with helping to resolve recognition claims but without any mandatory powers of enforcement. It did so in thirteen cases, recommending recognition in ten, of which five were not accepted by the employer. From 1971–4, under the Industrial Relations Act 1971 (IRA), the CIR's powers were extended by way of certain sanctions, although it still sought to encourage voluntary agreements. In this form, it dealt with twenty-seven references, making eighteen recommendations for recognition, of which four were not accepted by the employer. All but five of these cases concerned white-collar workers (involving around 75,000 workers). The relatively small number of cases and the preponderance of white-collar workers reflected a number of factors. The initiative for the CIR and its recognition functions did not spring from the union movement but rather government (Conservative and Labour) and some employers (see the Donovan Report 1968). The unions felt sufficiently strong at this point not to require legal or statutory assistance. Furthermore, they feared legal intervention, seeing it as a stalking horse for unwanted intervention in other areas of industrial relations. Indeed, the majority were not legally entitled to use the CIR as they chose not to register under the IRA because they opposed the Act's provisions. However, the mechanisms were used by registered unions in areas of traditional weakness, namely the service sector (retail, finance primarily) and amongst white-collar employees in manufacturing operations (see Kessler 1995 and Kessler and Palmer 1996).

The experience of ACAS between 1976 and 1980 under the Employment Protection Act 1975 (EPA) is more substantial. Under the EPA, ACAS was charged with providing voluntary conciliation where requested in recognition disputes. Under a referral by a union, ACAS was obligated to examine the issue, seek to resolve it by conciliation, and failing that, make further enquiries and prepare a written report setting out its findings and any recommendation for recognition. The Act provided for, in the event of employer non-compliance, further conciliation but where this failed, ACAS could make a legally binding award. ACAS dealt with 1,610 references for recognition. In 1,115 cases (70 percent) voluntary settlements were reached, in which the union was fully or partly successful in securing recognition in 518 cases. ACAS (1981: 32, 65) calculated this method brought 64,000 new workers under recognition (with 16,000 through final recommendations) while in the same period some 77,000 new workers were brought under some form of recognition by the more long-standing voluntary route. However, in only about a third of the statutory awards was recognition achieved (ACAS 1981: 92).

Whilst this represented a longer and more substantial experience than that of the CIR, the gains to recognition were similarly relatively limited. Again, unions were not desperate to use the means available as membership and recognition coverage (by establishment and workers) continued to grow in the period, although more use was made of references in manufacturing, probably reflecting the use by the previously non-registered unions. It may be the case that the presence of the procedure, threat of recourse to, and actual usage had a much wider, if unquantifiable, impact (see also Dickens and Bain 1986: 94). ACAS (1981: 100) concluded, after the statutory mechanisms were abolished in 1980 by the Thatcher government, that they "had no more than a marginal impact except in one or two sectors of industry" and that they had "clearly failed to achieve a major breakthrough that had been envisaged by their early advocates." However, the overall generally supportive tone of public policy towards unionism, of which ACAS was part, exerted a stronger indirect impact on employer attitudes and actions than direct regulatory mechanisms (see e.g. Bain and Price 1983: 20–1, Dickens and Bain 1986).

Mobilization theory

Broadly speaking, and following Kelly (1997, 1998) who draws on the work of Gamson (1992), Klandermans (1989), McAdam (1988), and Tilly (1978), mobilization theory involves identifying: the conditions and processes of workers' interest formation, the constructing of collective organization, opportunities to act, the cost/benefits of action, and the action itself. For each stage in this potentially sequential process, questions can be posed to investigate the presence or absence of certain features, processes and phenomenon. More specifically, the following questions are probed: whether there are collective or common legitimate grievances and injustices, whether these can be attributed to management, whether there are resources for, and courses of, action (e.g. ideology, time, personal assertiveness, leadership, unions) open to workers to use to seek redress. This section briefly examines the components and ideas that comprise mobilization theory.

Kelly (1997, 1998) postulates that the first stage in the potential move towards collective organization is the process of how workers come to define their interests: are they the same, similar, different, or opposed to those of the employer, and as workers, do they see their interests in individual, semi-collective, or collective terms? If workers identify these in collective terms, what is the unit of the collective: work-group, workplace, company, industry, or class? Central to this are senses of injustice and illegitimacy where workers' beliefs, values, and expectations are violated by employers. On this basis dissatisfaction arises. However, for grievances to develop denotes not just being aggrieved but believing in a rightful entitlement to make demands that are viewed as being reasonably attainable through some form of individual, semi-collective, or collective action. Within this thought process, attributions of the perceived causes of injustice and perceived solutions to grievances are made. If these are such that management actions are the cause, these actions could have been different and management has the power to change their decisions or actions, then a "constructive attribution" can be made. If, however, the attribution suggests personal negligence on the part of the workers or supra-company or national forces are at work, an "inhibiting attribution" has been made. Consequently, an appropriate and at hand personable force must be identified for collectivism in the workplace to begin.

Social identification "comprises the social categories to which [people] belong and the positive or negative evaluations of those categories" (Kelly 1998: 30) based on comparison with other social categories. These inform people's worldviews, but this does not suggest that the ways in which this happens and the components of this worldview are straightforward or internally consistent and compatible. These may or may not provide the ideological resources to help construct grievances, collectivism, and robust unionism. Organizational agency and resources are a critical part of the jigsaw in explaining the presence or absence of the ability to build an alliance of the aggrieved, i.e. a union. Crucial to this process are the agents of organizing and organization – that is the leadership malcontents or opinion-formers, who are prepared to carry out the task of organizing and representing as well as having the ability to do so. Preparedness concerns personal conviction, determination, and effort, while ability concerns characteristics like respect from, and profile amongst, co-workers as well as the capability to "frame" issues in a language supportive of the case. Any worker or workers considering seeking collective redress of grievance will normally make a calculation of personal and group costs and benefits between taking no action and taking action of whatever form (Kelly 1998: 34). Ignoring for the moment prospects of success and the avenues for individual redress, the questions these workers asked of themselves will center on how much effort, time, and anguish may be involved on the issue, is the issue of sufficient importance, and what penalties may management impose for taking action? A progression through the various facets of mobilization theory enables an understanding to be built up of why there is a paucity of organization and action.

Limitations of space here preclude an assessment of the emerging evaluations of Kelly's (1997, 1998, 2000) work (see e.g. Dabscheck 1999, Gall 1999, 2000a, 2000b, Martin 1999, Nolan 1999, Turner 1999) but many writers acknowledge the value of the framework he has put forward. Criticisms of his "mobilization theory" tend to focus on particular components without undermining the validity of his overall project. Consequently, it is constructively used in the chapters that follow to address salient issues within organizing recognition campaigns because it provides a framework (with a set of internal dynamics) to examine where and how campaigns arise, how they may proceed and with what outcomes. In particular, it helps provide a method for understanding the role and inter-relationship of workers, union members, activists, and FTOs.

Conclusion

This volume examines the struggle by workers to gain "organizational rights" to allow them to create some degree of workplace democracy through union recognition, as well as the actions by unions to determine their own destinies. These are relatively neglected areas of study in employment relations as a result of the recent domination of interest in management and HRM. The struggle for recognition should be regarded as both a "means" and an "end," which run alongside each other and are self-reinforcing. Most obviously, recognition is striven for in order to achieve higher wages, shorter hours, and so on. But it is also aimed at creating a process whereby workers have a semblance of equality of power with employers in order to create those higher wages and shorter hours and to control the employers' actions and behavior. It is, to use an analogy, both for substantive (material outcomes) and procedural (rights of process) goals. It is fairly clear that the presence of these elements of worker joint control may lead to increased material benefits, but less clear if achieving these outcomes reinforces the degree of worker support for joint control. This indicates the existence of instrumentality within workers' consciousness. Moving away from these workplace concerns, recognition remains the key element of any attempt to create industrial democracy under capitalism. It thus has both a democratizing and civilizing effect on society. The less recognition there is, the less democratic and civilized society is and vice versa.

Note

The term "organizing," for example, organizing model, and organizing approach, is used in this volume in a number of ways which have a wider array of meanings than the use of the term in the US literature on US unions generally has (see, for example, the work of Bronfenbrenner 1997 and with Juravich 1998). In Bronfenbrenner's work, she presents

> a comprehensive union building model which involves multiple elements ranging from strategic targeting, to rank-and-file leadership development of an active and representative organizing committee, to the use of adequate numbers of professional and trained full time organizers, to escalating pressure tactics in the workplace and the broader community, [and] to the use of member volunteer organizers.
>
> (E-mail from Bronfenbrenner, 26 April 2002)

Thus, care needs to be taken when making comparisons between Britain and the US, where in the former much debate has surrounded "organizing versus servicing," so that the degree of separation by a "common language" is not accentuated.

2 "Organizing the unorganized"

Union recruitment strategies
in American transnationals,
c. 1945–1977

Bill Knox and Alan McKinlay

Introduction

Union recruitment campaigns involve the transformation of a workforce's perception of themselves and of their relationship with their employer. Campaigning for union recognition mobilizes this changed perception in a struggle to reshape the institutions that regulate the employment relationship. Such campaigns necessarily challenge managerial prerogative. Securing and deepening representation from the formalities of recognition and annual contractual negotiations involves a milieu of activists and employee insistence that every managerial or supervisory decision be subject, at least in principle, to negotiation. One difficulty of case studies examining union recruitment and recognition campaigns is their tendency to be one-off snapshots, with little historic perspective. We believe that only by considering the long-run dynamics of union campaigns can we appreciate the contingent relations between recruitment, recognition, and representation. The unparalleled and prolonged stream of American direct investment into central Scotland between 1945 and 1975 is considered as the context for the case of union organizing in IBM and a number of other US branch plants. The "story" of IBM is one where in the 1950s, the unions had a toehold that they were unable to transform into a durable presence inside IBM. A union recognition ballot, triggered by a misplaced piece of union opportunism, encouraged by legislative change, was decisively lost in 1977. We also examine how, in other companies, collective bargaining was established: in some cases, unions were recognized from the arrival of the American plants while in others, collective bargaining was established after prolonged strikes. In all cases, however, formal recognition belied a long-term struggle by shop stewards to deepen union representation inside the US branch plants. The material for this research is derived from a number of sources: union, company, and government agency documentation, and interviews with union officials, supported by newspaper reporting.

Making "Silicon Glen"

In the first three decades after 1945, central Scotland was the recipient of the greatest flow of American overseas investment in the world (Dunning 1958: 58, Dicken and Lloyd 1976: 697). Major American firms such as Caterpillar, Hoover, IBM, Kodak, Motorola, NCR, and Timex all established significant production facilities in Scotland before 1970. The initial impetus to locate in Britain was to meet the fiscal requirement to increase dollar exports and minimize dollar imports. By establishing manufacturing subsidiaries, US companies ensured access to the domestic, Commonwealth, and, later, European markets. Initially, for companies such as IBM, British plants exported back to the USA to supplement their domestic production. In the most dynamic sectors, such as office equipment and calculators, American companies quickly dominated the British market. The reasons why US corporate investment was so concentrated in central Scotland were more diffuse: regional aid combined with a political willingness to accelerate Whitehall decision-making; and a ready supply of skilled engineers and labor accustomed to factory discipline, particularly "deep reserves of female labor."[1] The first wave of American inward investment was concentrated in mechanical engineering, slowly superseded by electrical and instrument engineering through the 1960s (Ashcroft and Love 1993). By 1975, central Scotland was the capital of the European electronics industry.

The American subsidiaries of the post-war period differed radically from those of the pre-1939 period. Above all, subsidiaries were no longer relatively autonomous plants manufacturing products for distinct national markets or under license from an American parent company. Post-1945 subsidiaries were branch plants increasingly integrated into regional or international strategies, orchestrated by American headquarters. Just as American productivity levels were the benchmark for British subsidiaries, local managements were also judged on how effectively they implemented corporate personnel policies (Firn 1975: 402–3, Gennard and Steuer 1971, Steuer and Gennard 1971: 97). Key American companies, such as IBM and NCR, had long-established labor strategies that combined corporate paternalism and scientific management. The coherence of this strategy hinged on the construction of durable internal labor markets.

American innovations in personnel management were introduced wholesale into branch plants (Richardson and Walker 1948), within which labor regulation was explicitly a *strategic* issue. The strategic importance of personnel was signaled by the universal development of personnel functions in American plants, although personnel management typically remained subordinate to manufacturing managers (Knox and McKinlay 2002). US firms used comprehensive labor contracts detailing every aspect of employment, including grievance procedures and rights to representation, irrespective of union bargaining rights (Forsyth 1972: 160, Dunning 1998). Similarly, payment systems were based on output, not craft status, and governed by production planners rather than by informal negotiation with supervisors. The legitimacy of the effort bargain no longer turned on the shared norms of the craft community but on the logic of a managerial system. Selection and recruitment were centrally controlled by personnel offices and geared towards a long-term strategy of constructing internal labor markets insulated from regional labor markets and from union regulation.

In NCR, personnel policy was highly centralized from 1904: systematic monitoring of employee attitudes and a series of management-controlled voice mechanisms aimed to reduce the salience of independent trade unionism. By the mid-1920s, NCR was convinced that trade unionism had been defeated (Jacoby 1985: 60–4). For the individual employee, the benefits of corporate welfarism increased with seniority. IBM, similarly, established innovative employment contracts and layers of communication with the workforce to forestall union organizing campaigns in the 1930s. Employment in IBM or NCR severed or eroded the ties between the individual and wider occupational community, arguably rendering union membership an irrelevance.

Union exclusion at IBM: strategy and tactics

[T]he individual was placed in isolated opposition to the combined forces of the mighty company.[2]

In the first few years after its arrival in Greenock in 1953, IBM was reliant on the traditional engineering skills of turning, fitting, and toolmaking as they installed new machinery and established flow line production. This reliance made it impossible to completely exclude union members. Indeed, IBM used union cards as a method of verifying the skill of new recruits. Equally, given the itinerant nature of much of engineering employment, skilled men hired by IBM retained their union cards to smooth their eventual return to heavy engineering. The AEU ruefully acknowledged that a union card did not necessarily indicate any deep affiliation to trade unionism, far less a willingness to build lay organization. Former shop stewards hired by IBM were criticized for their failure to recruit, their refusal to become "shadow" stewards, and their neglect of local demarcation rules. Nevertheless, there was an AEU presence inside IBM for the first eight years of the plant. Indeed, in 1952 the factory's main machine shop union density exceeded 60 percent, comparable to other large engineering plants, but plummeted to under 15 percent in less than four years. Although the AEU had five shop stewards, none of these men had any organizing experience and were isolated from each other inside the factory. Moreover, the novice stewards had only limited and irregular contact with the union. All five stewards had been publicly threatened by management and their intermittent reports to the union spoke of a growing sense of helplessness and despair. The union's support for these beleaguered

activists was grudging and unimaginative. Individual stewards were called
to meetings of the AEU District Committee to account for their failure to
build a durable membership base and were criticized for their failure to
attend subsequent meetings. The small group of AEU activists were unable
to develop even the most rudimentary form of workplace organization, far
less offer an ideological challenge to management.

The AEU's strategy was to negotiate a recognition agreement with IBM
without a parallel grassroots campaign. Negotiations by local and national
FTOs foundered on IBM's demands that the union relinquish control over
apprenticeship, training, demarcation, and workload. In compliance with
IBM's demands, the AEU's national leadership strongly discouraged any
local recruitment campaign, despite warnings by activists that its limited
organization and membership was evaporating. The AEU offered little
support to the stewards inside IBM.

The cornerstone of IBM's anti-union strategy was the development of a
robust, high wage internal labor market, based on individual mobility, where
the relevance of union membership diminished with seniority. Tactically,
IBM management was prepared to bargain informally with trade groups
until individual mobility eroded collective identity. In 1976, the Greenock
plant manager reflected upon the success of this patient, subtle strategy:

> No meeting had ever taken place [at] Greenock . . . to discuss the
> question of trade union organization. The company would object to
> this. At one time the company did enter into a discussion with the
> sheet metal workers . . . about trade union organization. [They] all . . .
> held union cards and there was a very strong sense of group identity
> amongst them. However, in the last five years all had been quiet on
> [that] . . . front. [S]ince the scope of their . . . job had widened, and
> they had been given technical responsibility, the demand for recognition
> had died. They were no longer a vociferous group. Very few of the "old
> school" sheet metal workers were left. . . . The new generation of sheet
> metal workers in IBM did not share the union aspirations of the older
> generation.[3]

Uniquely in the Greenock plant, IBM made one telling, formal concession
to address the issue of worker representation. Its works council was composed of one-third management nominees and two-thirds employee
representatives, chosen by ballot, if necessary. From the first, the purpose of
the council was to maintain a reliable downwards communications channel,
not to function as a consultative forum, far less as a negotiating body. Even
the AEU stewards' attempt to develop some organized presence inside
IBM by sitting as works council representatives drew criticism from the
union.

By late 1954, the AEU had effectively withdrawn from IBM as a collective, if insubstantial, presence. After discussions with members in IBM, the

AEU's local official was bemused to discover that "the members employed in the IBM were inclined to favour the [firm's] anti-union policy . . . and the avoidance of any trade union interference as it is called."[4] In part, this can be explained by the poor state of union organization in the region. Steward organization and authority had all but collapsed across Greenock's manufacturing base. Even where steward organization survived, this simply meant that the union was kept informed of the steady loss of steward bargaining power and the rapid erosion of job controls. In short, IBM recruits' experience of the vitality and relevance of union representation in the local labor market was, at best, ambiguous. The last rites were administered in November 1954 at a downbeat "mass" meeting attended by just sixteen IBM engineers:

> Vicious industrial relations, regimentation of workpeople by management amounting to terrorism. Discharged on the slightest pretext and flimsiest reasons without notice – even for divulging your wage rate. A general anti-trade union atmosphere definitely organized and intended by the firm. . . . Summed up by stressing the hopelessness of the situation and that we were not in a position to force the election of shop stewards. It was agreed that our members would attempt inside the factory to work quietly enrolling workers in the Union.[5]

From its arrival, IBM increased wages, reduced working time, and improved holidays in response to changes in the engineering industry. It consistently offered a significant premium over national and local collective bargaining settlements. The timing of IBM's contractual changes was designed to demonstrate the superiority of the company's non-unionism over collective bargaining. By 1961, the union had no stewards, a small but unknown number of members, and no knowledge of pay and conditions in IBM. The pattern of sporadic union organizing, followed by a hiatus, then collapse, was not unique to IBM. Three times between 1960 and 1966 the "girls" working in Sangamo Weston, Clydeside, built up union organization around specific issues, notably bonus disputes, but were unable to sustain workplace organization. They were mobilized around specific issues, rather than by a strategy to develop durable workplace representation. In Sangamo Weston, the absence of activists whose objective was to develop union organization and representation was critical. In IBM, similarly, the activists were unable to develop the critical mass necessary to maintain an organized presence. Nor could the AEU activists inside recruit on the basis of maintaining the protocols of the craft community. IBM systematically broke down or, more accurately simply ignored, job controls as they trained new recruits. To new recruits, whether they be unskilled or drawn from the ranks of displaced shipyard tradesmen, their employment security turned on IBM's success in overturning the demarcation rules that governed work allocation in engineering. Non-skilled IBM employees were acutely aware that their relatively privileged contracts would be unthinkable in manufacturing. There were, therefore, benefits from non-unionism for many whose skills were developed and recognized *only* within IBM's internal labor market. For the AEU, IBM "compelled" skilled engineers, some of whom remained union members, to train unskilled labor in skilled tasks: "the policy of this firm is to displace skilled labor with cheaper unskilled robots."[6] On the rare occasions that a steward recruited a few new members, the AEU proved insensitive to the immense difficulties of organizing inside IBM. Four new recruits were refused union cards because they were non time-served, yet they were doing tasks that were the prerogative of skilled tradesmen.[7] For over twenty years, unions made no attempt to recruit inside IBM.

The 1977 ACAS ballot on recognition was a watershed in the unions' relationship with IBM. The decision to approach ACAS for a ballot of IBM Greenock employees was an early attempt to test section 11 of the EPA as well as pursue a recognition claim of enormous symbolic importance. The decision to do so was, however, almost entirely top-down. More particularly, ASTMS's aggressive growth strategy placed the technical and supervisory union at the forefront of recruitment in IBM (Armstrong *et al.* 1986: 133–4). It had recruited around thirty new members. This, and ASTMS's pursuit of a foothold in the computer manufacturing industry, lay behind its approach to ACAS. AUEW and TASS followed, primarily to safeguard their strategic right to organize in IBM, despite their misgivings that ASTMS was "somewhat precipitate."[8] For ASTMS, the prospect of a successful recruitment campaign was secondary to the strategic imperative of establishing that it had a right to organize all workers in employers such as IBM, irrespective of their professional or skilled status. By the same token, the other unions' involvement was to ensure they also were legitimate players in any future unionization of high-tech industry.

There was little attempt by the unions to assess, far less develop, the potential for grassroots activism. ACAS background research revealed that there was no underground organization, or "shadow" stewards, and little likelihood that one would emerge. Its interviews with union members revealed that they were satisfied that wages and conditions were superior to those elsewhere but were dissatisfied with the secrecy and individualization of salary scales and appraisal systems. All union interviewees had more than five years' service and all had several promotions. IBM union respondents were agnostic about, but not hostile to, the value of the consultative processes and realistic about the prospects that the ballot would be a breakthrough. ACAS also interviewed fifteen current and former members of the works council to gauge the extent that it constituted a form of quasi-collective bargaining. The majority of its members had long service: 70 percent had over ten years' service. Only one had not been a union member previously, although only one was a current member. Council elections were always contested and 60–70 percent of the workforce voted.

Formally, the council's most significant functions were health and safety and communications from management but council members were unanimous they performed an important unofficial representational function. Such informal representation did not constitute collective bargaining, but council members accompanied, or acted as advocates for, individuals in the grievance procedure and exerted "a certain amount of influence" by calling managers to account for particular decisions, repeatedly if necessary. Only one councilor supported recognition. ACAS concluded:

> Some were at pains to make clear that they were not "anti-union" on principle, and that they were not opposed to union activity in certain areas outside IBM. As far as their own situation in IBM was concerned, however, they simply felt that union representation could bring no material benefits. They were confident that their terms and conditions of employment could not be bettered, and they were satisfied with the individual bargaining relationships they had with their managers.[9]

The works councilors had a realistic assessment of the voice mechanisms and recognized there was no groundswell of support for recognition. Indeed, they feared that recognition could damage job security, endanger current contracts, and "generally upset the present reasonably harmonious and satisfactory state of industrial relations in the establishment. Most councillors reported that the great majority of their constituents were anxious and fearful about the harmful consequences of recognition."[10]

Four unions claimed recognition at IBM, although they signaled that they were willing to accept individual representation as an interim settlement prior to full collective bargaining. The unions argued IBM's anti-union reputation and substantial numbers of lapsed members made support for collective bargaining viable. ACAS believed there was strong circumstantial evidence to support this: "IBM is an unusual company, there is considerable suspicion that employees have not revealed their wish to join a trade union for fear of consequences to their careers."[11] The AUEW, and its technical section TASS, claimed lapsed membership of around 500. Lapsed members were regarded as potential members, an unsatisfied demand for representation. This was an established and accepted union tactic in claims to ACAS (Kessler 1995: 61). The implicit assumption was that there was a natural connection between class location and union membership that was broken by IBM's anti-unionism. For the unions, IBM's acceptance of recognition and the prospect of individual and collective representation would trigger recruitment. But this seriously under-estimated the congruence between IBM's "personnel philosophy" and employees' daily experience of work and management. For IBM, even holding a union card did not necessarily signify a demand for collective bargaining. IBM management had "no clear idea of union membership" but estimated that it may be between one hundred to, perhaps, three or four hundred. In almost every case, however, membership reflected an individual's past employment rather than any dissatisfaction with IBM: "the vast majority would be mere card holders who were union members for an insurance, in case they had to leave IBM to work in another company."[12]

The unions exaggerated the practical appeal of trade unionism to IBM workers so lapsed membership was not a reliable proxy of intentions. IBM's "personnel philosophy" was to focus "on the individual, on the rewarding of individual effort and close employee–manager relations characterized by mutual trust" (ACAS 1977: 10–11). Individual performance was evaluated annually and salary was negotiated directly with one's immediate supervisor. In sum:

> The company expressed the fear that unionization would create a hitherto non-existent divisiveness between employees and management by shifting emphasis onto groups . . . [eroding] the unity and flexibility of its single status workforce [with] multi-unionism . . . result[ing] in fragmentation and consequent loss of flexibility.
>
> (ACAS 1977: 11)

ACAS's objective was to pursue conciliated agreement between appellant union and employer. It acknowledged the use of legislative powers to compel a hostile employer to accept recognition was an inherently fragile and unsatisfactory settlement. The ballot took the form of a workforce survey that attempted to gauge support for recognition among different occupations and locations. Prior to the ballot, ACAS undertook fieldwork to gauge what form of collective bargaining, if any, had the greatest chance of success. During this process, unions, employers, and ACAS also negotiated the precise form of wording of the survey. This was more than a technical exercise. In the IBM case, two key issues were the subjects of tripartite negotiation.

The first was the scope of the bargaining unit. The unions insisted that their claim was exclusively concerned with Greenock, the only IBM plant where they had a significant presence. IBM insisted that they would co-operate with the survey only if it included all UK employees. Without IBM's co-operation, a ballot was almost impractical. The compromise was a survey of all IBM's employees, but identifying Greenock separately. The second issue was the form of collective bargaining. The unions were aware that a ballot for full bargaining would win support from only the most committed trade unionists. Accordingly, the unions proposed the survey should determine support from current and prospective trade unionists for individual representation rights. That is, union representation for individual members after internal grievance procedures were exhausted. However, ACAS accepted IBM's argument that this option should not feature in the survey as it obscured the question about the viability of collective bargaining. Moreover, the open-ended nature of IBM's internal grievance procedures rendered individual union representation impractical. In effect, IBM was not just negotiating about the terms of the survey but also preparing the ground for rearguard action on the legitimacy of an unfavorable or close-run result. IBM also signaled that its opposition to specific survey questions would provide grounds for it to contest the result if it considered that necessary. Furthermore, IBM conducted two internal employee opinion surveys, presumably as ammunition for post-ballot negotiations. The negotiations over the scope and specifics of the survey lasted approximately eighteen months, a delay that left the unions struggling to hold onto their existing memberships rather than campaigning to increase their numbers.

When the survey took place, IBM refused the unions even the most basic workforce access. Not only were there no hustings or public exchanges between IBM managers and union officials, but the unions were denied use of noticeboards. For IBM, any union publicity would have to be met with counter-argument that would entail the company moving from its avowed "neutral position on the issue in communications to the workforce" (ACAS 1977: 9). IBM's neutrality masked its concerted campaign against recognition. A series of question and answer sessions between managers and television presenters, plant-level executive briefings, company literature, and management briefings to small groups further undermined the union case,[13] with their two key messages. First, any form of collective bargaining would jeopardize the flexibility that was the cornerstone of IBM's employment system. In an eve-of-poll edition of its company newspaper, workers were told "if you want to end the present IBM system and instead want to have . . . unions determining, at national level, your terms and conditions, then answer 'YES'."[14] Second, just to report that one was a union member may be recorded as a vote for recognition. IBM insinuated that that even union members should not declare their membership if they opposed recognition. The unions had no mechanism to counter IBM's position as company events did not permit any questions from the workforce. The survey process was also compromised by managers' intervention: the questionnaires were distributed by managers to their subordinates who had to complete and return them immediately. This provided intimate opportunities to erode whatever support there might have been for recognition. As one local union official put it, "if that was IBM being neutral, thank God they didn't oppose us."[15] The campaign did not generate a core of union activists. Indeed, such were the limits on the unions' campaign, there was little opportunity to consolidate existing union membership.[16]

However, the limits imposed on the unions' campaign do not fully explain the result: 90.2 percent at Greenock – the plant considered the most favorable ground by the unions – rejected collective representation for pay and conditions. ACAS concluded there was insufficient support for union representation and, therefore, that collective bargaining was unsustainable, so the claim was rejected. The survey revealed just fifty-two Greenock employees were union members, with more than half in ASTMS. Neither does the effectiveness of management's campaign alone explain this paltry number. Only a small number (8.1 percent) of non-union respondents signaled their readiness to join a union, if IBM recognized one. Around one-quarter of union members rejected collective bargaining, for fear of competitive multi-unionism and demarcation disputes affecting job security. In part, this reflected the reality of IBM's high wage regime in which job security hinged upon labor flexibility and retraining. Equally, for former shipyard employees particularly, trade unionism was equated with insecure employment and incessant demarcation disputes. Thus, for many, employment insecurity was partly associated with trade unionism, while secure, relatively well-paid employment was attributed to IBM. IBM had successfully projected the survey as being not just about recognition but about the very existence of its employment system.

In the aftermath, the unions attempted to massage the results to confirm their estimates of Greenock membership of 12–20 percent as realistic. This, as ACAS pointed out, was a forlorn attempt since IBM had the survey results and would simply turn such union sophistry into a further propaganda coup. ACAS also dismissed the union claim that it should attempt to broker a deal with IBM to deliver individual representation rights as implausible.[17] The unions were unable to salvage anything from the survey. Far from generating a crisis of legitimacy for IBM, the survey strengthened the ideological appeal of its "personnel philosophy." The form of the union claim – multi-union bargaining – was critical in *de*mobilizing all but the most determined trade unionists. There were serious flaws in the unions' approach, given there was no sharp deterioration in employment conditions that could be attributed to IBM management nor was there a cadre of activists inside IBM that could galvanize whatever grassroots support existed (see Kelly 1998: 27–30). The limited union membership inside IBM waned quickly. After the debacle, a departing ASTMS activist placed a sign above his desk: "one trade union card for sale – almost new."[18]

Dickson *et al.* (1988: 519–20) argued:

> IBM workers, despite the highly individualized non-union industrial relations system, are not generally opposed to the principle of trade unionism or collective action but regarded union representation as of no practical advantage in IBM, a conclusion that rendered any union recruitment drive futile.

We suggest this conclusion does not go far enough: the survey, particularly respondents' supplementary remarks, suggests that union representation was perceived not just as futile but as counter-productive. IBM's "voice" mechanisms were adequate: there was no workforce perception of a repre-

sentation gap. Indeed, employees contrasted the responsiveness of management and the openness of the employment system to their experience in
local shipyards and car factories. Thus, significant dissatisfaction and sense
of injustice were not generated. Accepting IBM employment was an implicit
acceptance of non-unionism by the individual. For the overwhelming
majority, relinquishing their union card was a small price to pay. For over
four decades, only individual union members remained in IBM. In addition,
there was no activist base and no sharp shift in employment contracts or
management practices upon which to base recruitment. Clandestine union
organization was not to return to IBM until 1997.

The durable anti-union strategies of companies such as IBM, HP, and
Motorola relied on relatively high wages and alternative employee "voice"
mechanisms, such as teamworking or works councils. Microelectronic
transnationals deliberately avoided any form of collective bargaining or
involvement in formal employer associations, at least in part to avoid any
pressure from other employers to accept union bargaining. Informal
channels of inter-firm communication were important for transnationals.
Motorola, for instance, was a founding member of the "East Kilbride
Personnel Managers Council" (Strathclyde Business School 1986: 12,
18–9). Such mechanisms were used to gather labor market intelligence but
also share information about legislative change and its impact on the
employment relationship. There were no similar bodies exchanging information among unions attempting to organize transnational plants. Transnational plants were treated by unions as the same as domestic employers,
in terms of the same occupational jurisdictions and same competitive multi-
unionism. The challenge of the transnationals stimulated no significant
organizational innovation within or between unions.

Recognition and representation in other American transnationals

> The manager, while not being opposed to trade unions, was not over-
> keen on them.[19]

Two routes to recognition existed in US branch plants. First, formal
corporate acceptance of collective bargaining in return for union assistance
in recruiting skilled labor, particularly as branch plants started operations.
Second, through a series of strikes for recognition. In both cases, however,
management strategy was to concede bargaining rights but limit these to
the factory level on matters such as annual pay and conditions negotiations. The objective was to minimize the erosion of managerial authority
on the shop floor by shop steward bargaining.

Caterpillar resisted recognition from its arrival in 1956 until 1960. Its
strategy coupled high wages with autocratic workplace management (Black
1983: 41–3). Pockets of high union density encouraged the AEU to include

Caterpillar in a recruitment drive in the region. In Cummins Engines and Sunbeam Electric, the AEU's presence at factory gates resulted in a surge of recruitment and the election of stewards but progress in Caterpillar was halting: there were no stewards or activists inside the plant to maintain contact with the union. Caterpillar's American management attempted to take the initiative by offering to recognize the AEU in return for union acceptance that workers would be regraded according to variations in demand and bargaining would only be with FTOs, shop stewards having no representative or bargaining function. The trigger for a recognition dispute was the dismissal of the leading AEU activist for organizing a meeting outside the factory gates. A second AEU activist was dismissed for insubordination, for insisting that management meet a group of engineers to discuss the crisis. This incident led to a walkout and the recruitment of 200 members. The strike committee, "many of whom had no previous experience, was now becoming an efficient organization."[20] The rapid escalation of the Caterpillar recognition dispute turned it into a *cause célèbre*. Both the union's Broad Left and right wing were forced to work together in the campaign. Even John Boyd, a notorious right-wing local FTO, was forced to take an uncompromising stand:

> I would sooner see the grass grow over this Company's plot of land than any British worker should submit to any such indignity and cruel dictatorship. It is a grave danger to the British way of life and must be eliminated from our midst.[21]

Caterpillar made a strategic retreat. The company joined the powerful Engineering Employers' Federation and installed the industry's collective bargaining machinery.

Recognition changed the strategic objective of US branch plants' personnel policies. Union exclusion was no longer possible and the objective was to minimize the union's role in shaping work organization or infringing on the day-to-day exercise of managerial power. Recognition was wrung from STC, East Kilbride, a manufacturer of complex telephone switching gear, in 1965 after a series of increasingly bitter strikes. All aspects of employment in STC were established by its (ITT's) European headquarters. The strategic task of STC's personnel management was to police ITT policy on the shop floor, rather than respond to local circumstances. Before this, all negotiations had taken the form of personal lobbying. Recognition introduced a framework of collective bargaining, but the substance of formal representation continued to be personal bargaining. This pattern of reluctant recognition followed attempts to maintain an essentially disorganized, personalized bargaining process was typical in all US plants.

In 1979, Hoover's experienced personnel director reviewed the development of its plant-level industrial relations between 1940 and 1970:

The [period] did not generate any significant industrial relations mainly because they were dominated by an environment of high pay and paternalism with stability in terms of growth and structure. As a result union activity was low and mainly contained in the skilled areas. The only real hiccup was in 1965 when a redundancy occurred but this did not generate militancy or a lack of identification with [Hoover].[22]

This pragmatic acceptance of a union presence did not signify acceptance of workplace bargaining, far less a pluralistic governance structure. In 1947 NCR, Dundee, traded-off recognition for assistance in recruiting skilled labor. NCR pursued a twin-track approach. On the one hand, it attempted to develop formal bargaining relationships with union officials that centered upon regular binding contracts for all employees. But, on the other hand, on the shopfloor it consistently sought to marginalize stewards. From its arrival in 1947 to the early 1960s, NCR successfully promoted the factory's works council as an alternative representative mechanism to that of shop stewards.[23] As the local AEU official caustically remarked, the stewards' argument that "the firm were attempting to crush the union . . . was a debatable point," particularly when NCR needed the union to resolve complex demarcation disputes.[24] For the AEU, the main challenge inside NCR was not outright employer hostility but its inability to exercise reliable discipline over its membership. It was at a loss how to channel volatile female members that regarded membership as secondary to a long tradi-tion of independence and militancy drawn from female employment in local jute mills (Gordon 1991). The women's favored bargaining tactic was the "wildcat," rather than reliance on formal procedure. As the AEU stewards acknowledged, it was difficult to represent constituencies so accustomed to representing themselves. Until the mid-1960s, wide variations in, and abrupt changes to, piecework prices compounded this inherent volatility.

In NCR, steward power slowly shifted towards the center through the 1960s. Ironically, this reflected the company's initial pragmatic acceptance of bargaining and marginalization of informal steward representation. Increasingly, the key union figure in workplace bargaining was the convener, not section stewards. The trend towards convener-led union organization was consolidated between 1969 and 1971, with the creation of a central joint management–union body empowered to settle work-study and bonus issues. The convenership also became a full-time post, with increased facili-ties and access to greater information about the plant's financial perfor-mance and its role in corporate plans. Equally, in response to convener pressure, NCR began to move all employees towards staff status. The success of the convener-led steward organization in NCR and its increasing distance from the regional AEU confirmed a growing "factory consciousness" (Batstone *et al.* 1979). This shift was to be vital to the successful joint management–union campaigns to keep the plant open and revitalize its product range over the next twenty years.

This factory-level institutional change was decisive in shifting the nature and trajectory of workplace bargaining: NCR was unusually successful in formalizing and centralizing workplace bargaining. Other US transnationals failed to transform the institutions of workplace bargaining and experienced continuous conflict over work organization and bonus payments. In the medium term, US managements' efforts to marginalize stewards were undercut by a combination of more complex product schedules and the use of bonus systems to counteract the resultant reduction in productivity. Small-scale disputes proliferated through the 1960s, as bonus systems designed for limited product ranges struggled to sustain their legitimacy. The growing complexity of bonus systems was critical in extending and deepening steward organization (Sloane 1967: 65). In 1966, STC lost an average of almost three working weeks per employee (CIR 1971: 7).

In Burroughs, Cumbernauld, the vehicle for an AEU recruitment drive was grassroots discontent over a lack of transparency in a bonus system, whose claim to equity was undermined by *ad hoc* supervisory adjustments. In 1968, bonus disputes averaged between 400 and 500 per week, with peaks of 700 complaints – or every one of Burroughs 2,200 manual work-force was personally involved in at least one bonus dispute per month. Managerial discretion was no longer cloaked by a factory-wide system that pretended to detached objectivity. Rather, as the integrity of comprehensive bonus systems became increasingly frayed, managerial prerogative was revealed and the legitimacy of steward representation entrenched. Intense, small-scale negotiations over bonuses built up a set of procedural norms that were predicated upon bargaining and mutuality rather than managerial prerogative. Over a decade, the stewards gradu-ally extended the scope, and increased the formalization, of factory-wide bargaining. Steward bargaining established a "tariff" for misdemeanors – lapses in quality, insubordination, and absenteeism. From having a marginal role in the early 1960s, stewards decisively shifted the frontier of control: all aspects of the employment relationship were the subject of collective bargaining. Nor was this simply a shift in the balance of eco-nomic power. Rather, as employers such as Caterpillar and Burroughs well recognized, the mobilization of small groups of workers against *specific* job times and task categories had two general effects. It laid the experiential basis for collective action against management, established robust custom and practice, and embedded the principle of mutuality. There were, therefore, instances of successful union recruitment and organization-building in US branch plants: mobilization stemmed from the creation of collective resources and exploiting moments during which managerial authority was over-extended and collective responses were possible (see Kelly 1998: 32–7). Workplace unionism overturned both management prerogative and any claim to objectivity in work organiz-ation or the bonus system.

Shifting the "frontier of control"

Workplace bargaining gradually undermined the integrity and ideological grip of American employment and payment systems in these plants. Initially, Caterpillar employees were graded by management, not by their skilled status. Like IBM, Caterpillar attempted to break existing ties between the individual engineer, the craft community, and the norms of the local labor market. Westclox, Dumbarton, similarly, used job evaluation and employee reviews to grade labor. For Westclox, the key to progression was not just skilled status but "consistent co-operative and reliable work over a period of time [and] other factors such as quality and knowledge of work, adaptability, time-keeping, etc."[25] There were no automatic triggers for promotion between grades nor was union representation permitted: labor grades were solely at management's discretion. Only IBM proved able to erect a self-contained internal labor market. The craftsmen at Caterpillar, for example, had skills valid outside the Uddingston plant that reduced their dependence on the corporate employment system.

As the 1960s progressed, contracts and earnings were no longer solely at the discretion of management. Rather, all aspects of employment were now negotiated, particularly through small-scale informal collective bargaining. In Caterpillar, formal recognition of the union was followed by a shopfloor war of attrition as stewards established their legitimacy as representatives. The withdrawal of good will was normally sufficient to force recalcitrant supervisors to deal with *all* stewards, rather than just whom they chose (McKinlay and Melling 1999: 237). Steward pressure shifted the frontier of control. Management discipline was calibrated and subject to procedural checks and balances. Adversarial bargaining "domesticated" the American model. But despite these advances, union organization remained fragile and volatile.

There were two clear alternative forms of steward organization in US plants. On one hand, highly unionized skilled men, often working in distinct enclaves such as the toolroom, were represented by their immediate peers. Stewards, normally middle-aged men with considerable union experience, represented small, relatively homogeneous trade groups. On the other hand, female stewards, much younger and often with little or no union experience, represented much larger constituencies with much greater contractual variations. Female labor was concentrated on highly routinized tasks or in assembly areas. Women played a marginal role in factory-wide steward committees. In Hoover, for example, some 60 percent of the workforce was female but over 90 percent of the stewards were male. There was no attempt by the AEU or the stewards to widen the bargaining agenda to encompass the particular interests of female workers. Nor did the AEU develop new strategies to deploy the skilled male workers' bargaining power to improve the conditions of other workers. In an exchange between union activists in Hoover, one experienced male steward conceded that they had not "overcome the 'foreignness' whereby members looked on 'The Union' as something apart from themselves."[26] One female Hoover steward went further, emphasizing the gender dimension that exacerbated the union's irrelevance to day-to-day shopfloor life: "the workers seem to regard the shop stewards as (dues) collectors. We have nothing to offer these women."[27] It is impossible to construct a reliable time-series of stewards–member ratios in particular plants. We can, however, provide snapshots. In Hoover, each steward covered a constituency of approximately eighty employees – but while four stewards represented the toolroom, two female stewards covered approximately 220 assembly workers.[28] Part-time women workers were barred from being stewards. While male toolroom stewards typically held office for several years, female assembly stewards often resigned and returned to their union office within a year.

Sectional bargaining undercut the construction of factory-wide strategies and could threaten the viability of union organization. In 1965, opportunistic bargaining by Caterpillar maintenance craftsmen resulted in the breakdown of steward organization, reducing the convener to an impotent spectator.[29] The close identification between union representation and skilled male workers in STC resulted in complex divisions inside the factory. Skilled male machine setters secured a substantial rise in bonus rates after a short work to rule which reduced the earnings of female machinists. This resulted in retaliatory action by the women machinists, contrary to the instructions of their male steward. As the local AEU official noted, "the action taken was against the shop stewards and not the management."[30]

Union organization throughout US branch plants in Scotland remained fragile until the mid-1960s when a sectoral shift towards comprehensive work study systems triggered a parallel increase in the strategic role of factory-level organization. The AEU estimated that its "solid core" of membership "who continue their membership indefinitely" was less than one in ten with the majority constantly "involved in the process of exclusion and re-admission."[31] Steward organization was no less precarious. In the Ranco factory in Uddingston, "Sister Dempsey did not feel inclined to carry the whole burden of negotiation and collection, and resigned. No one else can be found to take over the task" and within three months the factory was "disorganized."[32] Before union subscriptions were deducted through check-off, sustaining membership levels turned on stewards collecting dues. Steward organization was fundamental not just to workplace bargaining but also to the viability of the union itself:

> This is the position we are in. Our organization rests on the willingness of a very limited number of interested members, without whom our organization would disappear.[33]

The fragility of union organization was compounded by the chronic insecurity of routine mass production work. US manufacturers of consumer durables routinely laid off workers according to short-term shifts in demand without notice or consultation. In Ranco, sixty "girls" were laid off with 15 minutes notice, and told to return a week later. A lightning strike by 600 female assemblers secured the "girls'" reinstatement, and resulted in the election of stewards and an assurance that future redundancies would be preceded by consultation.[34] Just three years later, union organization in Ranco had again collapsed. The AEU's local official reflected on the union's failure to become entrenched inside US branch plants, even in plants where there was no overt management hostility:

> . . . the reluctance of members in some establishments to assist in organizing the unorganized; the fears held by some workers that union involvement would remove them from the job they were now doing; the almost impossible task of getting workers to become stewards, especially amongst the newly organized; the difficulty of uplifting contributions because no-one was prepared to take the contribution cards to the Branch. Some American firms were quite open in their anti-union attitude, but others whilst not welcoming the union would raise no objection to negotiating with stewards.[35]

Overall, a picture emerges of intense, small-scale negotiations over earnings being paralleled by emergent union strategies to extend the scope and depth of custom and practice, of developing informal protocols that hemmed in supervisory authority and defined legitimate task allocation and workloads. But, far from being a drive to consolidate informal bargaining, stewards in US subsidiaries also sought to shift the frontier of control by fleshing out domestic procedures that established a disciplinary tariff for misdemeanors. Managerial authority was now subject to informal limits and to procedural checks and balances. Mutuality trimmed managerial authority and eroded the ideological resonance of corporate welfarism. From the early 1960s onwards, improved earnings and conditions were no longer perceived as dispensed solely by management, but as the result of steward pressure. The attribution of improvements in employment contracts to steward bargaining and, conversely, of attempts to stem rises in bonus earnings to management, consolidated workforce support for workplace representation. But this process of encroaching upon managerial prerogative was neither uncontested nor always successful.

Conclusion

Of first-wave American inward investors, only IBM managed to sustain its anti-union strategy intact. Others made tactical concessions to unions early on. Tactical concessions by management granted unions a legitimacy at factory level that allowed the gradual extension of steward bargaining onto the shopfloor. Until the late 1960s, unions were extremely weak in American branch plants, irrespective of procedural agreements. Recognition did not necessarily equate with representation. In an era before check-off, structural weakness was a threat to union organization. Stewards, especially in routinized and feminized assembly operations, were incidental to bargaining, marginal to factory-level contractual bargaining and often an irrelevance to wildcat bargaining by particular workgroups. By the late 1960s, however, bargaining rights encompassed the smallest details of work organization. Just as there is no necessary link between union recruitment and recognition, so management's acceptance of collective bargaining does not necessarily result in any co-determination of terms and conditions of employment. The achievement of meaningful co-determination was the result of lengthy steward activity.

Formal recognition by management or acceptance of a procedural agreement did not necessarily signify a rapid transition to orderly workplace bargaining. Rather, the form of recruitment and recognition campaigns was important in shaping the development of steward organization and factory-level bargaining. Mobilization theory assists our understanding of recruitment and recognition campaigns but the nature of the transition to collective bargaining also established the trajectory of management–union and steward–member relationships in the long-run. Indeed, American companies were universally hostile to stewards and to informal bargaining. Typically, the employers' reluctant acceptance of recognition and formal bargaining was only the prelude to many years of small-scale confrontations as management and labor struggled to establish a balance between custom and practice and managerial prerogative. Formally, all American employers accepted the right of employees to belong to unions. In practice, the refusal to accept recognition was part of a strategy to fragment their workforces. Nor was this anti-unionism only an ideology. High wage strategies, deeply embedded corporate paternalism, open management styles, and extensive voice mechanisms were designed to provide incentives to forsake union representation. Compaq, Digital, Hewlett Packard, IBM, Kodak, and Motorola were not *non*-union but *anti*-union, this being an integral part of their corporate labor policies. Nonetheless, the demonization of American transnationals as harsh paternalist employers beyond the reach of union organization was both an excuse for failure and a rationalization of union neglect. More than this, it betrayed the unions' lack of engagement with the reality of employment in the transnational electronic sector, of relatively high pay, upward mobility, and adequate – if atomized – voice mechanisms. To claim that there was a material need for collective bargaining, that trade unionism was required as a counterweight to an autocratic management, or that there was a significant representational deficit, was not entirely credible.

In different ways, the unionization campaigns in Caterpillar and IBM confirm the importance of lay activist groups in promoting and sustaining unionization. The lack of an activist group and of adequate formal support in IBM and, conversely, the presence of a core of experienced lay union representatives and official support in Caterpillar goes some way to explaining the outcomes and trajectories of the recruitment and representation campaigns (Kelly 1998: 127). But mobilization theory goes only part of the way if we apply it exclusively to union campaigning. For, as Kelly (1998: 38) notes parenthetically, mobilization theory helps us to appreciate both the creation of sustainable collective action and its absence. During critical moments, managements such as IBM were able to maintain the legitimacy of managerial authority and mobilize a layer of workplace representatives in defense of a non-union employment relationship. In IBM, the moment at which unionization was most possible was during the early years. Within a few years IBM had laid the foundations of an internal labor market and sophisticated voice mechanisms that delivered on the implicit compact with the workforce: relatively privileged contracts and firm-specific upskilling in return for non-unionism. IBM's employment system proved so robust that it was strengthened rather than weakened by the recognition ballot.

Acknowledgments

Thanks to Dr O'Brien, Glasgow City Archives and John Quigley (AEEU) for access to union and employer records, and to John Harvie and Brian Quinn for assistance with local newspaper sources. Alan McKinlay also acknowledges ESRC support (Grant R000223271).

Notes

1 Phillips, Board of Trade (Scotland) to London, 7 February 1951 (PRO BT177/370).
2 Anonymous union member, ACAS, "IBM Inquiry," 3 December 1976, PRO CW2/33.
3 ACAS, "IBM – Management Interviews," December 1976, PRO CW2/33.
4 AEU, Greenock District Committee, Minutes, 18 August 1954.
5 AEU, Greenock District Committee, Minutes, 7 November 1954.
6 AEU, Greenock District Committee, Minutes, 2 March 1955.
7 AEU, Greenock District Committee, Minutes, 25 May 1955.
8 Butler, ACAS, Internal Memo, 1 March 1976, PRO, CW2/28.
9 ACAS, "Summary of Interviews held with Greenock Advisory Council," 28 February to 1 March 1977, PRO CW2/28.
10 Ibid.
11 Norcross to Kerr, "IBM," 9 February 1977, PRO, CW2/28.
12 Anonymous IBM manager, "ACAS, IBM Recognition Enquiry: Meeting with IBM Management," 26 July 1976, PRO CW2/32.
13 *Glasgow Herald*, 31 March 1977.
14 IBM (UK), *UK News*, 30 March 1977.
15 Interview, John Langan, former ASTMS official, February 2002.
16 Interview, John Quigley, AEEU district officer, January 2002.
17 ACAS, "IBM Inquiry," 2 June 1977, CW2/34.
18 Interview, John Langan, former ASTMS official, February 2002.
19 AEU, Greenock District Committee, Minutes, 16 March 1966, report on Sangamo Weston.

20 AEU, Mid-Lanark District Organizer, "Report on Caterpillar Strike," nd, 1961.
21 John Boyd, AEU, "A Personal Appeal," Caterpillar strike leaflet, 1961.
22 "Review of Cambuslang Operations," Hoover UK, October 1979, TD1383/2/174, GCA.
23 NCR, *Factory Post*, July/August 1949, p. 2.
24 AEU, Dundee District Committee, Minutes, 28 March 1953.
25 SEEA, CL66–430, 28 October 1966, GCA TD1059/7/66.
26 AEU, Shop Stewards" Quarterly Meeting, Mid-Lanark District Committee, Minutes, May 1967
27 AEU, Mid-Lanark District Committee, Minutes, 19 May 1954.
28 AEU, Mid-Lanark District Committee, Minutes, 13 January 1956.
29 AEU, Mid-Lanark District Committee, Minutes, 19 November 1965.
30 AEU, Mid-Lanark District Committee, Minutes, June 1967.
31 AEU, Shop Stewards" Quarterly Meeting, Mid-Lanark District Committee, Minutes, August 1967.
32 AEU, Mid-Lanark District Committee, Minutes, 30 June 1954.
33 Ibid.
34 AEU, Mid-Lanark District Committee, Minutes, 15 June 1956.
35 AEU, Mid-Lanark District Committee, Minutes, 10 June 1959.

3 Organizing in the offshore oil and gas industry in Britain, c. 1972–1990

A long burning flame or a spark that has gone out?

Gregor Gall

Introduction

Since its inception in the early 1970s, the UK sector of the offshore North Sea oil and gas industry has represented the largest sector of industry in Britain by numbers of workers employed, and has remained non-union and without union recognition. Given the preponderance of manual workers in the industry and their traditionally high propensity to unionize, as well as the period in which the offshore regulatory regime was established, under a "traditional" Labour government, this appears somewhat surprising, and contrasts markedly with the powerfully entrenched oil workers' union, the OFS, in the Norwegian sister sector. To take but one example, namely the extremely high levels of fatalities, epitomized by the July 1988 *Piper Alpha* disaster where 167 oil workers were killed, there would appear to be a clear need for trade unionism to protect the safety and interests of the workforce and regulate the activities of the powerful multi-national oil corporations through union recognition.

This chapter explores the various factors that have resulted in employer dominance, union marginalization and limited state regulation in the employment relationship in the offshore industry, summarized in the inability of the unions to gain recognition. Key amongst these are the preponderance of well-resourced US companies with their anti-union philosophies and practices, the weak nature of the workplace regulatory regime offshore, the physical difficulties involved in organizing a dispersed workforce offshore, the extensive use of sub-contracting and considerable inter-union competition. In particular, the chapter focuses on attempts by activists from a number of different unions in the late 1980s to organize an inter-union network to unite and galvanize the existing unions into action to secure recognition (and thus improve terms and conditions of employment). This involves examining the objectives and activities of the Offshore Industry Liaison Committee (OILC) before and after it became a bona fide independent union. The *Piper Alpha* disaster renewed the demands for recognition leading to widespread unofficial walkouts in 1989 and 1990. This represented the most opportune period in which to gain recognition. But outgunned and outmaneuvered by the oil companies, and aided by internal union divisions, the prospect of recognition slipped away by 1991. The OILC was then constituted formally as a union, since which it has made little headway, not least because of the large existing unions' attempts to marginalize it. The AEEU, with the GMB and MSF as junior partners, have secured between 1999 and 2001 limited recognition agreements, which exclude the OILC.

The chapter begins by examining the events, processes, and outcomes leading up to the biggest and most sustained campaign mounted by oil workers to date to secure recognition, namely the dramatic events of 1990 centered on a wave of strikes and occupations. This provides an introduction to, and background for, understanding the nature and form of the oil workers' most serious campaign for recognition. One aspect of this is to lay out the key characteristics of the offshore industrial relations landscape. Following these, the key battleground of the strikes of 1990 is recounted and assessed.

The material for this chapter is derived from a series of interviews with union officials from the main unions concerned (AEEU, GMB, MSF, OILC, RMT, TGWU) in 1999, 2000, and 2001, attendance at many of the oil worker meetings at the Trades Council in Aberdeen in the summer of 1990 (when the author was a post-graduate student), and secondary sources, i.e. newspaper reporting. These sources were then complemented by the OILC's (1991b) own detailed historiography *Striking Out!* and Woolfson *et al.*'s (1996) *magnum opus, Paying for the Piper,* which examines the political economy of the offshore industry. In a situation where the oil workers' struggle has gone unrecorded and unnoticed elsewhere (*pace* Sewel and Penn 1996, Terry 1991), these texts are important chronicles.

Characteristics of offshore industrial relations

In order to contextualize the battles fought by the oil workers for recognition, it is necessary to understand the particular nature of the forces operating in and on the industry, particularly with regard to the period of the 1970s and 1980s. Formally, oil operators and contractors adopted the position of being neither "for" nor "against" trade unionism, being happy to allow employees to be members of trade unions as well as to discuss various matters with national union officials. This represented a refusal to countenance collective bargaining and a willingness to talk without obligation. Bargaining and what would amount to meaningful dialog were unnecessary, the companies claimed, by virtue of the consultative committees they had established (Woolfson *et al.* 1996: 72–5). On top of this, the operators formed an employers' association (UKOOA) whose remit formally excluded consideration of industrial relations issues. In practice, this was a veil behind which the companies invariably operated union avoidance, union suppression, and anti-unionism practices. Three factors stand out here in their motivation and ability to do so.

The first is the almost complete dominance of an American "kick ass" style of management – unregulated, capricious, unilateral, and authoritarian (Woolfson *et al.* 1996). Long hours of work, relatively unrewarding rates of pay, instant dismissals (see ibid.: 63, 64, 222, 480), victimization (see OILC 1992 on blacklisting and *Socialist Worker,* 11 August 1990 on the Not Required Back system), and total subservience to orders proliferated. In the words of one US drilling superintendent: "There's only two can'ts – if you can't do it, you can't stay" (in Woolfson *et al.* 1996: 47). Nowhere in this offshore regime was there a meaningful place for trade unions. The dominance of American companies offshore is explicable by a combination of factors. In contrast to Norway, successive British governments were unwilling to establish a regime that favored indigenous capital. A sole nationalized oil company made little difference to this. Thus, there was a reliance on the experience, capital, and technology of US operators and contractors, who were keen to expand into new areas of production. The dominance of US companies here was supported by "*successive British governments* and the oil companies hav[ing] shared a common interest in bringing oil on stream as quickly as possible and in trying to maximize output" (Sewel and Penn 1996: 287, emphasis added; see also OILC 1991a).

In addition to over thirty operators, the second factor is that

> [A] distinctive, but not unique, characteristic . . . is the prevalence of sub-contracting. The main oil companies . . . constitute the field operators but during all the phases of the cycle [exploration, development, production and abandonment] most specialist activities, ranging from diving to construction work, from drilling to catering, are undertaken by sub-contractors. One consequence of such a client–contractor relationship is that it is not always clear who is ultimately responsible for the working conditions and terms of employment offshore.
>
> (Sewel and Penn 1996: 287)

The OILC (1991b: 19) and Woolfson *et al.* (1996: 88) suggest that over two-thirds of those offshore were employed by contractors and service companies, rather than the operators. However, the operators exercised a disproportionate influence over the contractors (Woolfson *et al.* 1996: 122), where there was significant competition for work, by virtue of awarding the contracts. Operators could, therefore, enforce considerable restraint on how the contractors operated their industrial relations. Furthermore, the operators could use the contractors as a buffer in dealings with unions (see also *Financial Times*, 14, 21 August 1990).

The third factor concerns the "practical" difficulties involved in organizing offshore (see OILC 1991b: 19–22). There are over 100 installations, each with a multiplicity of skills and trades groups on each. The impact of the physical separation of offshore workplaces from those on land highlights markedly the extent to which unions are dependent upon others, primarily the oil operators and contractors but also airport authorities, for access to the workforce. Moreover, if workers in dispute or sacked workers are physically removed from the platforms, they are not free to picket the premises. In addition to this, a new workforce (in a new industry) which frequently changed and moved about among different operators and contractors, rigs, and platforms created additional problems. Finally, the geographical dispersion of the workforce when onshore (based around north-east Scotland, central belt of Scotland, Merseyside and north-east England) further accentuated the fragmentation of the workforce. Against this, many were from unionized backgrounds (*Financial Times*, 7, 17 August 1990). Thus much of the explanation of what the operators and contractors did revolves around having no serious trammels, i.e. opposition and resistance, to their managerial prerogative. However, the prevalence of union "inaction" and internecine competition (see later) should not be discounted in explaining this employer dominance.

The first attempts at organizing offshore – a precursor to conflagration

The first attempts to "organize" were made between 1972 and 1974 by local north-east of Scotland politicians and trade unionists acting as opinion-formers. They sought through government regulation to improve pay and conditions, and appealed to trade unions to organize the industry. Following these efforts and the intervention of the STUC and the CSEU, a joint-union approach (the Inter-Union Off-Shore Oil Committee, IUOOC) to organizing was established (OILC 1991b: 73, Woolfson *et al.* 1996: 60–1). However, the fourfold increase in oil prices quickly strengthened the operators' position with the government (*vis-à-vis* the cost of imported oil and encouraging the fields to go on-stream as quickly as possible) and with the workforce. The former meant the companies could resist the requirements of minimum employment and health and safety regulation, while increased revenues allowed discontent to be ameliorated by increasing wages and improving conditions, particularly where labor shortages were acute.

Nonetheless, the growth in the level of production activity, the numbers employed offshore, and a more favorable regime under the 1974–9 Labour governments were *relatively* more conducive conditions in which the IUOOC pursued recognition. In 1974, the IUOOC invited the drilling and oil companies (operators) to talks on recognition, with the threat of stopping supplies getting to the rigs/platforms through strike action by NUS boat crew members (Sewel and Penn 1996: 294). That only two operators attended (ibid.: 293–4) reflected the lack of a credible offshore threat on, and to, the rigs and platforms and the unions' unwillingness to use onshore members in these companies' operations in a supportive manner (Woolfson *et al.* 1996: 62). However, one case of industrial action by a supply boat crew did lead to the company (Sedco) talking to the unions in 1974 and the same tactic was repeated successfully on a slightly wider scale against another American company, Odeco (Woolfson *et al.* 1996: 63).

More importantly, pressure from the UK government Department of Energy, under left-wing MP Tony Benn, ensured that those companies that showed a willingness to allow union access offshore would receive preference in the awarding of licenses (Sewel and Penn 1986: 295, Woolfson *et al.* 1996: 65–6). However, Benn was warned off making recognition a criteria for awarding licenses by senior civil servants (see Benn 1989: 516). Furthermore, the general industrial relations environment was made slightly more favorable by the repeal of the anti-union Industrial Relations Act 1971 and the enactment of the EPA (see Introduction). But the impact of these mechanisms was weak in this period and the statutory mechanism and the responsibility to further collective bargaining were both abolished in 1980 (Woolfson *et al.* 1996: 78–9, 80). The same weaknesses are true of the 1977 extension of the Health and Safety at Work etc. Act 1974 offshore with regard to union safety reps (ibid.: 80).

Nevertheless, a limited number of operators allowed unions to visit rigs and platforms, but used the clause "subject to operational requirements" to restrict the number of visits as well as the access to workers (ibid.: 70–1) while some (e.g. Shell and Occidental) signed agreements in 1977–8 covering representational (but not bargaining) rights for individual rigs/platforms. This was offset by the agreement of a memorandum between the operators (UKOOA) and the IUOOC on a procedure for testing support for recognition bringing no obvious gains (ibid.: 75–6). The picture of very partial gains and of one step forward, one step back resulting from limited legislative possibilities, modest union efforts, and employer opposition is repeated again and again in the rest of the 1970s and 1980s.

The catering contractors in 1978 signed an industry-wide collective bargaining agreement with the NUS and TGWU, as a result of pressure from the operators (Sewel and Penn 1996: 296, Woolfson *et al.* 1996: 98). The operators were motivated to do so by the increasing levels of competition amongst contractors which saw wage-cutting, and thus service levels in catering and cleaning falling markedly. Not unimportant either was the industrial action which applied pressure on the contractors. Meanwhile, the construction and engineering unions signed an agreement with construction contractors covering platforms before they began producing oil (the Hook-Up agreement). This reflected both the operators' and contractors' desires to avoid the costs of disputes (delays and settlements) with strategic groups of workers which could hold back the onset of production, particularly in periods of skill shortages (Sewel and Penn 1986:

294–5, 300, Woolfson *et al.* 1996: 88–9, 92). These relative advances were not made without inter-union strife, in particular over the NUS's success in gaining recognition on some vessels and rigs (Woolfson *et al.* 1996: 67, 70), which the companies then argued questioned the integrity of the unions' joint approach.

The end of the 1970s witnessed a major counter-balance to these limited advances. The "Winter of Discontent" of 1978–9, a revolt of public sector low-paid workers against the Labour government's pay restraint, created major divisions between the "two wings of the labor movement." Related to, and following this, May 1979 saw the election of the anti-union Conservative government in 1979. Both thus helped inform the increasingly difficult and hostile environment in which unions found themselves operating. However, in addition to these, the offshore unions had their own major debacle.

Beginning as an unofficial two-week strike by 500 workers covered by the Hook-Up agreement and concerning shift rotas, the strike re-started after negotiations with the offshore contractors' council failed to progress to the workers' satisfaction. Unlike the initial strike, the workers now had the support of their shop stewards and the unofficial strike spread to some 4,000 workers by January 1979 and continued into February. The strike's lasting impact among the oil workers was to open up, in a stark manner, divisions between members and their national union leaderships over tactics and strategies in the context of what was seen as a defeated strike (see Sewel and Penn 1996: 297–9, OILC 1991a, 1991b, Woolfson *et al.* 1996: 94). Put simply, "the men saw it not only as a defeat but as them being let down by their union" (Sewel and Penn 1996: 299), while Woolfson *et al.* (1996: 94) comment it "was to be a decade before the offshore workforce fully recovered its combativeness" following the strike. Both Sewel and Penn (1996: 298) and Woolfson *et al.* (1996: 93) argue the trenchant criticism of the strike from the national unions arose from the perceived undermining of their legitimacy as bargaining agents as a result of unofficial action.

The early 1980s were barren years for union organizing offshore. The legacy of the defeated unofficial strike was compounded by the conflict-calming impact of the growth in the number of relatively well-paid jobs in the industry when redundancies were legion elsewhere in manufacturing, and by some employers terminating recognition agreements (OILC 1991b: 32, 35). This inactivity was then concretized by employers' responses to a sharp downturn in the price of oil: cost-cutting, redundancies, and the ending of further exploration and development. Yet in 1986, the IUOOC was successful in extending the Hook-Up agreement to production and maintenance workers as a result of an agreement with the offshore contractors' council; the contractors were concerned to stop the damaging consequences of uncontrolled cost-cutting. But the agreement was subsequently nullified by the operators who refused to award any contract set on these terms (Woolfson *et al.* 1996: 96). Consequently, cost-cutting pressures were maintained on workers' wages and conditions.

In this period, the only fillips for the unions were the NUS and TGWU's ability to prevent the break-up of the catering industry agreement, the EEPTU's agreement with the Electrical Contractors' Association, and the southern sector agreement. Following wage cutting in an Occidental contract, some caterers sought to use this as an opportunity to respond to the downward pressure of tightening market conditions. Others feared the breaking-out of uncontrollable and destabilizing competition. The latter won out. Owing to the strategic importance of electrical work, the electrical contractors were permitted by the operators to sign the Scottish Joint Industries Board agreement in 1982, cushioned by its relative weakness compared to the Hook-Up agreement (Woolfson *et al.* 1996: 98). The Southern Waters Offshore Construction Agreement was signed after a bout of industrial action in 1985, but it was again weaker than the Hook-Up Agreement (OILC 1991b: 33, Woolfson *et al.* 1996: 102–3). Additionally, there was the short-lived creation by local union FTOs of a "rank-and-file" committee which held mass meetings and published the "Bear Facts" newssheet (OILC 1991b: 39).

By the end of the 1980s, both employment levels in the industry and the general level of economic activity began to rise again. But the operators remained determined to face down any attempts to use these conditions to leverage recognition from them, fearing for their consequent ability to control labor costs and the restrictions on their right to manage. Despite the majority of workers being union members on many rigs/platforms, employers, acting legally, simply refused to agree to workforce ballots to determine whether there should be recognition.

Drawing out the general lessons of this period, several points stand out. The unions found it very difficult to make any advance from a weak base. Membership density was poor, union organization weak, and willingness to take action low. Put another way, they had no independent and sizable resources to draw upon. Their divisions merely exacerbated the obstacles they faced. Moreover, they were unable to call on additional resources such as a statutory recognition law, pressure from the government, or other unions. Consequently, they remained reliant upon the employers for access and cooperation. To the extent that limited advances towards recognition were made, these accorded with situations where strategic considerations made the employers more willing to grant recognition and where effective industrial action was utilized. However, the granting of recognition on a limited basis (e.g. by platform rather than contractor) heightened sectional competition. Previously, the absence of recognition had united the unions but the failure of a joint approach to make headway increased the rewards for individual approaches which allowed the operators to play "divide and rule." Furthermore, the partial nature of the recognition granted meant that it was of limited use in building up union presence and strength elsewhere. Thus, the "steps forward" were often self-limiting.

Piper Alpha and its aftermath

Piper Alpha transformed the industrial relations landscape of the industry. It confirmed to many workers in a forceful and graphic way the rapacity of the operators and contractors and highlighted the inadequacy of the hitherto existing attempts by the national unions to obtain recognition (see e.g. OILC 1989, 1991a). Unlike the 1986 Chinook disaster which killed forty-two men, the *Piper* fundamentally changed the consciousness of workers: not only had "enough become enough" but readiness to confront the employers with widespread strike action emerged (see OILC 1991b: 41–2). Specifically, *Piper Alpha* re-ignited and re-energized the campaign to get a post-Hook-Up agreement, with strike action increasingly viewed as the necessary means by many union activists. "Cognitive liberation" (McAdam 1988) had taken place. However, the decision by national officers of the various unions not to sanction strike action widened an existing divide. The officers believed low membership density would make a strike ineffective while the logistical problems of organizing a legal ballot, namely the myriad of employers and the geographical dispersion of members, would make any action challengeable in law. But in the aftermath of a ballot among catering workers in early 1989 that secured an improved offer, the pressure towards industrial action further mounted. The demands for forceful strike action coalesced together in the formation of the OILC in February 1989 (see OILC 1991a).

Beginning in late 1987, an upturn in operators' offshore activity was paralleled by a general growth in economic activity. Increasing demand for skilled labor and some employment stability provided a conducive background in which activism was renewed, compared to an earlier attempt in 1984–5 when the oil price collapsed. Added to this was the feeling amongst oil workers of now "enough was enough." The opportunity for mobilization arose around the agreement between the union activists and the national officials from different unions to establish the OILC as a coordinating organization and the debate surrounding the unions' preparations for a new Hook-Up agreement.

The OILC organized nineteen successful short rolling strikes and sit-ins throughout the spring and summer of 1989 (Doran 1989, OILC 1991a:11, 1991b: 47, Sewel and Penn 1996: 308–10, Woolfson *et al.* 1996: 116–17). One of the largest strikes, involving 4,000 workers, occurred on the first anniversary of the *Piper Alpha* disaster and was spurred on by the use of foreign labor to replace strikers. Under pressure of the action, four contractors undertook to either engage in talks on recognition, sign recognition deals, or to hold ballots. However, these were all subsequently reneged on after pressure from the operators. Wage increases (of 11.7 percent) were paid with the intention of acting as a sop. Nonetheless, strategic and tactical lessons were learnt by OILC activists about industrial action; for example, staying on the production facilities rather than on the accommodation vessels, and some measure of workers' self-confidence returned (OILC 1991b: 49, Woolfson *et al.* 1996: 120). The OILC (1991a: 11) commented that the actions "sharply radicalized those workers taking part in challenging the very nature of the prevailing authority structure on their installations." Moreover, the notice of withdrawal from the Hook-Up agreement, in consequence of the reneging by the employers, made some common cause between different sections of the offshore workforce (Sewel and Penn 1996: 311) although the "one-table approach" of a common front between the unions also allowed individual unions to continue to pursue their own interests in their "spheres of influence."

The showdown has come: the other oil war

The improved weather conditions of the summer of 1990 precipitated one of the biggest shutdowns for maintenance and safety work in the history of the North Sea. The shutdown presented an opportunity to delay the resumption of production, potentially costing the operators vast sums in missed profits and, therefore, offering bargaining leverage. The pressure on companies to restart production intensified as a result of a price rise and reduction in output following the Iraqi invasion of Kuwait. However, any strategy to utilize this would require: (a) the absolute requirement that the maintenance could not be postponed; and (b) the enforcement of the introduction of safety mechanisms by 31 December 1990 by the government. If either of these conditions did not materialize, then the ability of the OILC to exercise leverage would be considerably reduced.

The strikes were preceded by intense and wide-ranging debates amongst members and activists both on and offshore about tactics, strategy, aims, and objectives. Without any formalized policies or structures, the OILC was run as a form of direct and immediate democracy; weekly meetings in various cities (Aberdeen, Glasgow, Newcastle, Great Yarmouth, Liverpool, and Middlesbrough) determined its direction while its leadership were drawn from the ranks of the long-standing activists. The first discussions focused on implementing an overtime ban to lay the basis for more forceful action. The advantage of a ban was that it could make some impact given the levels of quasi-contractual hours of overtime demanded by employers and workers would still be earning. However, the disadvantages were that its impact would be relatively slow to show and the habitual overtime worked to boost earnings would make many unwilling to carry it out. Furthermore, many workers favored strike action but some of these were then willing to work overtime to make up for lost earnings. These divisions meant the OILC could not move forward easily. Consequently, pro-overtime ban and pro-action activists mounted a more vigorous campaign to win over the majority, knowing that if there was no action soon the OILC would be seen as a spent force. The call to organize the ban caused confusion precisely because it was implemented before it had widespread support. On top of this, and in response, the maintenance shutdown was continually being put back.

Despite these difficulties, over a few months the extent of coverage of the ban was built up by activists campaigning in the face of smears, misinformation, and disinformation disseminated by employers, and the bribe of considerable wage increases from contractors (of up to 40 percent). There were still significant patches of non-coverage and discontent with and opposition to the ban, highlighted by the absence of both shop steward and workplace organization structures in many areas and a more cohesive union presence generally. However, the length of time that the overtime ban ran for without being particularly effective created pressure to unite the workforce by taking more hard-hitting action, namely a strike. Again, this was not without problems: there were both hesitation and division within the OILC leadership, manifesting itself in action twice being called and then stood down.

At this point the OILC was not "anti" the official unions – indeed it encouraged workers to join them. The national unions attempted to act as one body by adopting a "single table" approach as well as rescinding existing agreements in pursuit of a single offshore agreement and forming the National Offshore Committee. The OILC's role was to organize unofficial action in order to create leverage for the national unions to use, because the logistical requirements of holding legally balloted action in the circumstances offshore militated against the national unions doing so. To organize official but unballoted action would likely lead to fines and sequestration of unions' assets. In the OILC's own words, it "acted as the 'cat's paw' for the official unions" (OILC 199a: 11). A closer working relationship between the OILC, IUOOC, and national unions developed in this situation but this did not resolve all remaining inter-union problems (see OILC 1991b: ch. 9, Woolfson *et al.* 1996: 154–6).

Sensing the build-up towards more combative action, employers engaged individually, and in conjunction with each other, in counter-offensive and demobilization tactics. Blacklisting, delays in maintenance shutdowns, threats of lock-outs and dismissal for breach of contract, and provocation through mass sackings to strike pre-emptively all occurred. Prior to August, there were short mass strikes to commemorate those who died in the *Piper* disaster and a recent helicopter "accident." Onshore, a war of words was fought out in press before and during the strikes, particularly over allegations of intimidation (e.g. see *Independent*, 6, 8, 12 August 1990).

The first strike took place on 2 August with sixty-five platforms/installations affected. The OILC claimed some 4,000–5,000 workers were on strike. The operators, stating only 2,000 were involved, threatened dismissals unless workers returned to work, forced movement ashore for those refusing to return to work and lock-outs. Where lock-outs and sackings took place, many engaged in sit-ins, indicating that they had learnt the lesson of 1989, namely, that striking workers taken onshore have very little bargaining power. Around 1,000 were involved in sit-ins on Shell platforms. Others were allowed to return to work as normal, depending on operator policy, while some were allowed to leave the sit-ins to go onshore on half pay. Many upon returning onshore were pressurized into signing a no-strike document. OILC advised: "sign it and get back out offshore for more action." Several other features of the action are notable. Some new areas, platforms, and groups of workers took action while the operators attempted to shut down communication links between workplaces and with the OILC. Probably of greater immediate significance was the huge amount of work and resources needed to support those continuing their occupations.

The second strike on 5 August sought to carry on the fight, bolster those in occupation, and let new workplaces become involved. The OILC claimed around eighty platforms were affected with the numbers participating unclear. The operators claimed only 1,500 were involved. By this point over 1,000 workers had been sacked and the battle became one of staying on platforms/rigs rather than be isolated on flotels or onshore. The OILC acknowledged that after sackings, the number of those engaged in sit-ins increased at a slower than expected rate. The heart of the movement's strength was the East Shetland basin sit-ins. Elsewhere the workforce was less organized and less determined. Support from onshore operator and supply boat workers was weak, reflecting economic uncertainty, the restrictions of employment law, and low union density. In contacts between the national unions and operators, the unions requested a ballot on recognition to which the operators said they would not cooperate under duress. This further widened divisions amongst the unions as to the way to proceed (see Woolfson *et al.* 1996: 191).

The third strike took place on 9 August, being smaller than the last as many workers were now "on the beach," either having left occupations, been sacked, or been taken onshore to sit out the dispute. The operators claimed 750 took part while the OILC claimed 1,500. There was some unofficial sympathy action amongst onshore engineers. A split amongst contractors emerged, with the smaller being willing to reinstate and ballot on recognition. The larger effectively vetoed this. This provided no relief to the OILC. Pressure began to mount from some groups for an all-out strike because "there was no where else to go" as battle weariness of sit-ins began to bite and some workers began returning to work. However, others feared such a move would further expose the unevenness of support.

The fourth strike on 13 August saw further pressure building on the operators not to lose any more of the weather window. Furthermore, the action was costing the operators and government millions of pounds in lost revenue per day (*Financial Times,* 24 August 1990). However, so entrenched were the positions that no movement ensued. The OILC reported 74 of 105 installations in the northern sector took action with strong support in the south sector despite victimization. This could not counter-balance the shrinking numbers in sit-ins in the Shetland basin (then about 300), the problems in sustaining those left sitting-in, the increasing numbers on the beach, the lack of support onshore, and the isolation of occupiers and strikers. The leader of the OILC told a mass meeting "[W]e are in something of a stalemate. No progress has been made. We have to decide whether to withdraw or go over the top. What you have to decide is how rough you're prepared to allow it to get" (*Financial Times*, 15 August 1990). At this point, and without the prospect of employer cooperation on a ballot for recognition as well as their determination to ride out the action, the national unions began to organize their own ballot, even though the outcome would not be binding.

The 18 August saw the fifth strike with the OILC claiming 1,000 participants and the operators 600, while some 3,000 workers were "on the beach." Clearly the campaign had begun to falter. Moreover, OILC financial resources were nearly nil and the battle had become one to first secure reinstatement rather than recognition. Reinstatement became a precondition for everything else; workers earning again, activists not being victimized, and organizational regroupment. The loss of momentum accelerated with the granting of an interdict for Shell against the occupiers, precipitating them to leave. Significantly, this fifth strike was taken against the advice of the national unions (*Independent*, 18, 21 August 1990) although they would not publicly condemn the OILC (*Financial Times*, 21 August 1990). The only "bright" spot in the fifth strike was that many workers taking action were not union members.

As the national unions pressed ahead with the necessary cumbersome registration process for the legal ballot for industrial action to push for recognition, support was dwindling amongst offshore workers for further action. This was not ameliorated by the prospect of a softening on the Offshore Contractors' Council's line on cooperating with the organization of the ballot. This came to nothing – indeed it may have been an attempt to further disorganize the OILC by playing for time. In recognition of no progress being made there and little progress from the national unions, the sixth strike was held on 12 September. The OILC claimed around 500 participants, mostly in the south. Concomitant, open disunity emerged amongst activists as well as recriminations amongst workers. A further hammer blow was the government's announcement of extensions of time for the completion of safety work. The final action of the campaign was the calling for and then canceling of a two-day strike in the southern basin on 25 September. The prospect of some fillip from the offshore catering workers was dashed when their mandate to strike over pay after a 6:1 vote for was withdrawn following the prospect of a legal challenge to the validity of the ballot from an employer. The national unions' campaign to establish the registration system for a legal ballot was further delayed and delayed, with many activists suspecting foot-dragging on the unions' part. Indeed, many of the activists were unlikely to be able to take part in a ballot as they were not employed by virtue of being sacked. By the end of 1990, it was clear there would be no ballot and thus no official action despite the publication of the Cullen Report into the *Piper Alpha* disaster. The Report made relatively little comment and recommendation about industrial relations and trade unionism, feeling this to be outwith its remit (OILC 1991a, 1991b). Therein ended the most serious ever challenge to the employers in the North Sea. In its aftermath, the employers reasserted their control: wage increases of around 40 percent were granted between 1989 and 1991 (Woolfson *et al.* 1996: xx), new, longer contracts to enhance job security for "loyal" workers were instituted, and the blacklist was enforced.

Mobilization: necessary but in itself insufficient

Although the offshore oil workers engaged in a brave, large-scale, and protracted fight for recognition, they nonetheless failed to secure their goal of recognition and did so at the cost of widespread hardship, sackings, and victimization. Despite "decisively end[ing] a 25 year history of total control by the oil companies offshore" (OILC 1990), the impact of this defeat was severe: after 1990 no further similar mobilizations were enacted and the OILC was effectively disembodied for a number of years. Such a defeat largely explains the susceptibility to, and inability of workers and the established unions to resist, the spread of recognition since 1999 on the employers' terms, namely meek "partnership" agreements with the AEEU, GMB, and MSF and the exclusion of the OILC. This concluding section examines the contours of their struggle: its genesis and evolution, the relationship between the OILC and national unions, and the OILC's tactics.

By 1990, and particularly with the campaign of 1989 behind them, the majority of offshore workers shared the common experience of authoritarian management, continual risk, and the realization that change for the better would only come as a consequence of their own actions. Offshore workers began the campaign of 1990 with vigor and determination as the following shows:

> [The oil companies] will hope to isolate and break up the workforce and demoralize people. But they've reckoned without the determination of the workforce offshore. We've been treated like dirt for years but now we've got a real chance to win.
>
> (Unnamed oil worker quoted
> in *Socialist Worker,* 11 August 1990)

This trajectory has all the hallmarks of the process set out under "mobilization theory": interest definition and formation, attribution, development of grievance and senses of injustice, establishment of leadership and the pro-active "framing" of issues, calculations of opportunities to act with their associated costs, and mobilization itself (see Kelly 1998).

However, it is the particular nature of the mobilization that is of arguably greater interest and importance in this case. The OILC's strategy of one-day actions and only encouraging sit-ins where dismissals had been made *reflected* and *reinforced* the considerable unevenness, tensions, and differences within the offshore workforce. In turn, some of these replicated the different economic and industrial–political positions of the operators and contractors, and the different sectors (northern, southern). Many workers were keen to take action but far from a majority were prepared to take all-out action. But the series of actions over the period were unable to break the grip of the employers. As the series of actions progressed, more were sacked or taken to the beach, depleting the OILC's presence offshore and thus their main bargaining tool. All-out action only ensued as a result of employer action and thus in a selective, limited, and uncoordinated way. Without doubt the OILC needed to *lead* in a far more aggressive way – to seize the moment with all-out action (strikes, and sit-ins on production facilities) from the beginning and to continue with the utmost determin-ation and tenacity before the employers could intervene with sackings and try to disorganize the OILC. The employers' intention to deal with the forthcoming action in such a way was well known of beforehand. While this is convincing in the abstract, it was, as shown before, very difficult to realize in practice.

The OILC was between a rock and a hard place. To do take no action, for fear of alienating some workers from the OILC, risked alienating if not destroying its activist base, members, and supporters. If it went for all-out action early on, it might satisfy its own militants but alienate all other oil workers. A halfway house between the two risked alienating some of both groups, the non-OILC oil workers and the militants. The way to move forward was hampered by the objective reality that the willingness to act varied widely across the workforce. To further understand the unwillingness to pursue such an aggressive strategy requires more contextualization, principally surrounding the unwillingness of the national unions to provide meaningful official support. This is the one key feature of worker agency that may have had the power and resources to evince greater involvement in the struggle on the part of the offshore *and* onshore workforce. An anonymous FTO encapsulated the situation: "The OILC are doing our dirty work for us" (*Socialist Worker*, 18 August 1990). The OILC worked largely in parallel with the national unions – it organized the action they claimed they could not, and they undertook not to condemn the action. Indeed, something more akin to support was given but this close reciprocal relationship militated against the OILC campaigning to pressurize the unions into making the strikes official and to provide greater solidarity, a task admittedly not easy because of the existence of the Conservatives' anti-union laws. In the run-up to the strikes and during the exhilaration of the first strikes, to do so would have seem to be focusing energies and resources on the wrong target as well as "attacking the hand that feeds you."

Nonetheless, it was a necessary task in that the offshore workers needed, especially after the sackings and growing numbers on the beach, to find a way of pressurizing the companies. The most obvious recourses were to have widespread solidarity strikes by supply boat and catering workers as well as by onshore workers in the oil industry. But these actions could not be pulled out of a hat: they require long and patient campaigns led by FTOs to convince workers that they would be taking effective action and action which served their interests as well. The CSEU 1989 campaign for shorter working hours in the engineering industry in Britain is an example of such a campaign (see McKinlay and McNulty 1992). Ironically, as the OILC strategy ran into sand, the national unions took over, plowing in their resources at the point of downturn in the struggle. But, it seems, their strategy was to further wind down the struggle for recognition and make an exit from a bruising contest in which, although they were interested parties, by choice they played more the role of bystanders. This is likely to have been influenced by the national unions increasingly looking towards the re-election of Labour to government in 1992 and the hope of beneficial changes in industrial relations and employment law. In order for this to be a serious prospect, unions were encouraged not to "rock Labour's boat" with unsightly industrial action.

The preceding discussion focuses attention on the issues of strategy and tactics and particularly on the notion of what might be the most "appropriate" *modus operandi* in pursuit of stated union goals. All-out action may not be required or appropriate in all circumstances for, as the popular saying goes, "there's no point taking a sledgehammer to crack a nut." Thus, worker mobilization itself is required after the progression through the various "steps" laid out in the Introduction to this volume. But the form and character of that mobilization, in light of the employer response and the nature of the demands, are critical in determining whether the union will be successful. In the case of the offshore industry, seeking recognition from vehemently anti-union employers is potentially one of the most radical and far-reaching demands that a group of workers could make because recognition can go straight to the heart of management control and power. Granting or being forced to grant recognition entertains the prospect of ending employer unilateralism and moving towards co-deter-mination of wages, conditions, work tasks, work processes, and so on. In short, the whole gamut of issues over which management exercises control is opened up to contestation. To get to a point where this may be possible necessitates a degree of mobilization related not just to the numbers involved but also the nature of their activity and the use to which it is put. Thus, a far wider and more powerful mobilization deploying what would normally be described as more "militant" tactics would be required to effect this. By contrast, Woolfson *et al.* (1996) do little more than celebrate, albeit not romantically, the workers' struggle embodied by the OILC as a new form of effective trade union struggle on a par with the 1971 Upper Clyde Shipbuilders' struggle. Furthermore, they do not appear to recognize the import that the fairly dramatic changes in the balance of power between capital and labor since the 1970s have had on mounting such struggles in terms of the milieu of grassroots activists and worker combativity.

The story of the offshore workers' struggle for recognition is also one of the development of the OILC from a grassroots coordinating body into an bona fide independent union. The discussion and debate about the future of OILC after the 1990 strikes revolved around the issues of whether it should progress to become a new union or an offshore federation of the members of national unions. This debate revealed deep divisions between, and within, the OILC, IUOCC, and the national unions (see Woolfson *et al.* 1996: ch. 9). The AEU, EEPTU, and GMB reluctantly agreed to be part of an offshore federation under the auspices of the CSEU but the price of involvement was the exclusion of the OILC. Such a situation compelled those in the OILC to strike out as a new union. The AEU's view was that the OILC would either fail or if it grew it would reinforce employers' reasons for dealing with the AEU. In the absence of recognition, the OILC fought on safety, dismissal, and restructuring issues, and reflecting the (im)balance of power after 1990, in a defensive but dogged way. On occasions it organized its own demonstrative ballots on recognition. Its strength was that it took determined action against the odds and this reinforced the view amongst its supporters that the established unions had had their time. Its weakness was that it did not have the resources (primarily, members) to make headway against hostile employers, hostile employment law, and indifference amongst fellow unions. Put more bluntly, the established unions were the reason for the OILC's existence but also its nemesis.

But prior to this, through the OILC and its bi-monthly publication *Blowout* (which began in July 1989), offshore (production) workers developed and found a voice and an identity that was their own. The OILC became the direct and authentic representative of the offshore (production) worker – it was seen as being run by offshore workers for offshore workers. It organized mass meetings that brought the workforce together for the first time. It organized across, and within, the trade unions. In doing so, it reflected twin forces of a desire for unity amongst existing unions and the desire for a single offshore union as the *modus operandi* for effective representation offshore. This did much to overcome division and sectionalism, albeit temporarily. But without a more permanent and rooted structure the OILC remained, at this stage, a direct product of offshore workers' mood which goes "up" and "down," and which displays a sense of activity and then passivity, empowerment, and then dis-empowerment.

Conclusion

This historical case study indicates a number of important points. First, that employers of a certain predisposition in certain historical periods will not entertain recognition, seeing it as the surrender of managerial prerogative, and will use their resources accordingly. Second, to stand any chance of overcoming this, workers need not only to collectivize in sufficient numbers by building coalitions and alliances of the discontented, but also to adopt tactics which most fully deploy their industrial leverage. Third, and failing this, they and their unions become susceptible to "constrained forms" of recognition when hard-nosed employers with multi-site operations offer such terms.

Acknowledgment

Thanks are to Jake Molloy (OILC general secretary) in particular for providing access to OILC documents and publications, especially the authoritative *Striking Out!*

4 Trade union recruitment policy in Britain

Form and effects

Edmund Heery, Melanie Simms, Rick Delbridge, John Salmon, and Dave Simpson

Introduction

Aggregate trade union membership is widely acknowledged to be the product of several interacting forces (Mason and Bain 1993). Change in the macro-economic environment or in the composition of the workforce can either fan or dampen employee demand for union representation. Employers can depress demand through policies of union suppression or substitution, while the institutions of collective industrial relations supported by state policy can further inhibit or promote unionization. The actions of unions themselves can also help determine the level of membership. It has been variously argued that the level of union membership is influenced by the commitment of national leaders to a policy of expansion (Undy *et al.* 1981), the level of investment in recruitment (Voos 1984), the adoption of "union building" tactics in recruitment campaigns (Bronfenbrenner 1997), and the wider adjustment of union policy, such that it is congruent with the needs of a changing workforce (Hyman 1999). Seemingly, unions can directly determine aggregate membership, at least in part, through the supply of organization and representation. They may also indirectly influence membership by shaping the policies of employers and government, thereby removing some of the potential obstacles to unionization where demand from workers exists. Even those who have stressed the economic determinants of union membership have acknowledged that union activity can contribute to the aggregate total (Bain and Price 1983).

Given this consensus, this chapter examines national union policy on recruitment across the British trade union movement. While most workers who are actively recruited into unions join after an approach from a colleague or workplace representative (Waddington and Whitston 1997), national policy may nevertheless be significant in boosting and shaping recruitment activity at the workplace. By training activists and organizers, by promoting effective tactics, by attaching priority to recruitment and organizing, by publicizing successes, by targeting strategic non-union employers or key groups of workers, national initiatives may influence what happens on the union front-line (Charlwood 2000, Fiorito *et al.* 1995). Studies in the USA have identified the, often key, role played by external organizers in stimulating organizing and securing a successful outcome to campaigns (Milkman and Wong 2000, Voss and Sherman 2000, Zabin 2000). More generally, it is widely suggested that effective trade unionism in a decentralized system of industrial relations, like the UK's, requires the articulation of national and local activity. The focus of this chapter is very firmly on the national side of this equation. But this is not to minimize the immediate triggers to unionization or the actions of workers themselves in building trade unionism (see other chapters in this volume). National policy may stimulate and mold union recruitment but it is at the workplace that it is generally given effect.

Several aspects of national recruitment policy are considered. First, there is an attempt to gauge the extent to which national unions in Britain have adopted formal policies. We are concerned centrally here with the effects of ERA and the evidence for unions increasing their formal commitment to recruitment in the period since the passing of the Act. Second is the direction of policy and the extent to which unions seek to consolidate membership in organizations where recognition has already been achieved or expand into new territory. Again, there is consideration of the effects of ERA and the degree to which it has stimulated attempts to target non-union companies. Third are the methods of recruitment used or promoted by national unions. We examine the degree to which national policy follows three routes: the promotion of individual member services, the application of an "organizing" approach, in which membership is built around a core of lay activism, and the offer of "partnership" to employers as a means of gaining access to workers for recruitment. In so doing, we examine the evidence for these different approaches complementing or contradicting one another (see also Charlwood 2000, Heery 2002). Fourth is the nature of recruitment and organizing roles and the extent to which unions have both developed a specialist organizing function and redirected their generalist FTOs towards recruitment activity. This interest connects with the wider issue of management reform of unions and the extent to which organizational change can promote more effective union functioning (Fiorito *et al.* 1995). Fifth and last are the outcomes of national recruitment policy and the extent to which the latter has been successful in halting membership decline and securing new recognition agreements. We are also concerned with the extent to which increased recruitment may have stimulated inter-union rivalry, a definite possibility given the overlapping job territories of many UK trade unions.

The main tools used to investigate these questions are two surveys of national unions conducted in 1998 and 2001; that is before and after the passage of ERA. Survey returns were mailed to senior national officers in all TUC unions and non-TUC unions with a membership of at least 3,000. In 2001, fifty-six unions responded to the survey (60 percent; see Appendix

4.1 on pages 77–8) and these returns have been used for a cross-sectional analysis of current union policy. Of these fifty-six unions, forty-three (77 percent) provided a return in 1998 and this has allowed longitudinal analysis and an assessment of the seeming impact on national policy of legislative change. While the two surveys have provided our principal findings, they have been supplemented by an extensive program of inter- viewing with national union officers and the collection and analysis of union policy documents. We have also observed the regular meetings of the TUC's New Unionism Task Group, which has provided a central forum for the discussion and formulation of recruitment policy. Qualitative research, therefore, has supplemented and informed the interpretation of survey data.

Policy commitment

Union recruitment has been criticized in the recent past for its unsyste- matic and reactive character (Mason and Bain 1991), part of a broader penchant for "muddling through" in British industrial relations. To examine whether this was still the case the surveys sought information on the depth of formal policy commitment to recruitment and organizing. Several indicators were selected that were designed not just to identify the existence of policy but whether it was underpinned through research, specialization, budgeting, planning and review, communication, and train- ing. The aim was to establish if unions had put in place an apparatus for implementing policy and connecting national initiatives to the workplace. Data were also collected on the extent to which unions had developed a formal policy response to the new statutory recognition procedure.

The results are shown in Table 4.1, the first column of which indicates quite extensive development of formal policy. Thus, between a half and two-thirds of unions report a written policy, specialist national officer and executive committee, an annual budget, and recruitment targets that are subject to regular, quantified review. Similar percentages report the exten- sion of policy downwards through recruitment plans at regional and lower levels of organization, attempts to communicate policy through guides and journal articles and training for lay and full-time officers.[1] The only indicators with a clear minority of responses are those relating to research into worker attitudes and the response to ERA. Less than a third of unions had adopted a written policy on the response to be adopted to the new statutory recognition procedure, though half had arranged training for officers.

Comparison of the data in Table 4.1 with those from earlier research points to a clear shift towards greater policy commitment. Mason and Bain's (1991: 39) survey of 1990 indicated that, at that time, the presence of a specialist national officer, an annual budget, and "sophisticated monitor- ing" of recruitment were characteristics confined to a minority of unions.

Table 4.1 National union policy on recruitment and organizing 1998, 2001 (percentages)

	2001 All N=55	2001 Matched N=40–1	1998 Matched N=39–40
Regular discussion of recruitment at the national executive or equivalent	84	86	93
Senior officer whose main responsibility is recruitment and organizing	62	67	60
An executive sub-committee or working group that oversees recruitment	62	69	78
A written national policy on recruitment and organizing	56	67	61
Commissioned research into attitudes of employees towards membership	33	36	50
An annual recruitment or organizing budget	62	69	63
Quantified national recruitment targets	55	62	63
Periodic and quantified review of the effectiveness of recruitment policy	66	76	75
Recruitment plans at intermediate levels of union organization (e.g. region, trade group)	58	71	73
Recruitment plans at lowest levels of union organization (e.g. branch, workplace)	62	71	73
Head office monitoring of recruitment performance at lower organizational levels	53	60	78
Regular reports of recruitment in the union journal or magazine	59	57	68
A written guide to recruitment and organizing	53	62	63
Training for full-time officials in organizing methods	44	52	55
Training for lay representatives in organizing methods	56	69	78
A written policy on the union's use of the new statutory recognition procedure	31	41	n/a
Training for full-time officials in the new recognition laws	51	64	n/a

However, columns two and three of Table 4.1 present a less positive picture. They contain data from those unions that replied to both the 2001 and 1998 survey and indicate stability, not the extension, of policy in the recent past. There has been an increase in the proportion of unions reporting a written national policy, an annual budget, and planning and review procedures. But these changes are not statistically significant and are balanced by a decline in specialist executive committees, commissioned research, and head office monitoring.

This pattern of findings suggests that the key period for the development of union recruitment and organizing policy was the late 1990s, with the period since ERA witnessing some further elaboration. The interviews with union leaders supported this interpretation, with respondents in many unions reporting the adoption of formal recruitment policy in the period before 1998 (Heery *et al*. 2000c: 989). This period also saw the launching of the TUC's New Unionism initiative and the creation of the Organising Academy. It was in the period of "union exclusion" (Smith and Morton 1993) under the Conservatives, when many other policy options were closed off, that UK unions began to adopt formal recruitment policies in substantial numbers.

Policy direction

British trade unions have also been criticized for their conservative orientation in recruitment and neglect of attempts to draw new groups of workers into membership (Beaumont and Harris 1990). A striking finding from the Workplace Industrial Relations Survey is the absence of any attempt at recruitment at most non-union establishments (Millward *et al*. 1992: 69). To gauge whether this criticism is still warranted the surveys asked unions to identify their recruitment priorities along three dimensions. Following Kelly and Heery (1989), they asked whether recruitment was restricted to the consolidation of membership in workplaces covered by recognition or whether it also embraced attempts at expansion. Following Wever (1998), they asked if unions were pursuing a policy of "enlargement" and directing recruitment at groups who were often not targeted before (women, the young, and minorities). Finally, the surveys asked if part-time and contingent workers were the focus of recruitment, reflecting the increased incidence of "non-standard" employment.

Table 4.2 shows the percentages of unions reporting whether different categories of worker were accorded "high" recruitment priority in 2001 and 1998. The results for 2001 indicate strongly that consolidation in workplaces with recognition is the primary recruitment objective of UK unions. "Close consolidation," recruiting workers doing the same jobs in the same establishments as existing members, and "distant consolidation," recruiting the same type of worker but at new sites in the same organization, are the most frequently reported recruitment priorities. Just under half of unions,

Table 4.2 Groups accorded high recruitment priority 1998, 2001 (percentages)

	2001 All unions N=50–4	2001 Matched unions N=40–2	1998 Matched unions N=38–9
Employees in the same establishment doing the same work as union members	87	91	92
Employees doing the same work as union members but at different sites	72	74	82
Employees in the same establishment but doing different work to union members	42	41	36
Employees doing the same work as union members for non-union employers	47	42	35
Employees doing different work to union members and working for non-union employers	8	5	10
Workers in new industries (e.g. call centers, bio-technology)	24	24	18
Workers in new firms (e.g. inward investors)	18	18	18
Part-time workers	52	56	71
Workers on temporary or fixed-term contracts	44	44	55
Agency labor/sub-contractors	16	15	18
Students/trainees	39	41	26
Women workers	65	68	82
Young workers	54	62	71
Workers with disability	39	38	45
Gay and lesbian workers	42	43	47
Members of ethnic minorities	48	50	61

however, report a commitment to "close expansion," recruiting new types of worker at sites with recognition, and to "distant expansion," recruitment of workers in non-union companies. The focus of the latter, however, is very much on workers who share the characteristics of existing members (cf. Gall 2000c). Only a small percentage of unions report a strong commitment to breaking into new job territories and new firms.

On the second dimension there is evidence of union commitment to a policy of "enlargement." Thus, two-thirds of unions declare a commitment to recruiting women workers, a slightly smaller percentage claim young workers as a key target, and substantial percentages report targeting ethnic minorities, gays and lesbians, and workers with disability. Declared intent may not always be reflected in practice but the results indicate that many unions have embraced the need to represent diverse interests and identities at work (cf. Colgan 1999, Howell 1996). There is also evidence of many unions according priority to the recruitment of workers with "non-standard" contracts. Part-time workers, temporary workers, and students and trainees are particularly likely to be identified as recruitment targets.

Although the surveys in 2001 and 1998 show the same broad pattern of recruitment priorities, there are some intriguing differences that point to significant shifts in union policy under the influence of ERA. Comparison of columns two and three in Table 4.2 suggests that more unions are now adopting policies of expansion, targeting non-union organizations and new types of worker at sites with recognition. The only exception to this pattern is the seeming decline in the small number of unions that report targeting employees doing *different work* to union members at *non-union* sites. However, these results are misleading. If one adds together unions reporting a "high" and a "moderate" priority to recruiting this group then the figure for 2001 is 32 percent while that for 1998 is 18 percent. There is evidence of unions becoming more ambitious in their selection of recruitment targets over time.

The cost of this reorientation is a shift away from targeting women, minorities, and those on non-standard contracts: between the two surveys there is a decline in the percentage of unions attaching a high priority to recruiting these groups. The only notable exception is the marked increase in unions targeting students and trainees. Working students, in particular, have become a significant target of union recruitment in the past few years. The pattern of change in the data suggests that policies of consolidation have often taken the form of prioritizing the recruitment of minority workers neglected by unions in the past. As new opportunities for expansion have arisen as a result of ERA, however, less emphasis has been attached to this activity. Unions have become more focused on extending organization to non-union sites and particularly to those sites that employ workers who are similar to the existing membership.

Recruitment methods

It has been argued with increasing frequency that success in union organizing is dependent on the methods used (Bronfenbrenner 1997, Fisk *et al.* 2000). However, there is no consensus about which methods are most likely to yield results. One argument is that contingent, managerial, and professional workers are likely to be attracted by the provision of consumer, security, and labor market services that are consumed away from the workplace and which support workers through a mobile career (Osterman *et al.* 2001:

111–14, 117–19). A second argument is that unions must "organize the employer" and use the offer of labor-management partnership to obtain recognition and management-sponsored access to potential recruits. Such an approach might accord with the seeming preference of many employees for non-adversarial employment relations (Cohen and Hurd 1998) and, more controversially, endow partnership unions with advantage in a multi-union competition for recognition (Gall and McKay 2001: 104–6). Finally, adherents of the "organizing model" assert that enduring membership is built through reviving collective organization at work, which in turn requires the application of a series of "union-building" techniques and resort to alliances with community and other movements to overcome likely employer resistance to organizing campaigns. This approach has influenced recent organizing in the USA and Australia and has also informed the training at the Organising Academy (Heery *et al.* 2000b).

Evidence for the incidence of each of these methods of recruitment is shown in Table 4.3, which also presents findings on unions' use of the new statutory recognition and representation procedures. The most striking finding in the table is that all three approaches – servicing, partnership, and organizing – are present and being applied by considerable proportions of UK unions. Thus, with regard to servicing, a sizable minority of unions report that they "frequently" stress consumer services in recruitment, while smaller but non-trivial percentages emphasize security and labor market services. In addition, between a quarter and a third of unions report use of direct marketing techniques, like direct mail and subscription discounts, which target the individual union "consumer." Moreover, while direct email is a method used frequently by only a small percentage of unions, most (78 percent) now offer the facility to join through the union's website, another essentially individualized method of recruitment.

Employer-supported recruitment also features prominently. Half the sample report frequent recruitment at employee induction and about a fifth state that they have used partnership agreements with employers as a basis for recruiting new members. A similar fraction report that "partnership with employers" is stressed in the approach to new members, with a slightly smaller number emphasizing employer support for the union. Other data, not shown in the table, indicate that just over a quarter of unions have a "written policy of social partnership to secure recognition agreements from previously non-union employers." In most cases this is of recent standing, adopted in the three years prior to the survey.

Evidence for use of an organizing approach is spread across a broader set of indicators and tells a more complex story. Several techniques for building workplace trade union organization appear to have been quite widely adopted, including mapping, one-to-one and like-to-like recruitment, the use of events and grievances to promote a union campaign, and the involvement of activists through an organizing committee or in groups of volunteers directed at non-union sites. There is also evidence of an organizing

Table 4.3 Methods of recruitment 1998, 2001 (percentages)

Recruitment approach	2001 All unions N=51–6	2001 Matched unions N=40–3	1998 Matched unions N=41–3
Method used or message stressed "frequently"			
Individual servicing:			
Attractive consumer services	39	38	(81)[1]
Labor market services	15	17	–
Union stakeholder pension scheme	15	17	–
Membership cost effective	64	63	–
Direct mail to non-members	34	30	29
Direct email to non-members	6	5	–
Subscription discount	30	29	18
Recruitment incentive	26	26	12
Partnership:			
Presence at employee induction	50	57	44
Partnership agreements to encourage recruitment	21	24	–
Recruitment stresses partnership	20	21	24
Employer support for membership	16	19	17
Organizing approach:			
Rating of non-members (mapping)	27	34	5
One-to-one recruitment	81	88	71
House calls	4	2	0
Use of an organizing committee	28	31	22
Grievance-based recruitment	31	34	29
Raising union profile through petitions, surveys, displays, demos	52	55	45
Link-up with community bodies	11	12	3
Public campaigns for recognition	6	7	5
Like-to-like recruitment	35	40	33
Corporate campaigning	2	2	–
Direct recruitment by activists away from own workplace	26	31	–
Worker solidarity	37	41	31
Membership a democratic right	34	35	41
Participate in union democracy	33	35	29
Resolve own problems through collective organization	32	37	41
Need for "justice and respect"	39	44	33
Use of ERA procedures:			
Use of procedure to recruit	25	32	–
Use of procedure to secure voluntary recognition	28	37	–
Use of individual representation procedure to access workplaces	13	17	–
Legal support for membership	32	33	–

Note: [1]The wording of this question changed between 1998 and 2001. In 1998 unions were asked if their recruitment emphasized "attractive individual services," while in 2001 they were asked if it stressed "attractive consumer services (e.g. financial discount)."

message being used in recruitment. About a third of unions report frequently stressing collective values of solidarity, participation, and self-organization and a similar percentage report using a language of democratic rights and "justice and respect." Other elements of the organizing approach are less commonly used, particularly those that seek to extend union activity beyond the workplace (cf. Heery *et al.* 2000c). House calls, community involvement, public campaigns against anti-union employers, and corporate campaigns that target shareholders or consumers are not widely employed, though a small minority of unions does report that these methods are central. The data indicate an uneven take-up of the "organizing model" in the UK with greatest use of those methods that accord with the indigenous tradition of relatively active workplace trade unionism.

The final approach on which data are presented in Table 4.3 is use of the new statutory recognition and representation procedures. The findings echo those in Table 4.1, in that deliberate use of the new procedures is confined to a minority of unions. About a quarter of unions report that they have "frequently" used the statutory recognition procedure to secure voluntary recognition and encourage recruitment. A slightly higher percentage report that the new legal supports for membership and recognition have formed part of their recruitment message, suggesting that one of the main benefits of the new procedures is to raise the legitimacy of unions in the eyes of potential members. The least used element of the new legal framework is the right of representation. Only 13 percent of unions report frequent use of this procedure to gain access to workplaces for recruitment, despite union hopes that these regulations would furnish a fresh opportunity for organizing.

The other striking finding in Table 4.3 is that the three main methods of recruitment are increasing in frequency. It is not the case that organizing, partnership, or servicing is increasing in popularity at the expense of the other two. There is some evidence for a declining stress on member services but this probably reflects a change from a broader to a more specific question between the two surveys. What is apparent is that direct email, subscription discounts, and incentive payments for members who recruit their co-workers, that is recruitment methods that target individuals, are becoming more common. The same is true for recruitment at induction, an indicator of employer support for union membership. Several of the techniques associated with an organizing approach are also being used more frequently: mapping the workplace was a fairly rare technique in 1998 but by 2001 a third of unions reported that it was part of their basic repertoire. Other organizing methods that have become more common include use of an organizing committee, the use of events, petitions, and displays to raise the union profile and link-up with community bodies. What the pattern suggests is that unions are becoming more sophisticated and more likely to use systematic methods whatever broad approach to recruitment they adopt. It is notable in this respect that the "messages" stressed in recruitment, such as partnership with the employer or the need to resolve problems through effective organization, show less change over time than do the data on methods. It seems that we are witnessing a shift in technique, not in the philosophy, of union recruitment.

Evidence of continued use of different approaches to recruitment raises the questions of whether different unions favor different methods or if different methods are combined in the recruitment activity of a single union. To explore this issue, statistically reliable scales were derived from each of the four sets of indicators shown in Table 4.3. These were then correlated with one another to identify whether the various approaches to recruitment were being used by the same or by different unions.[2] If the latter, then one would expect a pattern of inverse correlation, if the former, one would anticipate a positive correlation. The results are shown in Table 4.4 and indicate strongly that individual unions are using a combination of approaches to recruitment. Thus, although a servicing approach is only weakly correlated with the other approaches, there are strong statistically significant associations between reliance on partnership, organizing, and use of the new statutory procedures. The association between partnership and organizing is particularly striking because these are often presented as opposing methods of recruitment (Heery 2002). Of course they may contradict one another in practice but many unions use both methods, perhaps because they apply partnership and organizing to different types of worker. An indication that this might be the case is the presence of a positive correlation (0.39, sig 0.006) between the "openness" of union structure (i.e. a job territory that straddles occupational, enterprise, sector, and industry boundaries) and a combined "score" for use of organizing and partnership. More open unions are more likely to report a combination of approaches.

Recruitment roles

The key resource that national unions can deploy towards recruitment and organizing are their paid officers. UK unions employ in the region of 3,000 union officers (Kelly and Heery 1994: 38) and the surveys sought inform-

Table 4.4 Correlation matrix of approaches to member recruitment

	Mean	S.D.	Alpha	Servic-ing	Partner-ship	Organ-ising	Use of ERA
Servicing scale	2.48	0.59	0.649	–	–	–	–
Partnership scale	2.56	0.84	0.747	0.260	–	–	–
Organizing scale	2.51	0.61	0.882	0.272	0.649**	–	–
ERA scale	2.42	1.03	0.900	0.347*	0.617**	0.684**	–

Notes: * Correlation is significant at the 0.05 level
      ** Correlation is significant at the 0.01 level

ation on two possible developments. On the one hand, they examined the extent to which there has been specialization of the officer workforce, such that an increasing number of unions employ dedicated recruiters or organizers. They also sought to establish the broad outline of the role these specialists perform and the extent to which they have been directed at securing new recognition agreements under the shadow of ERA. On the other hand, the surveys examined the extent and nature of the involvement in recruitment of the majority of generalist officers. The object here was to identify if recruitment is being "mainstreamed," with officers being encouraged through the union management system to attach greater priority to this aspect of their work. We were also interested in the relationship between these two organizational responses. Is it the case that specialization and mainstreaming are combined, perhaps with specialists and generalists performing different tasks? Or have unions differed in their deployment of officer resources, with some creating a new body of specialist organizers while others have concentrated on shifting the priorities of their existing workforce?

In 2001, twenty-eight unions (50 percent) reported employing "specialist recruiters/organizers who spend the majority of their working time on recruitment and organizing." There is strong evidence of specialization, therefore, and also evidence of specialization increasing over time. Among unions replying to both surveys, 56 percent reported specialist officers in 2001 compared to only 38 percent in 1998. This is a striking development over a short period and in part reflects the influence of the TUC's Organising Academy. There was a positive association (0.50, sig 0.000) between employment of specialists in 2001 and involvement in the Academy in the three preceding years.

Table 4.5 presents data on the activities of specialists that were regarded as "very important" by their employing unions. Direct recruitment of new members is the activity most frequently identified but in most unions it seems that the work of specialists extends beyond work of this kind and includes "organizing." Thus, three-quarters of unions stress the role of specialists in encouraging lay activists to recruit and two-thirds say they promote workplace organization and train activists in recruitment methods. Unions involved in the Organising Academy were particularly likely to report an organizing role for specialists, suggesting that the Academy has helped diffuse an organizing approach.[3] The table also indicates that in some unions their work spills beyond recruitment and organizing to include negotiation and representation. This is a minority pattern, however, and the main activity of specialists appears to focus on building membership and collective organization.

Comparison of the matched data for 1998 and 2001 indicates broadly similar patterns in the two years. Some changes are apparent but the small number of cases for 1998 means that caution must be exercised in interpreting the results. What they suggest is that there has been some de-

Table 4.5 Activities of specialist organizers, 1998 and 2001

	2001 All unions N=28	2001 Matched unions N=24	1998 Matched unions N=16
	Percentage saying "very important"		
Direct recruitment of new members	82	83	80
Encouraging recruitment by workplace representatives	79	83	100
Planning recruitment/organizing campaigns	75	79	94
Promoting workplace organization (e.g. identifying new representatives)	68	71	69
Training lay representatives in recruitment	64	67	50
Identifying workplaces with potential for recruitment	64	71	75
Involvement in union campaigns that seek to use ERA to secure recognition	32	38	–
Negotiating with employers over recognition arrangements	29	29	13
Representation of individual employees in grievance or disciplinary cases	26	30	25
Negotiation with employers of terms and conditions of employment	21	21	13
Involvement in union campaigns (other than recruitment)	11	13	25
Administrative support to union branches	7	8	27

emphasis of organizing, planning, and involvement in supporting branches and general union campaigning. This has been balanced by increased attention to negotiation, particularly the negotiation of recognition arrangements. It seems that the new opportunities for recognition that have appeared in the wake of ERA have altered the work pattern of at least some specialist organizers. In fact, the table indicates that about a third of unions have involved specialists in ERA campaigns. Clearly specialists in a substantial number of unions concentrate on "in-fill" activity where the union is already recognized. In a substantial minority of cases, however, they are involved in attempts to extend into non-union territory and the employment of specialists is correlated, albeit at a modest level, with a policy of expansion (0.43, sig 0.003) and a more active response to ERA (0.33, sig 0.016).[4]

The findings from questions on the recruitment activity of generalist officers are shown in Table 4.6. For a substantial number of unions, it seems that recruitment is not a "very important" component: encouraging recruitment by workplace representatives is the only item for which there is a substantial majority of positive responses. In many unions the work of officers continues to be defined mainly by activities, such as collective bargaining, joint consultation, and representing and advising individual workers (cf. Kelly and Heery 1994). It seems also that the involvement of generalists is more indirect than that of specialists. Direct recruitment is an important function but only in a minority of unions, while identifying targets and planning campaigns have greater relative importance. So does the negotiation of recognition agreements and this is reported as "very important" by a majority of unions for generalists but by only a minority for specialists. Moreover, this indirect role is becoming more pronounced. The matched data for 1998 and 2001 suggest that generalists are becoming less involved in identifying recruitment, targets, direct recruitment and the training of lay representatives. The seeming reason is that they are becoming more involved in the management of specialists who presumably are taking on these activities in their stead.

The surveys also gathered information on the techniques used by unions to support or promote organizing activity by generalist officers (see Table 4.7). It indicates that, while promotion on the basis of organizing expertise remains a minority phenomenon, a substantial body of unions has

Table 4.6 Organizing activities of generalist union officers, 1998 and 2001

	2001 All unions N=52–5	2001 Matched unions N=42–3	1998 Matched unions N=41
	Percentage saying "very important"		
Encouraging recruitment by workplace representatives	74	74	78
Promoting workplace organization (e.g. identifying activists)	57	61	61
Identifying workplaces with potential for recruitment	55	58	73
Negotiating recognition arrangements with employers	55	58	59
Planning recruitment campaigns	52	49	54
Direct recruitment of new members	47	47	59
Training representatives in recruitment	41	44	54
Managing specialist recruitment or organizing officers	27	26	7

Table 4.7 Techniques to encourage organizing by union officers, 1998 and 2001

	2001 All unions N=52–3	2001 Matched unions N=42–3	1998 Matched unions N=37–8
	Percentage reporting use of technique		
Briefing sessions on organizing	62	65	74
Requirement to identify recruitment targets	53	60	66
Regular monitoring of officers' performance as recruiters/organizers	50	49	34
Training for officers in organizing	50	50	63
Research support for officers' organizing activity	50	57	68
Assessment of organizing competence in selecting new officers	47	50	48
Requirement to devote a set proportion of time to recruitment/organizing	40	42	51
Promotion based on record of organizing	14	14	8

established internal management systems to encourage organizing. These include "softer" management techniques (e.g. briefing sessions, training, allocation of research support, and tests of organizing competence in officer selection) and "harder," performance-oriented measures (e.g. the requirement to identify targets and devote time and the regular monitoring of recruitment and organizing activity). Indeed, the latter technique is the only one, apart from promotion, that has increased in prevalence since 1998. Union management of recruitment and organizing is seemingly becoming more hard-edged. A more elaborate system for managing organizing, moreover, is associated with a more elaborate account of the generalists' organizing role. Unions that report that generalists are more involved in organizing also report using several techniques to support and direct that activity.[5]

To what extent are reliance on specialist and generalist organizers, alternative or complementary strategies? Analysis suggested that there is a weak positive association but that this is not statistically significant: the employment of specialists was correlated with more active involvement of generalists but only at a very modest level. It was not the case that unions that had failed to appoint specialists had been more active in directing generalist officers towards organizing activity. There was a strong association, however, between a particular dimension of specialist and generalist roles. In thirteen unions, it was reported that direct recruitment of new members was a "very important" aspect of the work of both specialists and generalists (0.604, sig 0.001). These tended to be unions that experienced difficulty in maintaining workplace organization because their members are mobile, often temporary or freelance, or include substantial bodies of part-time service workers. The roles of specialists and generalists converge therefore where there is an "organization gap" amongst the union membership.

Recruitment outcomes

So far we have examined union "inputs" in the form of recruitment policies, targets, methods, and roles. To conclude we want to consider recruitment outcomes and assess whether the increased investment of unions is resulting in increasing membership. National data on union membership indicate that the long decline through the 1980s and 1990s has been halted and there has also been a notable improvement in achieving recognition from employers (Gall 2000c, Gall and McKay 2001, Sneade 2001). It is apparent that trade unions have been performing better in organizing terms during a period that has seen the elaboration of national recruitment policy. We want to assess whether these two developments are associated.

The first task is to identify measures of union organizing success. Four have been chosen on the basis of the availability of data and the need to examine the separate dimensions of recruitment and recognition. In addition, a fifth outcome measure has been used, which taps the extent to which increased recruitment has had the perverse effect of stimulating greater inter-union rivalry. The five measures are as follows:

- *Membership change 1997–2000.* The change in total membership during the period since Labour's election to power for all unions surveyed in 2001. These and other membership data were taken from the annual handbooks of the TUC and, for non-TUC unions, from the records of the Certification Office. A total of thirty-six unions (65 percent) reported an increase in membership between 1997 and 2000. In comparison, the years before the 1998 survey (1994–8) saw only eleven unions (26 percent) record an increase in membership.
- *Female membership change 1997–2000.* An equivalent figure for the change in female membership, included because of the high formal priority attached to recruiting women by most unions. Thirty-eight unions (68 percent) recorded an increase in women's membership in 1997–2000 compared with only sixteen (38 percent) that did so between 1994 and 1998.
- *The number of annual increases in membership 1997–2000.* The purpose of this measure was to identify those unions experiencing a sustained increase in membership. Accordingly, unions were scored for each annual increase in the period 1997–2000. A quarter (fourteen unions) had the maximum score of three successive increases, while a similar proportion (23 percent, thirteen unions) recorded a score of zero.

- *ERA success scale*. The fourth indicator used data from the 2001 survey to examine the specific issue of union success in using the procedures introduced by ERA. It took the form of a statistically reliable scale (alpha=0.897) derived from two questionnaire items. The first asked unions to agree or disagree that, "The new procedure is helping my union secure recognition agreements from employers." Thirty unions (67 percent) replied in the affirmative to this statement, with 21 percent agreeing "strongly." The second item asked unions if, "The new right of representation is helping my union recruit workers in non-union firms." In this case, twenty-three unions (45 percent) responded positively, with eight (16 percent) stating that they agreed strongly with the statement.
- *Union competition*. The final measure also used data from the questionnaire to gauge if ERA was prompting inter-union competition. Unions were asked to judge the truth of the statement that, "The introduction of the statutory recognition procedure has intensified inter-union competition for members." Twenty-nine unions (53 percent) reported that it was true at least "to some extent," suggesting that union rivalry has increased to an appreciable degree as a result of the new statutory framework.

While these five measures encompass a range of recruitment outcomes, their deficiencies should not be ignored. The data on trends in membership are for a limited period and are influenced by a range of factors other than national recruitment policy, while the fourth and fifth measures are subjective and taken from the same source as the estimates of policy. It should also be noted that there is no measure of union "organizing," in the specific sense of establishing or strengthening collective organization at the workplace. The five measures reflect the limits of available data and the results reported below should be treated with due caution.

The independent variables included in the analysis consisted of three measures of recruitment policy and five controls that captured structural characteristics of unions that might influence membership trends and organizing success. The three policy measures were the employment of specialists, the scale measuring the adoption of an "organizing approach" and the scale measuring the commitment of unions to a policy of expansion. These were chosen because the level of inter-correlation was modest[6] and because they reflected distinct aspects of policy, specialization, method, and orientation. The five controls comprised union size (total membership in 2000), dummy variables for a predominantly private sector and managerial and professional membership, the percentage female membership in 2001, and a measure of union structure, in which unions were scored if their job territory embraced multiple enterprises, occupations, industries, and sectors.

The results of OLS regressions for all five outcome-measures are shown in Table 4.8. The first three columns present the findings for the measures of membership trends and suggest three primary conclusions. First, in many cases union membership growth is "received," rather than created, by virtue of an expanding job territory. Thus, membership growth in successive years and an increase in women members are features of professional and managerial unions and probably reflect the growth and gradual feminization of these forms of employment. Second, policy can be the product of membership change and not the reverse. There is a negative association between a policy of expansion and increasing membership, which suggests that crisis has stimulated policy innovation. However, another feature of union policy is positively associated with membership change. An increase in total membership is linked to the employment of specialists and the t-values for increasing women's membership and for a sustained increase point in the same direction. It may be that growing unions have the wherewithal or confidence to recruit specialists. It is equally likely, however, that investment in specialists pays off and the third conclusion that can be drawn is that those unions that have committed resources to recruitment have reaped some benefit.

The final two columns report patterns of association for the subjective reports of recruitment outcomes. They indicate that success in using ERA is associated with specific policy inputs: unions that report use of an organizing approach and a policy of expansion are more likely to report success in using ERA. There is also a positive association with the employment of specialists but it is not statistically significant. Union reports of inter-union conflict as a result of ERA are associated with a policy of expansion but not with other measures of union policy: it is unions that are seeking to extend their job territory that are experiencing most rivalry. However, expansion is not the strongest predictor of conflict. The percentage of women members exhibits a stronger association. Unions with a high number of women in membership are more likely to report inter-union rivalry, perhaps reflecting competition to expand into female job territories.

The measures of recruitment outcomes used in Table 4.8 are not ideal and do not cover all aspects of union activity. Neither have they been triangulated through a test of national policy using data collected at workplace level. Nevertheless, the analysis provides support for the belief that policy inputs can influence outcomes. The employment of specialists, perhaps the simplest indicator of union investment in organizing, is associated with membership growth and to a lesser degree with success in using ERA. The latter is linked much more strongly, however, to use of systematic methods of union organizing and a commitment to expand into non-union territory. These findings broadly parallel those of Charlwood's (2000) analysis. This used similar measures of union policy, taken from the 1998 union head office survey, and found an association with reports in the Workplace Employee Relations Survey of organizing success at non-union establishments. In combination, the two sets of findings point to the importance of national policy in extending trade union organization.

Table 4.8 Factors associated with recruitment outcomes 2001, OLS regression

	Regression 1 Membership increase 1997–2000		Regression 2 Female increase 1997–2000		Regression 3 Sustained increase 1997–2000		Regression 4 Success in using ERA		Regression 5 Inter-union competition	
	Beta	T	Beta	T	Beta	T	Beta	T	Beta	T
Union size	0.214	1.030	0.010	0.050	0.181	0.832	−0.177	−1.078	−0.036	−0.197
Union structure	−0.321	−1.238	0.128	0.503	−0.203	−0.747	0.295	1.421	0.346	1.525
Percentage women members	−0.083	−0.393	−0.037	−0.179	0.236	1.075	0.081	0.498	0.379	2.118**
Main occupation (1=managl. or profssl.)	0.181	0.740	0.525	2.192**	0.456	1.784*	0.141	0.758	−0.148	−0.690
Main sector (1=private sector)	−0.008	−0.036	0.364	1.653	0.218	0.926	−0.029	−0.173	0.074	0.377
Employment of specialists	0.364	2.133**	0.283	1.689*	0.181	1.015	0.217	1.596	0.017	0.115
Organizing approach	0.006	0.033	−0.019	−0.108	0.030	0.161	0.430	3.131***	0.064	0.407
Expansion	−0.386	−2.063**	−0.379	−2.064**	−0.138	−0.706	0.296	2.043**	0.326	1.972*
Adjusted R Square	0.164		0.070		0.086		0.517		0.377	

Notes: *Significant at 0.10; **Significant at 0.05; ***Significant at 0.01.

Conclusion

This chapter has used survey data from national trade unions to review recent developments in recruitment and organizing policy. Perhaps three broad conclusions can be drawn from the findings that have relevance to the wider debate over labor revitalization. The first concerns the origins of recruitment activity and its relationship to state policy. In social movement theory, which increasingly influences the analysis of trade unions, it is common to trace the birth and degree of success of social movements to the structure of opportunities afforded by the state (McAdam *et al.* 1996: 2–3, cf. Kelly 1998: 37). Following this line of reasoning, one would expect national policy to have emerged to exploit the opportunity for recruitment provided by the new statutory procedure for securing recognition. In fact, the pattern of change is more complex. Key developments in formal policy occurred before the new law was passed and, indeed, before Labour was elected to government. It was in a period of "union exclusion," of declining political opportunities, that UK unions turned initially to recruitment and organizing, a pattern that has also been seen in North America, Australia, and New Zealand (Heery *et al.* 2001). Policy has been refined and further developed under the influence of ERA but it was not the primary trigger. It seems that national leaders of trade unions turn to organizing, to the renewal of the structures of mobilization to use the term favored by social movement theorists, when access to other resources is closed off.

Not only is social movement theory being used to analyze union revitalization, but it is also argued that revitalization requires unions to act as social movements, mobilizing employees in "contentious politics" and campaigns for workplace justice (Hyman 2001: 60–2, cf. Kelly 1998). Transposed to the field of organizing, this prescription suggests that unions should apply a version of the "organizing model," in which membership is rebuilt or extended by mobilizing workers in activist-led, militant campaigns (Bronfenbrenner 1997). There is evidence of this prescription being followed in the UK and the data collected on methods used and on the roles of specialists point to an emphasis on "organizing" or "union-building" and not simply recruitment. As such, it supports Hyman's judgment (2001: 61) that the recent past has seen attempts by most European trade union movements to "recapture the role of a social movement." Equally apparent, however, is the uneven adoption of an organizing approach and the fact that it sits alongside other forms of recruitment that target employers and the individual union consumer. Unions, it seems, are assuming multiple identities and are pragmatic not principled in the methods they use. The question that is raised by this finding but which cannot be answered through a national survey is whether there are several ways to restore membership, not a single approach as suggested by advocates of the organizing model. Unions use a plurality of overlapping and even contradictory methods of recruitment and further research is needed to assess the effectiveness of each and the types of circumstance to which they are suited.

Our analysis provides some evidence for the efficacy of organizing unionism, in that reports of reliance on organizing methods are associated with reports of success in using the new recognition and representation procedures. Perhaps the most heartening, though most tentative, findings from the analysis are those that point to the successful outcomes of recruitment policy. There is evidence that investment in specialists is associated with increasing membership and application of organizing methods and a commitment to expansion have led to greater success in using ERA. The cost of a more active recruitment policy has often been increased inter-union rivalry but the main thrust of the findings is that organizing can work for unions and help reverse decline. As such, our research contributes to a growing body of work that has identified the independent effect of union policy on union membership (cf. Bronfenbrenner 1997, Charlwood 2000, Fiorito et al. 1995, Undy et al. 1981, Yates 2000). Clearly, the framework of public policy and the response of employers powerfully determine aggregate union membership but the research record indicates the distinct contribution of union action. It may be that British unions should and could accord higher priority to organizing and that much leadership-sponsored activity is ill-conceived, poorly implemented, or half-hearted (Carter 2000, Upchurch and Danford 2001). But the research lends support to the belief that unions are architects, in part, of their own destiny and that national policy can contribute to revitalization in the specific senses of restoring membership and winning new recognition agreements. Unions, it suggests, should be viewed as strategic actors that interact with their environment and can shape their own future.

Acknowledgment

Thanks to Jack Fiorito and Gregor Gall for helpful comments on an earlier draft, to all the trade union officers who completed our questionnaires and agreed to be interviewed, and to Frances O'Grady of the TUC for helping to boost the response rate. We would also like to express our gratitude to Cardiff Business School for research funding.

Notes

1 Perhaps unsurprisingly, the development of formal policy was a feature of larger unions (0.369, sig 0.006) and more open unions (0.402, sig 0.002), that have the wherewithal, incentive, and opportunity to engage in structured recruitment activity. The measure of policy commitment was a statistically reliable scale (alpha=0.853) based on the first fifteen items reported in Table 4.1. It should also be noted that this scale was not just related to the structural dimensions of trade unions. There were fairly strong associations between policy commitment and membership of the TUC's Organising Academy (0.507, sig 0.000) and a report that "We have learnt new methods of recruiting from unions in other countries" (0.541, sig 0.000). Policy development in this field appears to be a function of involvement in inter-union networks and union openness to learning from outside (Heery et al. 2000c).

2 Of course there are some important differences between unions. It was noticeable that recruitment on the basis of labor market services, such as provision of
information on job opportunities, was a feature of professional and managerial
unions. A stress on security benefits, such as stakeholder pensions, on the other
hand, was a feature of unions with a substantial freelance membership.
3 A statistically reliable "organizing scale" was computed from four items in Table
4.5, those referring to encouragement and training of lay recruiters, the identification of activists, and the planning of campaigns (alpha=0.843). This scale
was correlated positively with involvement in the Academy (0.57, sig 0.001). It
was also correlated at a fairly high level with a report that unions had been
"strongly influenced by the "organizing model" from Australia and the US"
(0.472, sig 0.013).
4 Expansion was measured using a scale derived from the data in Table 4.2. The
scale added responses to questions on the priority attached to recruiting in non-
union firms, new industries, and new firms (alpha=0.756). The response to ERA
was measured using the scale shown in Table 4.4.
5 Scales were created from the data in Tables 4.6 and 4.7 to perform this test. The
measure of the depth of officers' organizing role was created by adding all items
in Table 4.5 other than involvement in direct recruitment (alpha=0.858). The
measure of union management, on the other hand, was derived from all items
in Table 4.7 other than those relating to promotion and research support
(alpha=0.865). The correlation coefficient was 0.62 (sig 0.000).
6 Specialization was correlated with expansion at 0.43 and with use of organizing
techniques at 0.39. Organising and expansion were correlated at 0.35.

Appendix 4.1

List of trade unions that provided a return to the 2001 survey

ACM	Association of College Management
AEEU	Amalgamated Engineering and Electrical Union*
ALGUS	Alliance and Leicester Group Union of Staff*
AMO	Association of Magisterial Officers*
ANSA	Abbey National Staff Association*
ASLEF	Associated Society of Locomotive Engineers and Firemen*
AEP	Association of Educational Psychologists
AFA	Association of Flight Attendants
ATL	Association of Teachers and Lecturers*
AUT	Association of University Teachers*
BDA	British Dental Association
BFAWU	Bakers, Food and Allied Workers Union*
BSU	Britannia Staff Union
BACM-TEAM	British Association of Colliery Management – Technical, Energy and Administrative Management
BALPA	British Air-Line Pilots Association
BECTU	Broadcasting, Entertainment, Cinematograph and Theatre Union*
CATU	Ceramic and Allied Trades Union
Connect	The union for professionals in communications*
CSP	Chartered Society of Physiotherapy*
CWU	Communication Workers' Union*

EIS	Educational Institute of Scotland*
EMA	Engineers and Managers' Association*
Equity	British Actors' Equity Association*
GMB*	General, Municipal, Boilermakers and Allied Trade Union
GPMU	Graphical, Paper and Media Union*
GSA	Guinness Staff Association
HCSA	Hospital Consultants and Specialists Association
IUHS	Independent Union of Halifax Staff*
IPMS	Institution of Professionals, Managers and Specialists*
KFAT	National Union of Knitwear, Footwear and Apparel Trades*
MSF	Manufacturing, Science, Finance*
MU	Musicians' Union*
NACO	National Association of Co-operative Officials*
NAHT	National Association of Head Teachers*
NATFHE	The University and College Lecturers'' Union*
NGSU	Nationwide Group Staff Union
NUJ	National Union of Journalists*
NULMW	National Union of Lock and Metal Workers*
NUMAST	National Union of Marine, Aviation and Shipping Transport Officers
PAT	Professional Association of Teachers*
POA	Prison Officers' Association
RBA	Retail Book Association*
RCM	Royal College of Midwives*
RMT	National Union of Rail, Maritime and Transport Workers*
SHA	Secondary Heads' Association
SocAuth	Society of Authors*
SSTA	Scottish Secondary Teachers' Association*
T&G	Transport and General Workers' Union*
TSSA	Transport Salaried Staffs' Association*
UCAC	Undeb Cenedlaethol Athrawon Cymru*
UFS	Union of Finance Staff*
UNIFI*	Union for Staff in Financial Services
UCATT	Union of Construction, Allied Trades and Technicians
USDAW	Union of Shop, Distributive and Allied Workers*
UNISON*	Public Sector Union
WGGB	Writers' Guild of Great Britain

Notes: * Union also provided a return in 1998.

5 Employer opposition to union recognition

Gregor Gall

Introduction

With the arrival of the ERA, the issue of union recognition has now returned to the top of the industrial relations agenda in Britain. So too has the issue of employer opposition to it. This should come as no great surprise given the role of employers, in general, in the last twenty or so years in helping to account for both the more hostile environment in which unions operate and the decline of union membership and influence in British society. The imminence, presence, and use of the statutory mechanisms has created both a real and potential backlash against the tide of "managerial Thatcherism" that has increasingly come to dominate the way in which employers determine workplace relations in Britain. The backlash is "real" where a large number of campaigns for recognition have been won and are under way as well as where the statutory mechanisms are used and threatened, and "potential" where management may yet face campaigns and may tailor their behavior to meet this. Consequently, for the first time in over two decades the prerogative of management is being challenged in a significant manner, and with some legal support.

Employers, Kelly (1998) argues, will also make some of the same type of calculations as workers and unions, and their actions can also be seen in the same terms as mobilization theory suggests. This is particularly so in terms of definition of interests, opportunities to act, costs and benefits to acting as well as the acts of *counter-mobilization* themselves in order to defend their "right" to manage "their" operations in a unilateral manner. In doing so, employers will find the task involved somewhat easier than workers. Not only are they "primary" organizations and actors whose purpose it is to manage (Offe and Wiesenthal 1980), but they have also greater resources (financial, organization, ideological), and exist in an environment where their legitimacy to undertake the tasks of management is generally unquestioned and much supported by other agencies such as the government. The latter arises from the property relations in capitalist society as well as the deference to management expertise as a result of the social relations under capitalism.

Union campaigns may seek to cajole or force, by either voluntary or statutory means, employers to grant recognition for the first time or again following derecognition. This chapter is, thus, concerned with recent and contemporary employer counter-mobilization in the form of opposition and resistance to requests and campaigns by workers and unions for recognition, rather than employers' attempts to neuter or end existing and long-standing recognition agreements. The chapter may, thus, be said to looking at the "dark underbelly" of employment relations that is seldom exposed in a world dominated by the shiny practice and rhetoric of HRM and now of "partnership." This dark underbelly is further hidden from sight by the view, promoted by many media commentators, that the decline in overt conflict (i.e. strikes) is an indication that some forms of cooperation and harmony have emerged to displace the "old" class and union struggles of the past. Although not the subject of this chapter *per se*, the anti-union actions presented here are evidence of many employers' opposition to social justice, workplace democracy, and codetermination of the wage-effort bargain. Their actions revolve around the fulcrum of opposition to union presence and union rebuilding, given that unionism is the most effective mechanism by which workers can assert influence and power over the determination of the employment relationship.

The chapter begins by explaining the methodology used, before considering the conceptual issues involved and recounting evidence of past employer opposition to recognition campaigns. With this basis established, the evidence of the extent and nature of this employer anti-unionism is set out and analyzed, whereupon the implications and significance of this are discussed.

Methodology

The data is derived from a number of sources. First, material from the Labour Research Department – Trades Union Congress (LRD–TUC) *Trade Union Trends* surveys on recognition. Beginning in 1995, they are compiled annually from questionnaires to unions that cover on average 75 percent of the membership of TUC's affiliates. Second, eighty semi-structured interviews with regional field and national FTOs from the AEEU, BECTU, BFAWU, CWU, GMB, GPMU, IPMS, ISTC, MSF, NUJ, RMT, TGWU, TSSA, UNIFI, and USDAW who were involved with or responsible for recognition campaigns. These officials were interviewed in 1999, 2000, 2001, and 2002. Third, the determinations of the CAC, the body charged by the ERA with adjudicating on applications for recognition, were also utilized. By the end of 2001, 151 applications had been made, of which eighty-four were considered for validity and admissibility. The remaining sixty-seven applications were either withdrawn before being considered (forty-six incidents) or had not yet been adjudicated on. Generally speaking, applications are for recognition with employers that are hostile, as opposed to just reluctant, to granting recognition. These sources were supplemented by the monitoring of over thirty unions' journals and newsletters from 1995–2001, information gained from various union-orientated conferences (e.g. Institute of Employment Rights, LRD) on recognition, and surveying union-orientated publications like *Labour Research*, *Trade Union News*, the *Morning Star*, *Socialist Worker*, and various secondary sources (i.e. provincial newspapers through the Lexis-Nexis executive database) as well as websites like *laborstart* and *labornet* for the same period. The starting point of 1995 is taken because it is from this point that the influence of statutory recognition on employers can be traced as a result of it becoming clear the Labour Party was likely to win the next general election and legislate for statutory union recognition mechanisms. The end point for data collection was the close of 2001.

In presenting evidence of the most contentious types of employer anti-union behavior, only "corroborated" incidents are used. "Contentious" means occurrences or instances where unions allege unlawful activity or gross moral turpitude (e.g. dismissal for union activity, spying on workers) and employers counter with assertions of actions of legality (e.g. fair dismissal) and or reasonableness (e.g. protection of private property). Thus, rather than heavily relying on self-reported incidents by the aggrieved party (i.e. the unions) through interviews, only those incidents reported by unions which could then be verified by "independent" third parties (i.e. media or CAC reporting) are used. Whilst this does not guarantee absolute veracity, particularly given the decline of independent media investigation, it does, nonetheless, indicate that the allegations are not regarded as without basis, frivolous, and libelous. Moreover, where a union reports on such employer activity in its own publications, it is also deduced that this is not without basis either, thus being neither frivolous nor libelous. However, this has the effect of significantly reducing the frequency of these types and numbers of incidents of employer anti-union behavior that can be drawn upon. In incidents of less contentious and not unlawful types of employer anti-union behavior such as obfuscation, delay, and setting up non-union forums, all incidents identified in the data-collection are utilized.

Resisting union recognition: salient issues

Often a distinction is made between "anti-unionism" and "non-unionism" whereby it is assumed that the absence of a union presence is attributable to one or the other of these management policies. This distinction is sometimes alternatively posited as management policies of union *suppression* or union *substitution* (Beaumont 1987: 26, Blyton and Turnbull 1998: 267), or of *control* or *avoidance*. Some other schema exist for explaining the absence of union presence – for example the "good," "bad," "lucky," and "ugly" categories of Guest and Hoque (1994) using the presence or absence of HRM strategy and HRM practices as the explanatory variables, or Roy's (1980) classification of employer resistance to unionization and, by implication, union recognition, namely the "fear," "sweet," "evil," and "fatal" stuffs.

However, the dichotomy has a usefulness in distinguishing between employer activities which seek to provide positive benefits for non-membership in order to reduce the propensity to unionize and to seek/gain recognition in an attempt to improve wages and conditions and those which seek to impose costs on workers joining unions to reduce propensity to unionize and to seek/gain union recognition. But there are four caveats. First, it should not be assumed that there is a Chinese Wall operating between the two strategies (and attendant techniques). Thus, a single employer may use both at the same moment across space and time or either at different moments across space and time as is seen fit. This recognizes the dynamism and varying nature of the employment relationship. Second, the dichotomy cannot readily accommodate employer activities which seek to determine the form of recognition by virtue of which union is recognized, imposing "sweetheart" terms or establishing means to undermine the worth of recognition. Third, it should not be presumed that employer opposition to recognition reflect's their policy in the rest of their operations. Consequently, opportunistic or pragmatic employers may respond on a case-by-case basis to recognition campaigns where they arise and may oppose them even though they have recognition elsewhere or for other staff in their operations.

Fourth, and critically for our purposes in this chapter, it needs emphasizing that both "anti-unionism" and "non-unionism" employer actions are conscious and deliberate attempts to prevent and stop unionization and recognition. These are hard-nosed attempts, akin to Guest and Hoque's (1994) "ugly" type employer, who has a clear strategy of depriving workers of their rights and makes no use of HRM practices. This means employer policies and actions that may reduce, unintentionally or not as their prime purpose, propensity to unionize and mobilize prior to overt and conscious recognition campaigning are not particularly focused upon in this chapter. But it is recognized that there are gray areas between the two, primarily concerning identifying the relationship between employer action and intention with outcome, and identifying at what point unionization moves to recognition campaigning (which still comprises unionization). In this regard, Guest and Hoque's (1994) other categories differ, where these types of employers do not have these purposes in mind or these purposes are not to the fore. This results from Guest and Hoque's (1994: 2) interest in "developing frameworks and dimensions which allow . . . [the] study . . . of aspects of employment relations and human resource management without distinctive reference to the union issue." Thus their schema does not focus on anti-unionism *per se*. This is true also of McLoughlin and Gourlay's (1992, 1994, McLoughlin 1996) approach to studying employers.

Past employer opposition to union recognition

Employer opposition to recognition in Britain has a fairly long pedigree. In the post-war period until 1979, employer opposition to recognition in Britain was far from unknown despite a more supportive legal and public policy environment as well as stronger trade unionism (see McIlroy 1979). Among the most famous cases of suppression and substitution in this period are publisher DC Thomson, charity Barnados, computer manufacturers IBM and HP, retailer Marks and Spencer, and confectioner Mars. Between 1969 and 1980, CIR and ACAS case and annual reports record employer opposition ranging from opposition in principle, opposition to a particular union or for a particular group of workers, some of whom made threats to close down their businesses if forced to grant recognition, established staff associations, chose "appropriate unions," or argued individual bargaining or existing methods of communications or terms of employment were adequate (see e.g. Dickens 1978, Weekes *et al.* 1975: ch. 5). Others refused to accept (statutory) recognition awards or refused to bargain as obligated (Beaumont 1981). Furthermore, in this period strikes for recognition at photo-processing laboratory Grunwick, textile manufacturers Jersey Mills, engineering companies Con-Mech, Fines Tubes and Robert Arundel, Bristow helicopters, Grand Metropolitan and Trust House Forte hotels, and forklift makers Sandersons became union *causes célèbres*. Even after the advent of Thatcherism in 1979, workers continued to campaign for recognition. The evidence of continuing employer resistance into the 1980s can be judged, to some extent, from the 113 reported strikes for recognition between 1980 and 1992 (Gall 1994), of which the most famous was the Eddie Shah dispute (see Dickson 1984). The strikers came up against attitudes like those of Lord Charles Forte (1986: 123) of Trust House Forte hotels:

> I will not allow the unions to bully our staff or management, or tell us how to treat our employees. Moreover, I do not recognise or approve of the concept of the two sides of industry. It is the manager's sole responsibility to see that his staff are properly looked after and happy in their work.

These strikes arose in the main as a response to either the sacking of union activists whereupon the demands raised by the workers included not just reinstatement but also recognition or strikes to improve wages and conditions, out of which the demand for recognition was made. An analysis of the distribution of these strikes across industrial sectors finds that they were most common in the general manufacturing and, in particular, textiles and clothing, light engineering, and food production rather areas of the new private service sector (Gall 1994). In terms of company size, most employed less than 100 workers and the overwhelming majority of these employed between twenty-five and fifty workers (ibid.). In the early 1990s, the *Employment in Britain* survey showed 15 percent of employees reporting their employer was trying to discourage unionization (Gallie and White 1993: 42) while Abbot's (1993: 311) survey of eighty companies indicated that management in computing companies and pubs and restaurants were among the most opposed to unionization and recognition. Abbot (ibid.: 309–10) also suggested that small employers are more able to implement anti-union strategies as a result of managing smaller numbers and being in closer physical proximity. Well before the ERA, Richard Branson told BALPA in 1994 "I'll fold the airline if the [pilots] join unions" (in Bowers 2000: 177), which followed telling the TGWU in 1986 "If they join the union we will wrap up the airline" (in Bowers 2000: 154).

The case of the North Sea oil industry operators and contractors in the late 1980s, over and above the material in Chapter 3, illustrates many of a number of other tactics used by anti-union employers when faced by serious recognition campaigns under the period of the Conservative governments. Employers engaged in delaying tactics (endless meetings and correspondence with unions), promised independent ballots that failed to materialize, introduced arbitration panels for grievances, increased wages, and reinvigorated and extended their employee communication mechanisms (OILC 1991b). Other oil companies like Shell and Wood Group also established staff associations and works councils as well as engaged in victimizations and sackings (Woolfson *et al.* 1996: 188, 222, 480, 497).

Employers against union recognition: judging the size of the current phenomenon

In trying to make an assessment of the likely extent of employer opposition to recognition, a useful starting place is to map out the extent of recognition campaigns themselves. Table 5.1 shows those reported by the *Trade Union Trends* surveys (1998–2002) while Table 5.2 reports the findings of the CBI's (1998, 1999a, 2000, 2001) *Employment Trends Surveys* on employers' perception of recognition claims. Taken together these give an indication of the size of the canvas on which opposition to recognition could be based, where the CBI data gives the largest measure of likely recognition campaign activity and, as it were, within this the *Trends* data show the level of employer opposition to granting recognition where there is majority membership within the wider gambit of recognition campaigns. Thus, from Table 5.1 over 90,000 workers are being denied recognition despite having a density of 50 percent plus.

However, we can go further a little further, for a number of surveys have indicated the possible extent of current/contemporary employer opposition to recognition where they indicate data that shows opposition to recognition as well as opposition to unionization. The CBI's *Employment Trends Surveys* (2000, 2001) show that around a third of companies approached for recognition (which itself measures between 9 and 13 percent of surveyed

Table 5.1 Union recognition campaigns

Year	No of campaigns	Known no. of workers covered regardless of union density (from no. of cases)	No. of campaigns where union density is in excess of 50%	No. of workers where union density is in excess of 50% (from no. of cases)
2001	144	89,178 (93)	45	19,159 (45)
2000	149	34,870 (91)	47	5,835 (47)
1999	143	70,872 (n/a)	62	27,036 (62)
1998	106	59,680 (n/a)	50	23,984 (48)
1997	97	n/a	41	16,129 (38)
Totals	445	254,600 (184)	245	92,143 (240)

Note: Some campaigns are reported in a number of consecutive years while others have dropped out where union recognition has been gained. However, double counting is minimal.

Table 5.2 Employers' perception of union recognition claims

Year	Received	Expect/anticipate	Possible
2000	9%	7%	n/a
1999	13%	12%	n/a
1998	n/a	13%	19%
1997	n/a	10%	18%

Note: The surveys have covered between 671 and 830 employers covering with 2.0m and 2.8m workers in the private sector.

companies) rejected the approach. The CBI (1999b: 3) also found that 37 percent of respondents would "definitely" and 46 percent would "possibly" "minimise the coverage of union recognition" with 18 percent "definitely" and 45 percent "possibly" being prepared to "fight union recognition, if necessary through the statutory procedure." The Dibb Lupton Alsop surveys (1995–2001) show consistently high levels of opposition to the requirement to recognize a union (between 59 percent and 92 percent) by non-union companies and around two-thirds of companies have refused approaches. These surveys have covered around fifty non-union companies annually. The TUC (1997) found that 40 percent of workers questioned in it surveys responded along the following lines: "I can't join a union, my boss won't let me." In non-unionized call centers both LRD (2001) and TUC (2001a) have found not inconsiderable evidence of workers fearing dismissal for joining, or being active in, a union. Some callers to the TUC helpline claimed they had been sacked for holding union membership (TUC 2001a). Overall, these data indicate that employers are deliberately taking measures to prevent unionization getting to the point from which campaigning for, let alone gaining, recognition becomes possible.

Turning to relevant academic research, Heery (2000b) examined employers' responses to union organizing campaigns in 120 cases using union respondents, where just over half of the sites did not have recognition. From these, eight tactics were identified which were relatively common; "threat of legal action/police involvement against union," "denying organizers access to the workplace," "discouraging employees from joining the union," "distributing anti-union literature," "victimization of union activists," "use of management consultants to advise on avoiding unionization of the workplace," "improving pay and conditions to reduce demand for union membership," and "setting up or strengthening alternative channels of representation to substitute for the union" (Heery 2000b: 3). Bryson (1999: 85–6), using British Social Attitudes survey data, reports management in non-union organizations combine discouragement of union membership with making it a "non-issue." Further, he shows between 1989 and 1994 management were less likely to encourage union membership and more likely to discourage it. Finally, Oxenbridge *et al.* (2001: 6) report from their sixty case studies in southern England that around half of those employers who expected to be subject to the influence of the ERA were examining strategies for resisting recognition.

From these data, we can deduce that employer opposition to recognition is of a considerable extent. This has been recognized by various union leaders, such as the TUC general secretary who believed "a hard core of anti-union employers may need challenging through the CAC" (*Morning Star,* 11. September 2000). The TUC (2000) believe this, nonetheless, constitutes "a small minority." Furthermore, these anti-union actions must be held in regard to the dramatic increase in recognition agreements in recent years (see Introduction). Therefore, the evidence of anti-unionism is best seen as representing one current, albeit a small but significant one, amongst employers who have faced recognition campaigns. These points are important to establish, for the Chartered Institute of Personnel and Development (CIPD) (Emmott 1999) has stated it is not aware of any significant or widespread attempts by employers to evade the provisions of the ERA on recognition, nor does it expect a significant number to develop. This, it argues, is because while employers' organizations and many individual employers are against statutory recognition, the CIPD believes employers are either prepared to be flexible enough to adapt to the new law or they believe it will not affect them because there will be no demand for recognition by virtue of successful (non-union) employee relations. The chapter now proceeds to examine the evidence of contemporary employer anti-unionism.

The suppressionist strategy

The purpose of suppression is to kill off or sabotage existing or expected attempts at union organization and requests for recognition or at least prevent them from getting to a convincing or critical mass, which increasingly is being related to the stipulations set by the ERA on numerical membership thresholds (i.e. 50 percent+1). The strategy is based on intimidation and creating an atmosphere of fear and trepidation. The most obvious tools are the sackings, dismissals, and redundancies, or the threats of them, used by employers to disorganize and weaken the union presence and recognition campaign. Other methods include suspensions, harassment, and intimidation. These can be targeted at a number of sources: lay officers, union activists, union members, and potential union members. Generically, these actions seek to try to prevent or stop lay officers from being active in dealing with members' concerns, organizing meetings, producing publicity material, and recruiting new members. These actions are also meant to send signals to existing members about the response they face if they become active in the union and to say to potential members that the union and its activities are unwelcome. Together, these are achieved by a wide variety of means.

Such tactics leading to dismissal of union activists are understood to have taken place on forty-four occasions in non-recognized or derecognized workplaces through the means of stringent application of time-keeping and sick/absence policies, and monitoring of work performance. Two incidents exist of shop stewards being suspended for recruiting. Sixteen incidents exist of redundancies targeted at union members, while the less subtle threat of promising to shut the factory down if recognition is forced upon the employer is believed to have been made on six occasions. An array of other tactics is also being used by employers seeking to resist recognition. Management plants are being used at union meetings to find out how and when the union is planning to organize its recognition campaign in order to combat it. Other examples exist of videoing through CCTV, or super-visors or others workers being seen to note those that speak to union organizers at the gates to the company's premises and or those that speak to the union rep inside work. Such people are then spoken to by managers about their retrograde actions. These tactics have been reported on thirteen occasions. Six incidents exist of management distributing union resignation forms and there are seven incidents of workers being told they "can't" join a union. More common tactics include refusing the union access to company premises (25 incidents).

There is also some evidence of the use of anti-union consultants and legal firms in attempts to deter unionization and recognition. Some of these employers are using the American "union-busting" firms or "indigenous" law firms (9 incidents). Elsewhere "blacklists" are reported to exist (4 reports of) even though the use of such lists is outlawed under the ERA. Slightly more sophisticated methods which have been used include specific captive meetings and written communications warning about the "union threat" to the company's health and profitability and thus to wage levels and jobs (36 incidents in all).

Finally, companies have challenged "their" unions to ballots before the unions are in a position to properly contest the ballots, in the hope they will lose and this will stymie any future activity (19 incidents). Other methods detected include: the restructuring of the company by splitting up units on a legal–geographic basis; the changing of bargaining units; the contracting-out of certain activities to influence union density; and the introduction of personal contracts to take some members out of the potential for union membership and recognition (16 incidents). These all clearly have implications for the determination of membership interest and thresholds and the nature of the bargaining unit under the ERA (see below, pages 88–9).

The substitutionist strategy

The substitutionist strategy seeks to make the organization "an issue-free company" whereby the employer tries to supplant the potential union role by attempting to show that it is unnecessary, by means of resolving, or being seen to resolve, grievances and establishing "independent" and non-union related mechanisms for dealing with grievances and giving expression to employee "voice." Thus, employers seek to convince workers that there are no issues of contention at work, that should any arise they can be easily resolved to the satisfaction of both parties, that the presence of a union is unnecessary, and that there is a community of interests. In sum, there is no need for a union. The comments of the coordinator of the Pizza Express Employee Forum indicate the motivation: "[W]e will have failed if staff see joining a union as offering something the Forum cannot" (in Hewett 2000).

A common tactic is thus the "sudden" resolution of long-standing grievances, better than expected pay increases, and general improvements in working conditions (22 incidents). These are set in train after employers recognize they face a serious union recognition campaign. Another tactic is the promotion of the policies of "open door" of access to management and one-to-one communication (9 incidents). However, more noticeable are attempts to formalize and institutionalize non-unionism by establishing "consultative" or "representative" forums, where staff issues and grievances can be dealt with. At least 134 organizations were reported to have employed this technique to avoid union recognition. As many again are reported to have revived and reinvigorated their existing or dormant institutions in response to union recognition campaigns. A slightly more unusual example of union substitutionism is noteworthy – this concerns the seven reported examples of employers helping to or creating staff associations or staff unions to resist *bona fide* independent unions.

Central Arbitration Committee cases

The publication of the decisions by the CAC, posted on their website (http://www.cac.gov.uk), often provides details of how employers have sought to resist recognition under the new legal framework, albeit within the (prior) voluntary arena. Taking these and supplementing them with information on the incidents from the interviews from union officials (because the reasons for withdrawals and delays are not always posted), a number of issues have arisen. Resisting employers have sought usually to enlarge the bargaining unit by including other workers or supervisors to reduce union density (22 incidents). On occasion, they have sought to restrict the bargaining unit to a small number of staff to reduce the extent of possible recognition. In both incidences, arguments over the bargaining unit being compatible with "effective management" have been deployed. In other incidents, employers have requested and received extension to the periods under which they are obliged to respond. These have been used to give the employer more time to campaign against the union. A variant on this is the employer argument to have a ballot even where a union has a majority in membership in the bargaining unit. A number of incidents also indicate employers sacking or hiring workers to fall below the size threshold or reduce union density respectively. Finally, background information on employers' industrial relations shows that many have recently established or reinvigorated works councils/staff forums to avoid union recognition.

The efficacy of suppression and substitutionism

The example of the actions against the GPMU by the *Daily Mail*-owned Printworks in Gloucester is instructive. Having experienced years of hostility to requests for talks on recognition, the GPMU applied for statutory recognition in 2001 when it had 43 percent density. Because the company challenged the union submission at every turn (level of membership, bargaining unit, petition signed by 70 percent of the relevant workforce), it took four months before the ballot took place. In this time the company: (a) organized letters from workers resigning from the union and stating they were against recognition; (b) dismissed the shop steward (who was awarded interim relief at Employment Tribunal); and (c) made some casual staff permanent. Consequently, union membership fell to 36 percent and only 37 percent of eligible workers voted yes to recognition in the ballot. A similar process was acted out at Ryanair airline against BALPA. Well-planned, well-resourced, and aggressive anti-unionism can, thus, be effective.

But despite the general imbalance in power resources between employers and unions/workers, it would be wrong to assume that in all cases employers have been successful in their objectives. Thus, to consider only such employer activities against recognition and not union counter-responses would be to paint a partial picture. In the majority of cases employers' initiatives have been effective in maintaining non-recognition. Nonetheless, union presence (membership, organization, activity) has not necessarily always been consequently diminished, so possibilities exist that recognition may still be obtained from these bridgeheads. There are examples where elections to newly established staff councils have been successfully contested by unions, where employers have been taken to Employment Tribunals for unfair dismissals and where publicity campaigns have been maintained.

More importantly, there are nearly 100 cases where unions have been able to maintain a union presence and gain recognition despite employer resistance (consisting of dismissals, harassment, and the use of consultants, pre-emptive ballots, and company councils/staff forums). For example, BALPA has gained recognition in all but one of the major airlines in Britain despite the latters' widespread use of employee councils. The key to these successes is twofold: to build and maintain a high level of member-ship (well in excess of 50 percent+1) and to teach the employer that this membership can be mobilized in shows of strength to demonstrate the degree of conviction. This may mean organizing successful events like meetings, petitions, open letters, winning the elections to staff councils, and so on and doing so for some length of time. The ability to do this is attributable to a number of factors.

The first is the persistence of serious issues of collective grievance and injustice around which unions can organize. Here the unions have been able to continually keep actual members convinced and convince potential members that issues exist which are sufficiently serious to require a "union solution." The second is the absence of a large degree of workforce turnover. Workforce turnover can mean that recruitment has to "run just to standstill" and indicates that many workers are choosing individual exit strategies to deal with their dissatisfaction. The third is the maintenance of a small band of highly committed activists who are prepared to undertake what can be a long, hard slog to success where much personal time and effort are required. The fourth is a high level of union activity throughout the campaign to show that progress is being made in terms of recruitment and discussions with the employer. The fifth is that the union membership is well serviced in the campaign so that forward momentum in terms of union membership and credibility is maintained. The sixth is that the local or national union commits con-siderable resources, largely in the form of FTOs, to coordinate and staff the recognition campaign. Last is the generation of sympathetic publicity. Many companies appear to be susceptible to "bad publicity" in the local and national media and from local politicians where there is a strong base of union membership and support. Once the company or organization has become susceptible to these pressures, the services of ACAS are normally used to demonstrate in a ballot or membership audit that the union has majority support. In thirty incidents, threats or the use of industrial action have been important tools (cf. Millward 1994: 24). How-ever, most cases of employer resistance being overcome also appear to be attributable to the impending and eventual introduction of the ERA. In general, these conditions of success are reminiscent of the way in which Kelly (1998) talks about effective union or worker mobilization.

The re-emergence of single union and sweetheart deals

Single union and "sweetheart" deals are now back in vogue, after a period of absence since the late 1980s (see Gall 1993). Some employers have recognized the question they face is not one of granting or not granting recognition but to which union should recognition be granted and with what type of deal. This results from "irresistible" requests by virtue of the strength of union membership and organization, possible disruption to industrial relations, and likely poor company image resulting from an industrial dispute, or pre-emptive moves to ward against unwelcome unions campaigning for recognition. In this situation, the key questions become which union and deal best suit the employer's interests. Often the process of selection will involve inviting interested unions to outline the types of agreements they are prepared to offer, sometimes in the form of a "beauty contest," before selecting an appropriate union and appropriate agreement. What is meant by "appropriate" may be a union or an agreement that eschews traditional bargaining in favor of "business unionism" or "partnership." A couple of examples give the flavor of this:

> A spokeswoman at clothing retailer Ethel Austin told us that a number of unions had approached the company towards the end of 1999 but it had chosen USDAW as it believed it to be a less militant union.
>
> (IDS 2000: 20)

> We considered a number of unions but have chosen the AEEU as they are best for our workforce as one of the more progressive industrial unions.
>
> (Ross Richardson, UK Drilling Contractors' Association in AEEU *Offshore News*, Summer 2000)

Pressures for single union deals, in addition to employers' desires for simplified bargaining arrangements, have increased as a result of the ERA because, under it, only one claim for recognition can be made and because new claims for recognition cannot be made where there is already voluntary recognition.

With "sweetheart agreements," employers are attempting to set the terms by which recognition is granted whether this be with an "appropriate" or "inappropriate" union in order to lessen the influence of the union and maintain managerial prerogative. This may take the form of a weakened union presence where the union is unable to deliver membership benefits, the membership is passive, and the union lacks independence and has to continually struggle to assert its legitimacy. Ultimately, this could pave the way for derecognition and non-unionism. The most obvious means by which employers seek this are the explicit "no disruption" clauses or those which impose arbitration and, thus, lengthen the time by which it may be procedurally correct to ballot for industrial action. However, an array of other means is also being imposed by employers. These include initial pay freezes, representation for non-union workers in consultative forums, "partnership" provisions, and the absence of the normal bi-lateral channels for conducting collective bargaining in. All are the price to be paid for recognition and indicate that employers are continuing the fight against recognition even after it has been granted. There is a disregard for worker choice, be it for one union or another or for independent unionism. In total, some 120 examples of single union and constrained recognition agreements are known of.

Post-recognition battles

Already there is some evidence amongst new recognition agreements of some employers seeking to roll back the gains the unions have made through what is known in the US as "bad faith bargaining" or "surface bargaining." This represents rearguard actions to undermine, or indeed rescind, the earlier decision to grant recognition. The most common methods here are to offer no or low pay rises, no or slight improvements in conditions, and to continually ignore or delay responding to union requests for information and meetings. Here the employer is trying to show that not only has union membership no benefits but that it is a hopeless task trying to prove otherwise. For example, one employer "offered" a nil percent pay increase in the first year of bargaining, with the company's HR Director stating *after* the agreement had been signed that "trade unions are not necessary" (*Daily Record*, 29 January 1999). Another example of such tactics can be found in the first case of collective bargaining after re-recognition in the regional newspaper industry. Strike action was deployed successfully by the journalists in a Newquest center in Bradford following the company's 18-month period of intransigence over pay. Other tactics to undermine recognition include casualization and redundancies. The limited incidence of these tactics reflects the relative recentness of the agreements, indicating there has so far been little opportunity in which this may occur, as well as difficulty in halting, at this early stage, the forward momentum that unions have established.

Discussion

This chapter has presented evidence of a not insignificant number of reported incidents of employer anti-union behavior (over 600 in total) over the period, the volume of which is compatible with that which might be expected from the surveys examined above. Taken alongside the evidence (see Introduction) of the growth in new recognition deals, this suggests that this type of employer response to recognition campaigns is a less common feature of the current industrial relations landscape. This, therefore, contrasts markedly with the experience in the US where the position is the opposite. However, some commentators had expected more and even some Grunwick-type showdowns. The NUJ general secretary expected more resistance from regional newspaper employers (*Morning Star*, 14 September 2000) while the CIPD predicted confrontation in the newspapers and the voluntary sector (*Personnel Today*, 8 February 2000). Although this level of anti-unionism has not materialized, the existence of such practices belies the "soft" and "caring" approach advocated by HRM. Indeed, where HRM has "failed," stronger tactics have often been used. The incidences of anti-unionism reported in this chapter have increased annually during 1995–2001: most were located in 1998–2001, indicating that the imminence and presence of the ERA and the increasing number of union campaigns have stimulated employer response. Thus, employers are reacting to potential and actual "threats" rather than hypothetical ones.

The mechanisms deployed by employers in their attempts to remain "union free" have been shown to be those of time-honored tradition, primarily victimization (sackings and harassment) of activists and the creation of non-union workplace forums for the resolution of grievances and the expression of employee voice. In many instances, the public face of a company belies the anti-union actions it has taken. Take, for example, the statement by the managing director of Statex Press that "We were happy to have the GPMU representing individuals, but what we didn't want was collective bargaining. We want to reward staff on individual merit rather than award all staff with a flat 5 percent or 10 percent, because there's no incentive in that" (*Printing World*, 15 January 2001), which gives no hint that the company engaged in a sustained campaign to undermine the union. Statex was the subject of a CAC application by the GPMU for its nineteen members in a bargaining unit of thirty-seven. During the time that the application progressed, the company obtained twenty-nine signed letters from employees requesting a postal ballot and four signed letters from employees saying they did not want collective bargaining. The company obtained these letters by "talking" to employees in captive groups (whole workforce, small groups, and individually). It sought to present the letters to the CAC in its bid to dismiss the application, or if that failed, gain a ballot to decide on support for union recognition, presumably in order to give itself further time to campaign. In the event, the CAC awarded recognition through a membership audit.

Turning to the types of employers that have engaged in resistance to recognition, a number of features stand out. First, there are those with certain identifiable predispositions against, and aversions to, unions and union recognition. The most obvious are those companies which are from the US or have US ownership, companies and organizations which are headed by their founders or Thatcherite "entrepreneurs," and charities (see Simms, this volume). Put in flamboyant language, these type of employers may view a recognition campaign as "an economic heart attack," according to a US union-busting consultant seeking business in the UK (*People*

Management, 25 May 2000). Second, there are those organizations whose management believe they have had "bad" experiences of industrial relations, comprising assertive unions or industrial action (such as newspaper employers and some offshore oil contractors). Third, while the distribution of these employer activities is widespread across the economy, a picture does emerge of employer activity much being less pronounced in particular parts of the service sector (hotels, restaurants, retail, distribution and wholesale, business services) while far more so in general manufacturing, general printing, newspapers, and the offshore oil industry. This would seem to reflect the combination of the location of union activity/union recognition campaigns and the attendant employer response to remain "union free" as a result of an anti-union *Weltanschauung*. Fourth, there is a concentration of employer resistance by workforce size. Those small and medium-sized organizations, commonly with between 21 and 250 workers, show the greatest signs of resistance, deploying the less sophisticated means of staying "union free." This accords with previous research which has established the predominantly anti-union view of small employers (Rainnie 1989, Scott *et al.* 1989).

The source of ideological anti-union predispositions can vary for different employers. For US companies, unions "cause" concern as a result of demands for wages and conditions being seen to damage profitability (see e.g. *Observer*, 4 June 2000). This appeared to motivate the mostly US companies attending an anti-union seminar in 2000 in Britain: McDonald's, Dow Chemical, Fedex, Otis, Chevron, Gap, Omega World Travel, Transworld Airlines, Nasdaq International, and Tower Records. For the founding Thatcherite "entrepreneur," unions are seen as a threat to running the business as a personal fiefdom. In this regard the manager and founder of Synseal windows, which employs 250 workers, stated

> This company is my company. I started it I built it and I own it. I'm not prepared to tolerate their [unions'] intrusion. They've got nothing to offer. We have made it clear to our workforce that if the new legislation created a situation where we were required to unions then I would have to consider closing the company.
>
> (*Channel 4 News*, 6 June 2000)

while other employers have made similar, if more terse, statements; "I will not recognize any union at Pricecheck. If staff don't like it, then they don't have to work here" (Manzoor Chaudhary, owner of Pricecheck supermarkets, *Morning Star*, 5 May 1999) and "I'll have no union at my companies!" (John Cauldwell, chairman and chief executive of call center group Cauldwell Company, *Stoke Sentinel*, 24 April 2001). Usually this notion of the personal fiefdom also accords with a number of other compatible features found in anti-unionism: the companies being recent start-ups and relatively small in the number of workers employed. Commenting on these types of employers, the GPMU deputy general secretary said

There are still far too many firms where employers take a diehard, over-my-dead-body attitude to people's natural rights. I have come across several who would rather go out of business than recognise the union: one man told me he would burn the place down before he was prepared to negotiate with us.

(*Printing World*, 18 September 2000)

Lastly, with regard to charities, many of the boards of management have views which combine not seeing themselves as employers because of the voluntary and charitable nature of their activities, coming from professional backgrounds that are not "union-friendly," *and* believing that all employees are motivated to carry out their jobs as a result of a strong feeling of vocation, where they are "at one" with the employer and are not overly concerned about wages and conditions. This could be described as a left-wing form of unitarism.

Authors such as Bronfenbrenner *et al.* (1998), Fiorito (this volume), Friedman *et al.* (1994), have documented the use of similar anti-union tactics in the US to those used in Britain; sackings, intimidation, harassment, disinformation, management plants, spying, captive meetings, threats of closure and employee participation programs, carried out with a view to frustrating recognition campaigns and producing low union win rates in certification elections. Management consultants were heavily used. They also detail the use of disputes over bargaining units to reduce union support and non-cooperation with the US statutory recognition body, the NLRB, to lengthen the period of the recognition campaign in order to provide more opportunity to frustrate and exhaust the union supporters. Where recognition is won, the widespread use of "surface" or "bad faith" bargaining and decertification has also shown to be used to nullify and revoke it, where penalties for such "unfair labor practices" are so negligible as to fail to constitute a deterrent. The direct relevant aspect of this "US dimension" is the importation of such techniques into Britain by US companies operating in Britain. Of the best-known reported examples are the on-line bookseller Amazon, and the book retailer Borders (*Guardian*, 11 September 2001, *Observer*, 24 January 1999).

With single union deals and constrained agreements, unions are now experiencing a re-run of many of the unresolved dilemmas of the 1980s, and before (cf. Hyman 1975). Is the choice they face whole tracts of non-unionism or accepting constrained recognition? Can constrained agreements be used as a staging post to full recognition or will unions be compromised by them? Would employers not be able to demand such terms if unions jointly agreed not to offer them, or are the employers sufficiently strong to compel the offering of such terms? Is it "morally" right that workers can have the choice of which union to join in effect decided for them in advance by an agreement between the employer and a union? These questions are now posed much more starkly and forcefully in the period of the ERA. With the weak central authority of the TUC, agreement amongst unions will not be easily forthcoming on these issues. The issues here of inter-union competition and thus less effective use of union resources, while of importance, may be of lesser significance than employer opposition.

Conclusion

Given the nature of the data collection, it is impossible to gauge exactly how representative the incidents here are of wider employer behavior – the self-selecting nature of the incidences means there is no sample from which to calculate this. That said, the actual extent of employer anti-union actions is no doubt greater than was captured. This is not likely to be the case with the types of actions, given that a wide range of tactics was highlighted. While the explicit employer anti-unionism documented here cannot be held to be the sole, or even, major factor in preventing unions from extending recognition coverage back to anything like approaching 1979 levels, it is nonetheless an important one. Other factors may include union organizing approaches, amount of union resources, worker attitudes, and the compositional and occupational nature of different workforces. But the mobilization of employer resource to maintain unilateral control over the employment relationship where recruitment and recognition campaigns do exist is important to explaining their outcomes. This chapter has shown employer actions to resist recognition are far from unsuccessful.

Note

For further examples and analysis of employer anti-unionism see Gall (2002) and Gall and McKay (2001).

6 Union organizing in a not-for-profit organization

Melanie Simms

Introduction

There is now broad agreement that the actions unions take in relation to organizing and recruiting new groups of workers have an effect on membership levels (Price 1991, Undy *et al.* 1981, Bronfenbrenner and Juravich 1998). There is also recognition that most British unions have, to date, not put sufficient resources into organizing in the expanding private service sector where there are large numbers of workers who are currently not represented in unions (Heery *et al.* 2000a). Thus, there has been discussion about the challenges facing unions attempting to organize these "new" groups of workers and the potential difficulties in representing their interests in an attempt to "enlarge the playing field" of unionism (Wever 1998). A fairly clear divide can be identified between authors who primarily write about union revitalization in the private sector (e.g. Heery *et al.* 2000a) and those who study union organization and the possibilities of renewal in the public sector (e.g. Fairbrother 2000). As a result, an implicit debate has emerged between the two with the former identifying a key role for union leaders in the process of renewal and the latter arguing that renewal can only come from an active rank-and-file membership.

Interestingly, however, little attention has been paid to the "third sector," comprised of not-for-profit organizations, voluntary organizations, and charities. The sector employs nearly 500,000 workers in Britain, representing around 2.2 percent of the workforce (Passey *et al.* 2000), and has been expanding rapidly. It should, therefore, be of prime importance to trade unions seeking to expand their influence. A number of large household name charities dominate the sector, where the largest 10 percent of organizations generate almost 90 percent of the sector's income (ibid.), lending a strategic importance to gaining union recognition in these organizations. Importantly for the prospects of establishing trade unionism in the sector, it exhibits characteristics of both the public and private sectors. Many of the occupational groups have public sector equivalents, some public sector experience, and express a strong loyalty to their professional group. Furthermore, in 1999 over 30 percent of the income to the third sector was in the form of government contracts and grants and this is increasing (ibid.). This is particularly important given the evidence that public sector professional workers are most likely to be union members and that women's union membersip as a proportion of total female employment is growing whist the proportion of male members is declining (TUC 2001b). This suggests that there is little evidence that these workers are inherently resistant to trade unionism and it may be that they are particularly "unionate." However, there are also interesting parallels with the private sector. Managers in not-for-profit organizations are increasingly being recruited from the private sector (Cunningham 2000) with little experience of dealing with unions and much of the organizational restructuring that has taken place across the sector has been influenced by the private sector. Consequently, there is an opportunity for unions to respond to this agenda and to use experiences in both the public and private sectors in dealing with third sector organizations.

Work organization in the sector also exhibits a number of interesting features. Employers are heavily dependent on employees being committed to the objectives of their organization. This commitment is expressed in altruistic terms, placing greater emphasis on achieving the objectives of the organization than on, for example, earning a high salary. However, many employees recognize the organization's values are not exhibited in their employment practices. Employers here typically exhibit a unitaristic approach to employee relations, often relying on their employees' commitment and altruistic instincts to achieve objectives.

It is, therefore, possible to identify three employment relations scenarios. First, employers often emphasize the service delivery aspect of work and the caring values of the organization. Employees express commitment to these values and this "altruistic unitarism" could limit the scope for unionization. Second, a perceived mismatch between the values espoused by the employer in relation to clients and those acted upon in relation to employees may provide an opportunity for unions to mobilize the workforce around the attribution of a perceived injustice (Kelly 1998: 30). Third, the shared values of employees and employers may allow an opportunity to develop a "partnership" approach where a union can represent workers' collective voice within the organization's decision-making structures. Voluntary sector organizations, therefore, provide interesting cases from which to develop existing analysis and knowledge about the prospects for union renewal.

This chapter examines an attempt to organize a predominantly female workforce of a large national charity in order to develop an understanding of the ways in which a union can represent and negotiate on the issues of importance to these workers and deal with organizations which are often reluctant to recognize unions as the representative voice of the workforce. Cunningham (2000: 202–3) is relatively optimistic about the opportunity for unions to organize in this sector, albeit with potential difficulties given employer preference for restrictive disputes procedures, the level of employee commitment to their organization, which could limit the scope of unionization, and the influx of employees from private organizations into the sector. This optimism seems to stem from the similarities between third sector and the well-organized public sector in terms of the occupational groups, work organization, and attitudes towards employment. This study suggests Cunningham is right to be optimistic about the opportunities for union membership when unions are prepared to invest time and resources into an organizing campaign in this sector.

The chapter also provides insights into how unions are attempting to organize "new" groups of workers. The "organizing model" has received considerable attention within the British union movement although there is limited evidence of diffusion of the organizing techniques developed by US unions in recent years. Nonetheless, the techniques of using organizing committees and issue-based campaigning have diffused most extensively (Simms *et al.* 2001) and are certainly evident in the study where the union established an activist-led campaign around issues that are workplace based and specific. The union relied on the establishment of an organizing committee (or, more accurately, a network of activists) made up of union members who attempted to recruit and mobilize their colleagues. However, this approach has so far failed to build up enough support across the geographically dispersed workplaces for the union to break through significant management resistance to union recognition. The campaign is, therefore, an interesting study of how a union can establish a collective voice and redress in a workplace without formal recognition. Further, the study provides an example of how a large general union has developed an organizing campaign within the framework of the provisions for statutory union recognition and an increasingly juridified employment relations environment.

Data was gathered through a number of methods. A series of in-depth, semi-structured interviews were undertaken over a three-year period with key officials and decision makers within the union, the specialist organizer, key activists, and other employees. In total, twelve actors were interviewed at least once during that period, although often twice or more. Organizing strategy discussions were observed and recorded, ranging from short discussions to residential strategy meetings, totalling some 25 hours. Supplementary data was gathered from union documentation as well as informal discussions with less active members, evidence from a number of documents produced by the employer, and secondary sources such as newspaper articles.

The chapter begins by providing a background profile of the employer and of the union before moving to describe the previous union attempts to gain union recognition in the organization. It then examines the reasons for the current union recognition campaign, namely the presence of active members with a background of trade unionism, the new rights granted by

the ERA, and the decision by the employer to review employee participation structures by introducing a works council to replace the consultative
forum. The next section considers the issues around which the union has
attempted to collectivize and mobilize the workforce. In the final section,
the chapter identifies some of the specific effects of the ERA on the union's
organizing and union recognition campaign.

The employer profile

The organization is a national charity which provides support services for
people with disabilities and has a high national profile in lobbying for
improved services for the physically disabled. It has three core activities:
providing care assistance, campaigning nationally on behalf of people with
disabilities and their families, and raising funds for the activities of the
organization through a network of charity stores. The organization is
highly effective in its campaigning activity and the delivery of support
services but the market for second-hand retail is becoming very competitive
with many large charities running these shops and increasingly competing
with budget clothes stores. Consequently, the retail operation is not creating the desired income levels to help to fund the charity's other activities so
the organization is under pressure to restructure and has initiated a
controversial program involving redundancies to deal with this. It employs
around 3,500 permanent staff and approximately 500 "casual" staff. Over
three-quarters of the employees are women. The main occupational groups
reflect the organization's main activities: shop managers, care workers, and
administrative, secretarial, and clerical staff, together accounting for
around half of the workforce. Other groups of staff include managers, field
workers, and development workers, teachers and lecturers, shop van
drivers, and a range of support staff.

Employees are based all over Britain. Typically, shops will employ just
one or two full-time employees in a management or supervisory role. The
staffing for the shops comes primarily from volunteers who offer a few
hours a week of their time. Regionally, the retail arm will employ a driver
or bag collector who distributes and collects bags of second-hand goods
from households in the area. The organization also has a considerable
number of residential homes. Many of the workers in the regional divisions
are groups which have not traditionally been represented by unions,
although others such as teachers or specialist care workers have traditions
of professional organizations and unions representing their interests in the
public sector. The charity's headquarters is in London where the
campaigning and administration take place. Unlike the other employees,
these staff work in a traditional office environment with a standard working
week. Many are graduates and continually express their commitment to the
objectives of the organization and their keenness to promote the rights
of people with disabilities. In general, this workforce is typical of the

occupational groups that unions need to organize if they are to become more representative of the labor force.

The charity has consistently been very reluctant to engage with the union. The chief executive has a private sector background and has little experience in dealing with unions. Additionally, the personnel managers have little union experience and advocate a view of HRM which allows employees to express their views but which offers little scope for genuine negotiation. Consequently, the behavior of the charity has been to tolerate a limited role for the union by, for example, allowing union representatives to attend grievances and disciplinaries, but to resist union recognition attempts. This means that where line managers tolerate union activity, the union does have a visible presence within the workplace and active representatives, but where there is greater resistance from line managers, the union can do very little to establish its presence.

The union profile

MSF is a large, general union which recruits and organizes mainly non-manual staff in a wide range of industries and sectors, including a long-standing interest in organizing within the voluntary sector. It thus has a strategic interest in prioritizing a number of large, national charities for recruitment and organizing because of their high profile and household name status, and it recognizes that little concerted effort has previously been given to organizing workers here. It is hoped that if recognition deals can be reached in key organizations within the sector, other large not-for-profit organizations will follow suit. The campaign, therefore, has a strategic role in the union's future development. The union's focus on representing predominantly white-collar and professional staff means that it is well placed to represent voluntary sector workers who fit the profile of other groups represented by the union.[1]

Due to financial difficulties, resulting partly from membership decline, the union has attempted to encourage a greater focus on organizing "new" groups of workers. To this end, it committed itself to sponsoring several trainees through the first year of the Organising Academy and to employing specialist organizers. It has also recruited a number of temporary organizers in order to give a boost of resources and expertise at a particular point in a campaign. In this campaign in question, a temporary organizer was employed on a short-term basis to take responsibility for the project in 1999. She was employed for an initial period of six months and was eventually employed for a full year on this campaign.

MSF has made several attempts to win union recognition at the charity over the past fifteen years, beginning in the late 1980s with moves by a core of members, many of whom were speech therapists, to involve the union in issues of concern to the workforce. There has been a small group of members throughout the organization since that time and a number of other unions have a small membership. As a result of its members' presence, MSF has been involved in a series of issues with the employer reluctantly opening a channel of communication with its representatives and officials so members can be represented in grievance or disciplinary proceedings. This situation has been reinforced by the ERA rights on individual representation by underpinning the union as the legitimate representative of its members. Despite these advances, gaining union recognition remains a key objective because without it the opportunities for collective representation and collective bargaining are restricted. An important aspect of the campaign has been the way activists have used the language of organizing (e.g. "equality" and "respect") to identify a mismatch between the employer's espoused values and the way in which employees are managed in order to develop support for the union with some degree of success.

The organizing campaign

The most recent attempt to gain union recognition was prompted by three developments. First, an activist at the headquarters has been instrumental in building a membership core and has consistently argued for resources from the national union to support the union recognition campaign. Second, the ERA has been an important factor in the timing of the campaign. Third, the charity reviewed its employee participation and involvement procedures as a result of a perceived weakness of the national consultative forum which had been in place until 1998 and which was seen as being ineffective. Combined with organizational restructuring which changed the constituencies on which the forum was based, an alternative employee participation structure was felt to be needed. The review process prompted the union to reassert its preference for union recognition rather than a staff forum or works council as a mechanism for employee representation.

Prior to the launch of the current campaign for recognition in 1998, MSF had made little attempt to develop its membership other than to "recruit, service and walk away" (interview, lead union organizer). But with the growing interest of management in trying to establish a works council, the workplace activists requested more support from the union and this led to the involvement of the specialist organizer. The additional resources and expertise that she brought allowed the officers and activists to rethink their approach, resulting in greater emphasis being placed on developing the members and activists in order to build and sustain a union presence and gain union recognition. She had previous organizing experience in Britain and Australia and was particularly keen to build membership using issues that were directly affecting the workforce. The campaign attempted to create lay member structures to give activists the skills to develop recruitment and representation plans, and to help employees identify the issues around which they had a collective interest and could challenge management by acting together with the help of the union. This approach has been argued to be positively associated with unions successfully winning "first contracts" in the USA (Bronfenbrenner and Juravich 1998). Further, Kelly (1998) argues that identification and attribution of collective grievances are crucial in the process of mobilization.

Challenging the works council

The existence of non-union forms of employee participation has posed a significant challenge to unions' workplace presence and organization (Terry 1999, Lloyd 2001), and this case is no exception. Works councils can threaten workplace unionism by offering an alternative voice to employees who perceive an injustice, attribute that injustice to their employer, and develop a sense of collective identity (Kelly 1998). Lloyd (2001: 315) argues that for a union to establish itself in a workplace with a non-union employee participation channel, workers must hold negative views of the utility of non-union voice mechanisms in the process that Kelly (1998) identifies of addressing issues and resolving injustices. The replacement of the consultative forum with a works council was recognized by union activists to pose a significant challenge to their efforts to establish an independent union, but after much debate, they chose to engage with the works councils and it is important to consider this decision in detail.

In the early 1990s, the charity set up a forum for the representation of staff views. The National Consultative Forum (NCF) had no formal negotiating rights, but did have the right to express views on a narrow range of subjects such as the future of employee representation. A number of union members had sat on the NCF in a personal capacity and had presented a union perspective on issues discussed. In the late 1990s, the structure of the organization changed and the representational basis of the NCF no longer existed. The management team reviewed the represent-ation mechanisms and decided to ballot staff in 1998 on the form of preferred representation. Three options were presented: to re-establish the NCF, to establish a national works council supported by local councils, or to engage in full union recognition. MSF ran an active campaign urging employees to vote for recognition of a union(s). The organization's litera-ture preferred a system of works councils because of low union density (less than 10 percent) and a works council system would allow the voices of non-union members to be heard. The ballot result was 66 percent for union recognition, although it remained unspecified as to which union(s) would be recognized. However, with a poor turnout (15 percent), management rejected its outcome, saying it was unrepresentative of the workforce's views, and implemented the second option. Activists and officials, feeling the decision was particularly harsh, continued to campaign for the result to be recognized.

The issue of whether the union should participate in the works councils generated the most controversy because its existence has faced the union with significant dilemmas about how to proceed with its union recognition campaign. Many activists believed that it would give the works councils legitimacy (and undermine the legitimacy of the union) if the union was to field candidates for election to a body which it argued should not have come into existence. However, an alternative perspective has become dominant since then: that the union should engage with the works councils and attempt to use them as a forum for putting forward collective issues and the union perspective. As a result, the union fielded candidates for both the local and the national councils and now has a won a significant presence on them; just under half of the seats are held by union members, most of whom speak from a union perspective.

This has created a difficult situation where many of the union activists try to balance their potentially competing roles of being a union and a works council representative. A headquarters representative explained the dilemma of the dual responsibility:

> You are a union rep. You are on a works council. You don't want the works council to succeed for ideological reasons, but on the other hand none of us want to sit there and be deliberately obstructive because we want to improve things.
>
> (Interview, union and works council representative)

The activists felt that the works councils are based on an illegitimate inter-pretation of the ballot, yet in recognizing the impact of the absence of union recognition, the councils present a useful forum by which to express the members' collective views. Activists also perceived dangers to building union support using the works councils:

JOANNE: [The works council] is the only thing we've got and we want it to work.

SAMANTHA: But ironically if you are too successful you will make the works council a success and we will be stuck with it!

JOANNE: It depends what you mean by success. What would you see as successful with the works council and would that achieve the same things as the union?

SAMANTHA: Well exactly. [The organizer] said that even if you do make a massive success of the works council, it's still not going to have the same rights as the union. It would be OK, but we could do even better. And I think that's important and we need to make sure we don't lose sight of that.

JOANNE: I think what will be difficult will be to get people to join the union at the same time as telling them what you have been doing in the works council. I think you are going to have to keep those things quite separate otherwise there could be conflict. A bit of a conflicting message.

The danger of this "conflicting message" was still being debated a year after the establishment of the works councils: the union argued about the legitimacy, whilst the works councils had some degree of success in pursuing some of the arguments put forward by employees and union representatives. This, in turn, raises the prospect that the works councils may be seen as a more effective channel of communication than the union.

An example of the union's success in challenging management policy came when union members argued against a proposal to have a confidentiality clause on the works councils' discussions. This was argued to be unhelpful to the objective of improving communication with staff. The non-union representatives supported the union view and management dropped the proposal. The union representatives linked their success to having had the support of experienced FTOs who warned against such clauses and publicizing the case as a union "victory." If, however, more significant examples of the works councils representatives exercising influence over management develop, it is possible that the concerns identified above become realized. To avoid this, activists have been encouraged to engage with the councils as a way of establishing and developing an on-going relationship with management and despite the potential hazards, this approach seems to have had some success. But whilst this has been a crucial issue for union activists and officials, there is little evidence that it has had any significant negative effect on building broad-based support for collective representation through the union. Nonetheless, the works councils clearly do represent a form of "substitutionism" and to date there seems to be relatively little return from union representatives' energies in constructive engagement.

Issue-based campaigning

The issues around which a sense of collective interest and grievance are built up are important in understanding the alleged advantages of the "membership-led" approach to unionism. Issue-based union campaigning is argued and implied respectively to be a key element of Bronfenbrenner and Juravich's (1998) "organizing model" and of Kelly's (1998) mobilization theory. This study presents an opportunity to examine this where the union primarily used concerns around pensions, working time, and the proposed reorganization of the works council. In support, issues of health and safety, management style, and unreasonable expectations were raised throughout the campaign. The works council reorganization posed important problems to the union, including the prospect of dividing union members, supporters, and potential members. The organizer, therefore, considered it particularly important to build a collective response to other workplace issues. But the recognition campaign was notable because the issues addressed by the activists have not been confined to traditional workplace industrial relations issues such as those mentioned above.

An early union "success" related to the organization's pension fund. Concern existed amongst a number of groups, including the charity's auditors, that payments were not being made into the pension fund within the time prescribed by law. The charity was therefore asked to explain what had been happening as failure to make prompt payment is a criminal offense. The union played an important role in ensuring the issues were heard in full by organizing a postcard campaign to draw employees' attention to the issue and to allow them to express their concern to management. The postcards, numbering 150, were collected by the union and then forwarded to the chief executive asking for a review of the procedures. Postcard responses from members and non-members gave the organizer the names and addresses of potential members who were interested in what the union was doing. Alongside the postcards, the pensions regulator, OPRA, held an inquiry, establishing there was evidence of late payment. This led to publicity in a number of national newspapers and industry journals. MSF produced publicity material for potential members to reinforce the message that by campaigning together, workers could be successful in achieving collective improvements: a key technique associated with organizing success (Bronfenbrenner and Juravich 1998). This approach also illustrates Kelly's (1998: 32) arguments about the importance of leaders in identifying, consolidating, and expressing collective grievances. While the issue affected the majority of workers, without union involvement it seems unlikely that it would have moved beyond an issue of individualized and atomized interest.

Working time has been another on-going issue, largely in respect of residential home staff's hours. Residential care inevitably includes some night duty and requires some staff to sleep on the premises. Prior to the campaign, the government issued regulations for compliance with the European Union Working Time Directive. The regulations recognize the health and safety implications of long working hours, seek to limit total working time, introduce compulsory rest periods, and regulate days off and holidays. Although there are "loopholes" in the regulations, MSF used the regulations to help promote a debate on working hours and the rest hours of staff, using the campaigning tools of newsletters, posters, and other publicity material.

In many of the residential homes, staff working time has been reviewed to bring it into line with the regulations. While this review may have happened independently of the union, the union was able demonstrate its relevance and influence by stressing that the review had occurred more speedily and more extensively than would have been the case without it, and that without MSF, employees would have had to argue for this to be carried out on an individual basis. Again, the union objective was to demonstrate to members and potential members that the union could be more effective in improving the working conditions than non-union means.

More general health and safety issues such as lifting clients with mobility difficulties and guidelines about driving minibuses have also featured, not because the charity is particularly negligent here but because with clear law on management's responsibility in this regard, MSF viewed these as "winnable" campaign issues. Making small improvements here can help reinforce the message of union and collective effectiveness. It is notable, however, that despite the redundancies implemented as part of the organization's restructuring program, this was not an issue around which the union developed a collective campaign. There seem to be a number of reasons for this.

MSF has not solely focused on such traditional workplace issues for, in this case, its activists at headquarters have taken a broader approach. A successful petition campaign to get the local council to build a pedestrian crossing outside the headquarters was mounted following the charity's move to its current headquarters in 1998. Many of the people who use the building have physical disabilities, be they visitors or staff. Another example was the campaign to remove Nescafé products from the building, given their selling policies to under-developed countries. While this has been less successful, it again highlights the attempt to build a broader base of support for the union by extending the scope of traditional union activity. In the absence of formal recognition agreement to define the union's remit, one activist believed this kind of activity generated legitimacy:

> They [the broader campaigns] work because people see that we are not only interested in getting membership, we are interested in the wider issues. I think we have built up quite a lot of credibility there and people see that we are interested in other things.
>
> (Interview)

while another argued:

> We don't know about such and such a standing order. What we focus more on is more about the issues. I've been to [some] regional meetings which were dominated by middle-aged men who had been there for years. And you feel very ostracized by that. It all seems very much governed by process rather than content.
>
> (Interview)

This illustrates one difficulty of unionizing "new" groups of workers and the organizing approach more generally, namely that in developing issue-based approaches and attracting groups which have previously been under-represented, existing union structures may be unsuitable for representing their interests. Thus "new" groups of workers may need to develop new forms of representation (e.g. McBride 2000) or may have different interests from more traditionally unionized groups. In this regard, Hyman (1992) argues that differentiation of worker interests has long been a feature of union development, and Leisink (1997) develops a case for unions to create agendas which differentiate between the wide range of interests of "new union constituencies." This study suggests that at least some newly organized groups of workers perceive more "traditional" workplace interests as forming only part of a broader union agenda. Whether traditional union structures can adapt to this challenge is a vexed issue because it will help determine if unions are able to organize amongst "non-traditional" workers.

The language of organizing

A significant feature of the campaign has been MSF's attempt to use the charity's own espoused values to build support for itself. The increasing importance given to stressing union membership as a "human right" and the wish of the employees to be treated with "dignity" and "respect" at work in organizing campaigns (Sciacchitano 1998) may productively chime for unions with the dominant discourse of voluntary sector employers. But Cunningham (2000: 203–4) suggests that the nature of work in the third sector and the effect of employees' "ideological commitment" to shared goals with their employer could hinder unionization. This study suggests support for the former as the union has been effective in using the employees' commitment to the charity's campaigning values "equality," "caring," "support," and "advocacy" to highlight the inconsistencies in the employer's behavior towards its clients and employees. Thus, the lead organizer noted that "[The charity] is spinning a very strong line about the rights of the clients. So that helps [us to organize] because it allows us to talk about our rights." The union consistently used this lexicon in organizing meetings and in literature to members and potential members, whether this be MSF's objective of "making society fairer," its commitment to equality of opportunity by, for example, having a national disabilities officer, or the notion of equality in relation to what was felt to be lacking in the workplace environment. One headquarters union representative further explained:

> Our organization's core value is equality. You can't just have disability equality and forget the rest ... You are going to have to also deliver equality on all other things which means gender equality, which means age-based equality, paternity rights.
>
> (Interview)

The lexicon used has been useful in developing a sense of collective grievance. Where these common values are not being upheld in the employment relationship, MSF has been able to use this disparity to develop support for the need for an independent union in the workplace. This supports the finding in the USA that the language of "respect," "dignity," and "justice" in organizing campaigns is an effective way of mobilizing union support (Sciacchitano 1998) and challenges Cunningham's (2000: 203–4) view that employees' commitment to the organizational values may constrain the possibilities for unionization, indicating dual commitment can exist. Further, there is no evidence of the language of (union–management) "partnership" being used because of the charity's reluctance to engage with MSF. Indeed, it likely that the union's forward and robust approach may have increased management hostility. But it is possible that in other voluntary sector organizations the "partnership" approach may prove more fruitful.

The Employment Relations Act 1999

MSF has consistently campaigned to gain union recognition in order to formalize its right to represent the workforce and to bargain collectively on their behalf. It has done so by encouraging management to recognize it voluntarily because this method holds a number of advantages over statutory recognition (see Introduction). As the details of recognition provisions became clearer from 1999, the union had to decide whether to pursue a claim for statutory recognition if voluntary recognition was not forthcoming as well as how to use the legislation if the charity persisted in refusing recognition. These decisions hinged around the union's preferred bargaining unit and in using the legislative context to open a formal dialog with management.

The statutory procedures compel the CAC to determine the bargaining unit, with regard to a number of principles, if the two parties cannot agree on one. The bargaining unit can be any group of employees within the organization which can be shown to form a cohesive work group, e.g. a staff grade, or employees who work in a particular location, or all staff working for an organization. The union has the right to make the first proposal and to then put this to management. The procedure progresses to the next stage if management has no objections. If there is disagreement, the CAC will rule on an appropriate bargaining unit, where maintaining "effective management" is a key consideration. In choosing a bargaining unit where the union can demonstrate majority support, the union has various choices. Membership and activism was strongest, for example, in the headquarters and some of the residential homes where members have frequent contact with each other. Amongst the shop workers and drivers, membership was lower as these employees are isolated and have little opportunity to meet each other, let alone a union organizer. The choice therefore became whether to build up to a claim for recognition on a geographical basis, starting with the regions and areas where the union was strong, or to attempt to organize across all workplaces, thereby risking that overall aggregate membership may be brought down by the retail division.

The issue was debated at several meetings of the activist network and a consensus emerged for keeping all of the employees together because of the importance of acting collectively. It was resolved to thus focus on bringing together groups of employees who had not previously been targeted for membership, such as the delivery van drivers. In doing so, the challenge became more difficult than if the union had decided to focus resources on the areas where it was already strong. By late 2000, the difficulties of this strategy were becoming evident with the union still having recruited only 10 percent of the workforce, although membership has reached between 30 amd 40 percent in areas such as the headquarters. The influence of the legislation is evident, even in the absence of a statutory claim. This case suggests that the task of organizing, gaining, and sustaining membership across this kind of large and diverse "multi-divisional" organization takes on an added significance under the ERA. If this continues to be so in this case, MSF may feel compelled to make a claim(s) for the bargaining units where they have membership strength. In doing so, they risk having these selective bargaining units rejected in favor of one that covers the whole workforce. Crucially, this approach may also divide the membership, isolating the members in bargaining units which have not been targeted.

The legal right to representation in grievances and disciplinaries where there is no union recognition may give unions a way of setting out their wares to potential members, servicing existing members where effective representation for problems at work has been established as being the key reason why people join a union (Waddington and Whitston 1997), and opening a formal channel of communication with management. In the multi-divisional organization, this right is of greater immediate significance in supporting workplace unionism and aiding the campaign for union recognition. MSF thus trained a cohort of workplace representatives to undertake this work, although these are currently concentrated in the stronger areas of unionization. As a result, some of the pressure on the FTOs responsible for the campaign was eased as the activists were able to take on much of the day-to-day work of sustaining MSF's workplace activities, freeing up the FTOs to concentrate on the campaign's more strategic aspects. These new workplace representatives are now identifiable to managers and staff alike, helping normalize the union's presence and role and overcoming perceptions that union activists are "troublemakers." Nonetheless, without recognition, the union still faces considerable difficulties in sustaining its presence in the organization. There is little enthusiasm from management to grant union recognition but recent changes of personnel on both management and union sides may lead to some progress.

Thus, the ERA's recognition provisions have provided little help to MSF's campaign primarily because of the charity's structure. The provisions may only be of help once MSF has been able to build a substantial membership across the heterogeneous workforce. Indeed, the legislation may in fact legitimate the employer's decision to not recognize a union with a significant, but minority, membership by establishing the threshold-cum-principle of simple majority union membership or majority union support. However, other legislation has proved more helpful, notably on working time, health and safety, and pensions. Thus, an unrecognized union can make an impact in a workplace by pursuing internal grievances and, if necessary, employment tribunals and legal cases. There is evidence from this case that increasingly "juridified" employment relations can provide unions with some opportunities to establish their presence in workplaces.

Conclusion

The uneven pattern of unionization has been an important barrier to MSF achieving union recognition. The headquarters staff are particularly well organized for a number of reasons. First, resulting from their work skills, these staff are often experienced campaigners and are able to use this to recruit and campaign for the union. Second, through working in the same building with regular working hours, these workers find it easier than others to meet regularly to share information and ideas and to develop the campaign. Some residential services staff, by contrast, work shifts and find it difficult to bring people together to discuss union issues. Third, the headquarters workers included a number of key activists who have an ideological union commitment and are prepared to put considerable amounts of their time into the campaign. Thus, many of the initiatives developed by the union were led by this group of workers. This suggests two possible conclusions. One is that greater union resources and effort need to be invested to help boost membership beyond its current low level of around 10 percent. Another is that structure, location, and associated constraints may heavily influence the outcomes of organizing campaigns. This case suggests some support for both. Membership growth and development was particularly strong during the time the organizer was employed and if membership is to reach 50 percent plus, MSF may need to make a longer-term investment of resources, particularly to develop organizing and campaigning skills amongst a broader group of members and activists.

It is, however, possible that, even with this, the charity's structure and the factors associated with this will continue to constitute barriers to MSF's aims. It may, for example, prove impossible to build collective organization amongst the atomized shop workers. If this is the case, it suggests that Bronfenbrenner and Juravich's (1998) position about the universality of the organizing approach needs questioning. The study suggests that whilst issue-based organizing may be effective in building union support and activism, with the current statutory recognition procedures, it is more successful in achieving union recognition in smaller bargaining units with greater homogeneity amongst the workforce. The structure and characteristics of the charity's workforce may be too diverse, dispersed, and inimical for this approach to be effective. But with management hostility ruling out a "partnership" based approach, there seems little prospect of an alternative but to continue the current strategy. In this the works council may be used given its greater reach to all employees but this risks showing the works councils to be more effective at representing employees than the union.

Overall, this study does give some support to Cunningham's (2000) qualified optimism regarding the scope for unionization in this sector. He is correct to suggest individual representation rights, combined with other legal provisions such as health and safety legislation, allow unions opportunities to establish a presence in this sector. There is also some basis for his skepticism about the opportunities presented by the statutory recognition procedures. Perhaps more importantly, this study allows an insight into the ways in which the union's actions help or hinder their union recognition campaign.

In the face of employer resistance, significant and long-term investment of union resources is necessary in order to build and sustain union activity but this is inevitably risky as union recognition is not guaranteed. Although there is evidence that when such an investment is made the presence and effectiveness of union activity can be established, MSF still has a difficult decision to make about whether or not to continue to invest in the campaign. Thus, the future of the campaign remains uncertain.

Recent developments suggest that the union's strategy in the charity may change. A new FTO has responsibility for the campaign and the charity has made some key personnel changes within its managerial structure. This means that approaches by the union to develop a more consensual approach to union recognition may yet be possible. Indeed, the relationship between the two parties seems to be improving and management is increasingly willing to meet with senior FTOs to discuss the union's future role within the organization. Additionally, the union has merged with the AEEU in January 2002, becoming Amicus. Given that the AEEU was foremost in developing a partnership approach to target unrecognized workplaces and is the dominant partner in Amicus, this may have some impact. That said, it is not clear whether Amicus will be prepared to invest the required significant level of resources to develop the issue-based organizing campaign.

Until the union is successful in gaining a formal recognition, its legitimacy to speak on behalf of its members will continue to be questioned by management, particularly in the absence of a majority membership. Despite the importance of union recognition in enabling a union to operate effectively, the local activists have still had a number of successes. There is therefore evidence that a union can perform an important, if limited, role in a non-recognized workplace. The emphasis MSF has placed on small but collective victories accords with Kelly's model (1998) of mobilization in demonstrating to both employees and managers that collective action can address grievances. However, the overall degree of effectiveness has been limited where there has yet to be any significant and fuller mobilization against management. The union has not yet been tested or tested itself by attempting mobilize and do so with a successful outcome over an issue which challenges more fundamentally the managerial prerogative. This would test the robustness of its members and support.

Cunningham (2000) also raises issues concerning the difficulties organizing groups of workers such as young workers and women. It is notable that the preponderance of relatively young and female workers does not seem to have posed any particular or significant difficulties in establishing MSF in the workplace, especially given the flexible and issue-based approach developed by the union in this campaign. However, some activists have expressed concerns about how this approach to workplace trade unionism fits with some of the broader union structures and there may yet prove to be a mismatch between the two approaches to unionism, those of the local union and national union. The wide agenda identified by these employees as being important for building support for the union amongst a workforce that is predominantly young and female and which has a broad notion of the role of the union within the workforce suggests that unions organizing in this sector may face a challenge in developing an agenda which appeals to these workers by embracing some of their less traditional collective interests. That this confronts traditional union structures, policies, interests, and *modus operandi* should not be underestimated. Union structures have developed to focus primarily on work-related issues and these findings suggest that if unions impose a solely work-related agenda on these "new" groups of workers, they may see this as overly prescriptive and too limiting. Furthermore, it is evident from this case that the union will have to invest considerable effort before many of these members feel comfortable dealing with the formal procedures that most unions use to deal with regional and national business. It may well be that the most significant barrier to organizing new groups of workers in the voluntary sector concerns representing their interests within the wider union.

More generally, whilst this case does point to some of the difficulties in organizing workers in the not-for-profit sector, there are important notes of optimism. The most significant of these is that whilst workers in this sector do identify with their employer's objectives, they also clearly identify with the values of unionism, collectivism, and collective action, suggesting evidence of "dual commitment" (Guest 1992). This is particularly evident in employees' discussion of a mismatch between their employer's espoused values and the ways in which they are treated as workers. This has given, in turn, MSF the opportunity to use this to build support for the union using the language of "respect," "rights," and "equality." Thus, the barriers to establishing union recognition in this sector maybe more structural rather than attitudinal. Crucially then, there is evidence the union movement has a significant opportunity to expand into the voluntary sector as long as some of the structural barriers can be overcome.

Note

1 MSF is one of at least four large unions competing to organize voluntary sector workers. The relationship between these unions is not, however, a focus in this study.

7 Organizing in electronics

Recruitment, recognition and representation – shadow shop stewards in Scotland's "Silicon Glen"

Patricia Findlay and Alan McKinlay

Introduction

For much of the past two decades, unions in Britain and the US have faced a difficult economic and political climate, with union and member experiences reflecting retrenchment and survival, not expansion (Aronovitz 1998). More recently, however, recruitment and organizing have been resurrected on union agendas in both countries (Beaumont and Harris 1990, Nissen 1999), addressing the possibility that non-membership results partly from inadequate recruitment strategies (Mason and Bain 1991, Bronfenbrenner et al.1998).

From the US experience, new approaches to organizing operate at four distinct levels. First, unions commit additional resources to organizing. Second, rank-and-file activists in individual workplaces are identified, developed, and supported as they engage in "bottom-up" campaigns for recognition, using a range of organizing tactics. Third, union officers adopt "transformational" leadership styles, with initial high levels of personal contact and support followed by grassroots activists increasingly taking greater responsibility for union affairs. Last, organizing is taken outside the workplace through the use of activists from unionized workplaces, alliances with community groups, and external pressure groups. Issues of governance, fairness, and dignity are the primary emphases here. In both countries, it is increasingly acknowledged that union tactics matter (Bronfenbrenner et al.1998).

In non-union workplaces in the UK, recruitment and organizing priorities have also been reshaped by the ERA's statutory recognition procedures. The implications of the legislative framework are complex (Towers 1999a, Wood and Goddard 1999). There may be a world of difference between formal and effective recognition but symbolically the ERA provides a more supportive legislative framework for union recognition and regeneration and a springboard from which to challenge unfettered managerial prerogative in the workplace (cf. Zeitlin 1985).

Non-union workplaces pose a particular challenge to both recruiting and organizing. Union membership exists in non-union firms, yet little is known about why individuals join unions where recognition is absent and unlikely, and where membership appears to offer little material benefit (Findlay 1993). It might be argued that at least tacit employer co-operation is necessary to sustain union presence and servicing. From a rational choice perspective, the return to membership without recognition is limited. Further, without a critical mass of union members, union recruitment and activism is less likely to be socially constructed in the workplace.

Yet workers in unorganized workplaces do attempt to organize. Literature in the US has identified factors associated with successful recognition campaigns (Reed 1989, Freeman and Kleiner 1990). Yet little of this work assesses the impact of the campaign on workplace actors and activity. Unsuccessful organizing campaigns may significantly affect the attitudes and behaviors of both parties. Successful recognition campaigns provide only a starting point from which new workplace relationships maybe reconstructed in a new context. Notwithstanding the practical difficulties of moving from recruitment to recognition, recognition itself can add up to "something or nothing." Employers may thwart the objectives of formal recognition, promoting the view that unions deliver little. Additionally, or alternatively, unions may be unable to develop the skills and capabilities of new workplace activists to prevent this happening.

Even with a more accommodating legislative framework, unions still face significant challenges in achieving adequate recruitment, turning recruitment into recognition, and turning recognition into effective trade unionism. There are risks at each stage. In addition, strategies adopted at one part of the process may have implications for subsequent developments. According a high priority (and significant resources) to recruitment impacts both on the relationships and the services offered to existing members, creating a potential tension between "organizing" and "servicing" models of union activity (Fletcher and Hurd 1998). Furthermore, recruitment strategies in unorganized workplaces set the tone for future relationships between the union and its members. Shaping the expectation of members and potential members in terms of levels of activism and forms of representation may well define the possibilities of any post-recognition scenario in the short to medium term.

The role of lay activists is crucial in relation to recruitment, recognition, and representation in non-union firms. Effective trade unionism requires more than members: it requires activists whose workplace activities sustain and develop the objectives of trade unionism in their immediate setting and in unions at large. These activists must be identified, encouraged, and developed. While some research on recruitment and organizing has focused on TUC or individual union level (e.g. Carter 2000), we wish to evaluate the organizing process from the "bottom up" by considering the experience of *shadow stewards*. Shadow stewards are individuals who, in the absence of recognized shop stewards, act as unofficial representatives of their immediate workgroup, and whose role may prefigure official steward activity. As Kelly (1998: 127) notes, "The transformation of a set of individuals into a collective actor is normally the work of a small but critical mass of activists whose role in industrial relations has been seriously understated." Shadow stewards are likely to play a crucial role in union organizing. Given the relative sparseness of research in this area, detailed case analysis is a necessary prerequisite of developing a strategic approach to the organizing process (Burawoy 1998). We examine three recognition campaigns involving the AEEU and ISTC in Scotland's "Silicon Glen" – at IBM Greenock (IBM), Chunghwa Picture Tubes UK (CPT), and Fullerton Computer Industries, Gourock (FCI).

The electronics industry in Scotland and worldwide is commonly associated with the absence of trade unionism (MacInnes and Sproull 1989, Findlay 1993; see Chapter 2, this volume). A combination of entrenched employer opposition and limited engagement by unions has resulted in a multinational and indigenous microelectronic sector almost bereft of union organization. The main corporate employers have consistently pursued ideologically driven *anti-union* strategies, alongside a "sophisticated paternalist" approach to managing employees, including non-union channels of employee representation. However, the effectiveness of these channels is open to question (Findlay 1992). Intense competitive pressures on indigenous companies, largely concentrated on tight margin commodity production and low value-added operations, have generated a number of "black hole" workplaces regulated neither by unions nor by consistent HRM policies (Guest and Conway 1999). These "black hole" employers are more openly hostile to trade unionism, although they offer few positive incentives to employees to remain non-union.

Yet pockets of union membership exist throughout the sector. Here, we present data derived from semi-structured interviews on national and local organizing strategies with thirty-five union-side "players" in the electronics industry, including national and local union officers, specialist recruitment and organizing officers, shadow stewards, accredited stewards, and union members. Additional data was derived from non-participant observation of union recruitment, organizing, and branch meetings. This provided important insights into the organizational capabilities of new stewards and the expectations of their memberships. Each case illustrated important dimensions of organizing and resulted in distinctly different outcomes. We will consider each campaign briefly before drawing together the key themes.

A marginal voice: the AEEU and IBM

IBM is one of the best-known companies in the world. Until relatively recently, the company had a reputation as a sophisticated paternalist employer, offering relatively high wages and good conditions of employment

(Dickson *et al.* 1988). These relative benefits were not lost on its Greenock workforce:

> When I first entered IBM I thought that although there was still a place for trade unions . . . there was nothing really wrong . . . I was getting, on average, between 15 and 17 percent wage rises every year. I could hardly say to anybody . . . "Hey we should get organized because they keep giving us too much money here!"
>
> (AEEU steward C, 2001)

Many employees were aware that favorable employment conditions were part of a company strategy to keep unions at bay. While IBM claims not to oppose union membership, it has consistently opposed recognition in Britain. In 1974, an ACAS workforce ballot registered a four-to-one majority against recognition, following the company's offer of a month's tax-free pay if the workforce rejected recognition. A sophisticated management, extensive corporate paternalism, and an elaborate in-house system of employee representation (Dickson *et al.* 1988) undercut the appeal of trade unionism. Various company voice mechanisms exist. "Open Door" allows any employee to challenge any contractual decisions taken by their line manager. Each challenge is progressively raised to the next managerial level until it is withdrawn or resolved. "Speak Up" is a confidential voice mechanism. In theory, the plant's "Advisory Council" offers the possibility of collective voice through elected plant representatives.

IBM maintained its favorable employment conditions intact until the early 1990s, when a shift in competitive strategy towards the production of "commodity" PCs brought with it significant change for employees. A salary freeze was introduced in Greenock in the early 1990s, followed by the withdrawal of a range of additional payments and rewards. Core staff were confronted with reduced incremental pay rises, unilateral changes in shift patterns and work organization, and an increase in the volume of contract labor. Despite IBM's public stance on unions, there have always been a small number of union members at Greenock (Knox and McKinlay 1999). Primarily, these are engineers and electricians who retain membership in case they have to leave IBM and work elsewhere. This was a trace element of trade unionism, a hidden residue rather than a platform for any concerted union recruitment campaign.

Deteriorating terms and conditions in the early 1990s stimulated some employees to raise issues through the Advisory Council. The Council's inability to deal with their concerns became increasingly obvious, however:

> I did start it with a genuine belief. I thought when it got to higher management they would be genuinely interested in what was happening . . . I spend three very frustrating years getting absolutely nowhere fast . . . It was really used as a stepping stone into management . . . We

were bringing up issue after issue and it was just being utterly swept
under the carpet.

(AEEU steward C, 2001)

The lack of meaningful consultation on significant changes in employment
contracts was critical to the formation of a small group of shadow stewards.
A number of craft workers, ex-public sector workers, and former employees
in heavy industry identified themselves to each other through their shared
trade backgrounds, their willingness to offer advice to employees, and their
readiness to question managers during departmental briefings. This
resulted in an approach to the AEEU for support in 1996. Initially, the
group wanted information with which to challenge IBM management, and
this was provided informally by a FTO. Through word of mouth, additional
IBM workers began to attend these meetings. A union branch was established in 1996/1997. It has a membership of about fifty, although the
number of activists is considerably smaller. Recruitment appears to be
closely related to deteriorating terms and conditions, suggesting that
members join for practical reasons, despite limited scope for union
effectiveness. Yet despite this deterioration, the vast majority of IBM
employees have not joined a union, perhaps reflecting their continuing
relatively privileged position in the local labor market.

The shadow stewards are unable to recruit openly in IBM, relying on word
of mouth and approaches made by employees to them. Given constraints
on their opportunities to act (Kelly 1998), covert distribution of information is a significant part of their strategy:

> I tend to leave leaflets lying around, in the canteen, smoke rooms.
> They absolutely hate that and if they ever caught me at it, they'd be
> forced to do something about it. Recently they've begun to train
> cameras on the location of leaflets, and put up signs saying "IBM
> property only."

(AEEU steward A, 2000)

Although the shadow stewards are "unofficial, sometimes cloak and dagger"
(AEEU steward B, 2000), they deal with many similar issues to conventional
stewards. Most members are production workers who have been particularly
hit by the recent changes. One particular source of contention is the system
of individual contracts, and, in particular, individual performance management and reward, which are seen to be arbitrary and lack transparency and
consistency. Similarly, the individualist nature of in-house voice mechanisms
remains controversial:

> Departmental or site meetings are convened for annual reports on
> plant and corporate performance. Anyone can challenge managers from
> the floor but this is an intimidating forum for individual dissent.

(AEEU steward A, 2000)

To challenge a managerial decision via Open Door is visible and risky for the individual. As one AEEU member notes "it's an Orwellian open door, simply because anyone that uses it is discriminated against. The last figures I saw, about 4 years ago, 12 people used Open Door and 2000 used Speak Up" (AEEU steward A, 2000). From 1998, the shadow stewards deliberately raised their visibility in the plant, challenging managers at large "Speak Up" meetings. In 1999, twelve activists received written warnings for insubordination as management clamped down on public dissent.

Given their unequal position in terms of security and reward relative to their core counterparts, temporary workers at IBM (who are mainly directly employed by the company) have every reason to seek union membership and protection, and thus provide an important recruitment opportunity. Further, given that issues of fairness and consistency of treatment have been central to the motivations of activists at IBM, the recruitment of temporary workers seems an obvious step. Yet the activists are reluctant to expose such vulnerable individuals in any way, and this has acted to limit their recruitment efforts amongst the temporary workforce. This has not prevented them, however, from arguing on their behalf within the company, and successfully winning for them parity on annual bonus payments.

There are costs in associating with the union. Aside from the disciplinary action, individual activists believe they have paid a heavy price in career and financial terms. One key activist has been "redeployed" from a relatively skilled job to a high-speed assembly line, where salaries are one-third less, with his earnings red-circled until the others catch up. Given this, the branch leadership is exceptionally protective of other, particularly young, activists. Inside IBM there is a well-established group of experienced union activists, with a clear strategy and realistic objectives. They do not expect to achieve union recognition in the short term, far less to negotiate on terms and conditions. Rather, they hope simply to compel IBM to accept that the union has a legitimate voice:

> The worst trade union in the world, the weakest trade union in the world, would be a thousand times better than what we've got at the moment. If we gave them a no-strike clause for a thousand years it would be better than what we've got at the moment. Collective bargaining is what we need.
>
> (Interview, AEEU steward A, 2000)

The IBM activists have considered the strategic opportunities presented by ERA and the development of European works councils (EWC). Consideration is being given to identifying a bargaining unit that maximizes membership in the hope of triggering a workforce ballot. While there would be little hope of achieving the 40 percent vote threshold, the electoral process would help legitimize a union presence. This would be a major symbolic breakthrough for the union but there are no illusions about the practical impact: "We would have a notice board" said one activist with heavy irony (AEEU member B, 2000). A similar logic was applied in relation to IBM's EWC. Plans had been made to stand two AEEU candidates in 2000 in order to have access to the hustings. Unfortunately, the AEEU failed to deliver the nomination forms and leaflets necessary, and the candidatures did not proceed. This raises questions regarding the AEEU's support for the shadow stewards. From an initially hesitant response, the union has worked to contain, and not facilitate, the activists' requests for a concerted recruitment campaign. No tailored leaflets have been produced. There is no concession in dues for IBM members. In part, this is simply pragmatism over returns on resources. Strategically, however, the union calculates that it is better to hold what it has, rather than to engage in a risky recruitment drive. Yet this drastically constrains the potential of the activist group:

> I make no bones about it, we need the AEEU to get up off their butts and recognize that there is potential. We've shown that there is potential and now we're saying to the union "come on, we've done our bit, let's see you take if from here and push on a bit towards that end goal," which is recognition.
>
> (AEEU steward C, 2001)

Precarious gains: the AEEU and Chunghwa

CPT UK, part of the Taiwanese conglomerate, Tatung, established a manufacturing plant in Bellshill in 1995 to manufacture tubes for televisions and computer monitors. The work process was based on highly automated, flow-line production. High levels of automation were efficient only if there was a high volume of standardized production. The labor practices of the parent company centered on tight supervisory control, corporate paternalism, and a hostility to trade unionism. Tight labor control was a prerequisite of competitiveness in the fiercely competitive market for consumer electronics and computer peripherals. Initially, Taiwanese practices were moderated by the British management team, which stressed the need for workforce co-operation. From its inception, the plant struggled with employee relations problems relating to line discipline, supervision, and health and safety.

The combined effect of the Asian economic crisis of 1998 and a collapse in demand from IBM was catastrophic: expansion was put on hold as the parent company repatriated all available funds. On the shop floor, long, automated production lines designed to mass-produce a single product had to be reconfigured with minimal capital investment to form shorter loops that allowed for greater product variety. Mechanized transfer was replaced by human effort. Highly orchestrated tasks became more varied and improvised as production-planning systems buckled under the strain. In addition, the plant's experienced British management team was replaced with

Taiwanese managers. All decisions were referred back to the parent company, causing delays that added to the daily crises on the shop floor. Direct control of labor could not deliver the daily innovations and routine improvisation necessary to compensate for this perpetual crisis in production flows. Efficiency and quality standards fell dramatically. With no mechanism to harness workforce commitment or to sustain innovation in work routines, line supervisors intensified the pressure on individual workers. Job specifications became open-ended as operators struggled to compensate for reductions in technical support. Shift patterns were altered unilaterally by management. Supervisory interventions became frequent and discipline harsher and more arbitrary. Driving the line further, however, limited the space for planning or altering work organization. The shop floor was locked into a vicious downward spiral of declining production performance and intensifying supervision, with obvious negative consequences for workers, for which management was clearly held responsible (see Kelly 1998).

There was no consultation regarding these changes in employment contracts, work organization, or management style. The workforce indicated through internal surveys that they had no effective "voice" mechanism. While CPT had instituted a Staff Representation Committee (SRC), this body was solely consultative. In the manufacturing areas, the overwhelming opinion was that Taiwanese managers' absence from the SRC and the neglect of issues raised by the elected representatives rendered this body irrelevant. In the three main production areas particularly, a CPT internal survey indicated that "many staff's daily experience of working for CPT [was of] a chaotic and poorly organized" factory. Discipline on the lines varied wildly, with company procedures ignored or applied arbitrarily according to many of the employees surveyed. The picture inside CPT was of uncertainty, chaotic production flows, and arbitrary first-line management.

In 1995, the company had rejected partnership overtures from the AEEU. There was no follow-up AEEU campaigning. But in 1998, around thirty workers, largely former AEEU members from a closed electronics factory, began to discuss unionization and contacted the AEEU to enlist its support for a recruitment campaign. None of this group held official steward credentials, yet they began to function as shadow stewards. The increasing uncertainty over job specifications increased these shadow stewards' visibility to their co-workers and management. Their activities were largely motivated not by the changes *per se*, but by the lack of prior consultation, once again highlighting perceptions of fairness and justice in mobilizing workers (see Kelly 1998). Their authority increased as they attempted to compensate for the absence of credible consultation. The AEEU did not initiate the campaign, but responded by providing recruitment material. The CPT workforce is drawn from a wide geographical area which, combined with complex shift patterns, made it difficult to organize off-site recruitment meetings. But within six months, some 40 percent of the 800 blue-collar workforce joined the AEEU. The workforce at CPT was offered free union membership until recognition was achieved. The initiative continued to lie with experienced shop floor activists rather than the union recruitment campaign. As shadow stewards, the activists did not bargain with management but confined themselves to recruitment.

For the activists, the key to recruitment was not that financial gains would necessarily follow from recognition, but rather that wide disparity in supervisory practices would become subject to a negotiated code of conduct. Supervisors on each line settled all aspects of workplace discipline. There was no central code of conduct, no factory-wide process for imposing – or appealing against – particular disciplinary decisions, and no central monitoring for consistency and equity. Poor wages were also a significant issue in recruitment. Given the role of particular supervisory experience, the recruitment pattern involved groups of individuals from specific lines joining the union together.

Against this background, shadow stewards used the failure of the SRC to demonstrate the need for an independent trade union. AEEU membership rose rapidly to over 50 percent in the manufacturing areas. CPT's own employee attitude survey registered this upsurge in union membership and the support for recognition even among non-unionists. The company concluded that given current and projected union membership, they would be compelled to accept recognition once ERA's provisions were in place. In October 1999, local CPT managers made a tactical retreat by agreeing to recognize the AEEU, subject to the approval of the parent company. However, as of February 2002, the parent company had yet to ratify the decision. The union was given access to the plant to recruit in March 2001. Access to represent members only followed ERA's provisions on individual representation in 2000. As the company's own disciplinary procedures appear to be given scant regard by management at all levels, the demand for individual representation is enormous.

The conditions that prompted CPT employees to unionize continue to exist. Wages are still relatively poor, production organization continues to be chaotic, and there are significant health and safety issues arising. Significantly, arbitrary supervision continues to prevail in many areas of CPT:

> These section chiefs are young guys who are out to make a name for themselves. They're bullyboys who don't know the first thing about procedure. They'll sack somebody then they'll go to Personnel and say "Have I done the right thing?"
>
> (AEEU officer B, 2001)

The AEEU scaled down its campaign following agreement to recognition in principle and membership dwindled, although there has been some resurgence since the replacement of the FTO responsible for the plant by a new officer in January 2001. The primary union activity being undertaken there continues to be individual representation in grievances and disciplinaries. Yet this, in the absence of an active steward group, has huge implications for the role of the FTO, and there has been no transfer of responsibilities from the officer to lay representatives.

> Basically, my mobile is switched on 7 days a week, 24 hours a day. You don't get a minute's peace . . . I think I've actually created a monster for myself, because now when I'm servicing these companies they think it's alright to phone me at 11 o'clock at night. . . . I'm never away from the place, doing appeals and disciplinaries. Actually, I should move my office up there.
>
> (AEEU officer B, 2001)

The AEEU could submit an application to the CAC but there is anxiety on two fronts. First, there is concern over losing a possible ballot, and second, given the precarious commercial position of the company, the AEEU is reluctant to be made a scapegoat for plant closure. There are FTOs within the union who believe that the union has erred in accepting the company's word on recognition in principle. There has been no gain in formal channels of employee representation and key AEEU activists have left. Without the support of a robust formal recognition of collective bargaining, the informal representational activities of the shadow stewards have now declined sharply. The union acknowledges how difficult it is for union members to operate in the absence of formal recognition.

From recognition to representation? FCI and the ISTC

> It's the sense of being powerless: that bad things can happen and all they can do is complain in the canteen and that's it. They want to be empowered so they can at least have some type of voice which can grow in strength.
>
> (ISTC officer A, 2000)

FCI is a sub-contract manufacturer with seventeen factories in Scotland, centered on its Gourock plant. It performs a range of labor-intensive operations from engineering components to final assembly, testing, and despatch. Effectively, FCI is a labor-only sub-contractor for IBM. Until 1997, FCI's contract with IBM linked profit to employment and volume of production. Assembly was group-based and production targets easily attainable: assemblers were able to compensate for poor management planning and control the pace of their workload as the inherent slack in the production system reduced the need for tight supervision. However, a change in ownership and senior FCI management coincided with a shift in the IBM contract to promote efficiency and quality. FCI moved to tighten labor control by restructuring the labor process. Sequential lines replaced individual product building. Consequently, employees lost control of their pace of work and total workload. Impromptu movement from the line became impossible, as supervisors moved to increase control of the process through increasingly intense, harsh, and arbitrary practices.

> They used to sack a whole line if one of the valuable parts went missing. Hire and fire, hire and fire: throw them out, start some again. "I don't like you, 'you're bagged.'" Always in front of the line, so people could see the fear factor at work.
>
> (ISTC steward A, 2000)

FCI also moved to reduce labor costs. Wage rates of core workers were raised by 40 percent by consolidating overtime and shift premia. Continuous production replaced the existing shift system. The real consequence of these changes for assemblers, however, was an average loss of £20 per week. Lastly, 300 permanent employees were made redundant, replaced in part by agency workers on lower rates. The sharp deterioration in earnings and intensification of discipline, and significantly the unilateral nature of FCI's actions, were crucial in generating a shared sense of grievance amongst shop-floor workers.

FCI management was hostile to trade unionism. In 1997, FCI bought a plant in Livingstone where the AEEU were recognized, closing the plant shortly after and transferring both contracts and employees to Gourock. The AEEU were derecognized with an undertaking that they would be the "preferred" union should the company ever reinstate recognition.

The catalyst for shop-floor protest was the withdrawal of a customary ten-minute break. Lacking any formalized representation, 80 percent of the workforce signed a petition to pressurize management. FCI hastily launched a works council, with elected works councilors, to head off impromptu strikes. They also, however, made it clear that this was not a negotiating body, and the works council immediately lost all credibility. Four of the councilors had organized the petition and were also now in contact with several unions, including the ISTC. Management's response to the situation only inflamed matters: "I paid £21 million for this company – a shed, a shower of alcoholics, druggies, and single mothers" was the managing director's contribution (ISTC member B, 1999). He made it clear to the workforce that "there would be no union in his factory so long as he had a hole in his arse" (ISTC steward B, 1999).

Once the petition and company "voice" mechanisms failed, workers turned to direct action. During an extraordinary two days, the workforce struck inside the factory and confronted senior management *en masse*. The small group of ISTC members, under a dozen, remained on the margins of this protest, too weak to affect events and uncertain of the support for unionization. However, continued discontent inside the factory was paralleled by an intensive ISTC leafleting campaign. The campaign was imaginative and confrontational. Some 300 workers joined ISTC within a month of these events, simultaneously exhibiting both solidarity and a rejection of employer unilateralism.

Management opened talks with the AEEU, based on their previous undertaking (Walsh 1998). Despite the AEEU's *prima facie* case for pursuing recognition, it quickly withdrew, calculating that recognition would embroil it in a long, messy, and unwinnable struggle to secure decent conditions in FCI. More generally, the attitudes of the labor aristocrat underpinned the AEEU's disdain for unskilled, unorganized, undisciplined workforces:

> Not to downgrade anybody, but the calibre of people in there is low. Because the job's so cyclical . . . you're getting people who left school . . . very early with little qualifications who're doing work just to get a wage or because the dole has told them to. It's hard to retain those people because those kind of people will leave the union on the spur of the moment, on a whim.
>
> (AEEU officer B, 1999)

A company-organized ballot, intended to demonstrate the lack of support for trade unionism, returned a huge majority in favor of the ISTC. Management signed a recognition agreement with the ISTC in January 1999. In return, ISTC agreed to step back from their aggressive recruitment campaigns outside other FCI factories until the Greenock agreement had bedded in. The agreement was wholly procedural. Activists, along with plant and HR management, expected the agreement to be fleshed out gradually to include substantive issues. For FCI's executive management, however, enough had been conceded, and there has been little formalization of factory governance since.

ISTC membership data indicate that recruitment was based on explosive growth centered on specific events (notably the petition and recognition agreement), with consolidation and slow growth occurring later. The first wave of recruits was largely male, aged between 25 and 39. Consolidation spread membership to mature women and younger men. Approximately 65 percent of FCI's core workforce were recruited within six months. Despite efforts, the ISTC has made little progress in recruiting young women and contract labor. Membership offers little protection to agency contract labor in the absence of bargaining rights. Union activity remains a largely male affair, reproducing much of the paternalist characteristic of FCI management.

In the pay negotiations, management's offer of minor improvements in wage rates and a reduction in the qualifying period for pensions and attendance bonuses did little to satisfy shop-floor discontent. Stewards feared that management intransigence was a test of the union's strength. The unionized workforce rejected the wage offer by 95 percent in a ballot. Sentiments among the workforce were running high – "he's heard our

bark, now it's time he felt our bite" (ISTC member A, 1999). But as the first
one-day strike approached, support dwindled. Unaware of this, management made minor improvements in the wage offer, whilst simultaneously
writing to all workers warning that any strike would jeopardize attendance
bonuses and offering a shift on triple time to those ignoring the strike call.
In addition, rumors spread through the factory of the potential disciplinary
costs of striking. Faced with an increasingly divided membership, the union
negotiators were forced to sue for peace before their weakness was revealed.

These negotiations offered the salutary lesson that union discipline and
organization requires more than a membership card. Other important
weaknesses were revealed, particularly in the organization of the action.
There was no consideration of orders or output levels, and hence of what a
strike would cost the company. There was no attempt to expand involvement for the organization of the action beyond the stewards, for example,
by co-opting members representing each workgroup onto the committee
for the duration of industrial action. There was little sense that the branch
activists could or should play a decisive role in the process. For the core
activists, recruitment had been an intensely emotional, and ultimately
successful, experience. It delivered recognition, however, at a pace that left
little time for new stewards to develop the skills of effective representation.
Their inexperience as organizers or negotiators is a significant weakness.
Only *after* recognition have stewards confronted a new reality of compromise
and ambiguous mediation.

Stewards have been pitched in at the deep end, spending up to fifteen
hours a week on union business and dealing primarily with grievances
about work intensity, supervisory behavior, and discipline. They acknowledge their limited influence on labor process issues. Given the size of their
constituencies, face-to-face contact is not an effective means of communication. Whilst off-site monthly meetings with members take place, these are
largely dominated by immediate issues. There is no systematic reporting
from different sections of the plant, and few of the formalities of lay union
organization. The stewards remain heavily dependent on the local FTO,
and inexperience leaves them exposed to constant criticism from the
membership, with few tactical methods of preventing criticism of the
company from becoming criticism of union representation. Ironically, the
incipient collectivism that made unionization possible itself generates
expectations of a return on membership. This makes for an uneasy relationship between stewards, ISTC officers, and the branch membership.

The stewards' main concern is to formalize and calibrate the disciplinary
procedure, by using the grievance procedure to challenge supervisory
excesses. In the three months after recognition, there were forty-five formal
complaints against supervisors. Stewards are fleshing out a procedure that
allows for hearings, appeals, and representation. These challenges strike to
the heart of FCI well-honed harsh managerialism. The union has had some
success in redrawing the frontier of control, but the formalization of the

disciplinary process is extremely hesitant. Relations with FCI's management are little better. Management has not attempted to normalize or stabilize relations. There are monthly meetings with the personnel manager, but these provide few answers to the stewards' concerns. Stewards perceive that their access is to management at a level that has little information and influence. Yet small gains have been made – plant-level management, contrary to the executive strategy, has been drawn into co-operation with shop stewards, and there is a measure of informal collective bargaining.

The stewards have negligible facilities in the factory. They are not permitted time off during working hours and meet only briefly at shift changes. Few supervisors allow any informal use of company facilities to support steward activities. This leaves little opportunity for the stewards to develop any coherent strategy and thus they are largely reactive. Yet, the ISTC has established a durable organization inside FCI. Gains have been made, particularly in relation to supervisory behavior. The effectiveness of the ISTC's agreement may be gauged by the recent interest among FCI supervisors in union membership. Whether or not these gains are sufficient to carry the membership remains to be seen.

Themes and issues

The dynamics of union organizing in hostile environments have been outlined. IBM's resources and its consistent managerial opposition to unionization act as an obstacle to the development of effective trade unionism. While widespread grievances appear to exist, these often remain focused on individual managers, rather than management *per se*. IBM's focus on the individual has, for many, reduced collective mobilization. At the same time, IBM's relatively privileged employment conditions increase the potential cost of organizing against management. In FCI and CPT, union recruitment has proceeded successfully as a shared sense of collective injustice has developed. Yet, relatively unfettered managerial prerogative prevails in these companies, and there is little likelihood of significantly improving the economic prospects of these highly insecure workers. Important lessons can, however, be learned from these cases.

Activist-driven organizing

All three recruitment campaigns resulted from approaches by lay activists to unions, not the reverse. Collectivism at grass-roots level was translated into formal union activity rather than being generated by union organizing campaigns. At FCI, embryonic, if fragile, organization was in place before any union campaign, and the ISTC acknowledge being ". . . in the right place at the right time" (ISTC officer, 1999). As Aronowitz (1998: 8) suggests, "it's not that unions 'organize' workers who would otherwise remain dormant. In many, perhaps most, instances, workers organize themselves." The core activists who initiated recruitment had a wide range of prior union experience. The CPT activists were largely drawn from a previously recognized factory. None had previously been shop stewards. In IBM, activists had been union *members* in previous jobs, although only one had held office. Some FCI activists had been union members before, but described their membership as passive. Only one respondent had any significant experience of political or community activism. In all cases, therefore, inexperienced activist groups with low levels of organizational capability conducted recruitment and representation. Given this, union support, education, and development become crucial to the success of shadow steward activities. This raises important issues in relation to the leadership capabilities of unions at both workplace and officer level, particularly in light of the crucial importance of leadership in workforce mobilization (see Kelly 1998).

Despite differences between companies, the nature of each workforce's grievance against their employer was similar. Changes in the labor process and in reward stimulated opposition and activism. The manner of these changes called into question the governance process in each company, undermining the legitimacy of non-union consultative processes for large numbers of workers. Weak company-regulated consultative processes were discredited as "voice" mechanisms, reflecting negatively on the "fairness" of management in dealing with their workers (cf. Kelly 1998), and was critical in stimulating efforts to build an independent union presence. Improved contracts and earnings were important but of secondary importance (cf. Bronfenbrenner and Juravich 1998).

Recruitment

The AEEU followed relatively traditional approaches to recruitment, involving leafleting within plants (and outside at CPT) by FTOs, members working in other companies, and retired members. Only the ISTC used innovative recruitment tactics, combining targeted leaflets with publicity stunts to attract attention, and setting up small organizing committees early on. No such body existed at CPT, whilst the IBM activists were constituted as a union branch, with official branch structures and leadership. All three, however, fell considerably short of the approach described in the US literature on organizing, and at FCI and CPT activists continued to be heavily dependent on their servicing FTO.

In FCI and CPT, membership growth was explosive and arose in response to specific events. A more gradual pattern characterized IBM. In each, similar demographic patterns emerged: older male workers joined first, followed by younger men, then older women. Young women were most resistant to joining. The perennial problems of encouraging women to identify their interests with those of male dominated trade unions affected all three cases. As one young woman activist noted:

I'm a young lassie, they're all middle-aged men, and they're all ex-shipyard workers and stuff like that. It's kind of an unwritten thing that they have more authority than you, so when I speak out it's as if they're views hold more weight.

(AEEU member A, 2001)

Recruiting contract labor in IBM and FCI remains problematic. While the use of contract workers threatens to undercut members' terms and conditions, family and neighborhood ties combined with the natural sociability of the workplace produce a strong solidarity between core and peripheral workers. At IBM, the main reason for not recruiting contract labor more actively relates to concerns amongst core and periphery staff not to compound the already enormous insecurity of their employment. At FCI, recruiting agency-employed temporary workers to the ISTC in the absence of any agreement with their employers is both difficult for the union and high risk for the temporary workforce.

For the core activists who initiated recruitment and established basic organizational infrastructures, the overarching objective of union organization and representation was to give employees a voice and promote greater fairness in the workplace. Activists were realistic about the prospects of recognition delivering rapid and significant improvements in terms and conditions. At IBM new members' motivation was to seek protection from arbitrary managerial decision-making. The evidence from FCI and CPT suggests that members joined in order to improve their earnings or contracts. Here, there appears to be a gap between activist and member expectations of what union representation can deliver. The scope of the research did not allow an exploration of the extent of this gap and its consequences for union and management strategies. However, there have been some signs of a developing union consciousness at FCI: a proposal to contract out the security function generated strong support for action. Unions are often more successful in actions based around the pursuit of dignity, justice, and fairness than in those dealing primarily with pay and rewards (Bronfenbrenner and Juravich 1998).

Recognition

None of the campaigns relied directly on the ERA to pursue recognition. For IBM activists, recognition was neither a real nor realistic objective. Yet, there is little doubt that the imminent arrival of statutory provisions influenced members and management at FCI and CPT. At FCI, recognition was achieved by traditional means but management's acceptance of recognition was conditional on an informal agreement with the ISTC that delayed the pursuit of recognition in other FCI sites, raising issues of union democracy. At CPT, the agreement in principle to recognize was also voluntary, albeit in the context that a CAC application was likely to be successful. Yet, this agreement has discouraged senior FTOs from making an application. CPT's prevarication on the substance of recognition has fueled concerns that a more effective union strategy would have been to force the employer's hand.

Representation

The form and pattern of union representation differs markedly across the cases. While all activists stressed that some form of collective voice was now in place, in FCI employee "voice" was institutionalized, in CPT there was limited informal engagement, and in IBM it was a marginal, dissenting presence inside established management-controlled consultation processes. In FCI, recognition delivered only the most basic facilities for shop stewards: there is no guaranteed facility time, and supervisors retain discretion over the stewards' mobility and access to FTOs or personnel managers. While some progress has been made in delivering substantive change, the experience of the pay negotiations is a stark reminder both of the union's and members' organizational capabilities, and of the power of management to thwart effective collectivism.

At CPT, recognition in principle has been paralleled by erosion of shadow steward representation activities, despite continued disorganization in the labor process and in the management of employees. Local FTOs have responded to this representational deficit with greater interventions themselves. In effect, a net loss has occurred in terms of the representational and leadership activities of stewards inside the factory. AEEU activists inside IBM have no legitimate presence or rights at plant level. Campaigning has delivered only the most precarious of gains in terms of plant level union infrastructure. The AEEU's unwillingness to mount a campaign for union nominees on the EWC and IBM's use of its disciplinary code against shadow stewards have thwarted the possibility of shadow stewards acting as official union representatives. However, the silencing of the activists' public voice inside the company's consultative mechanisms has paralleled incremental gains in recruitment and activist organization, despite the limited AEEU support, and representational activity continues through clandestine individual interventions.

Employers' responses

The harsh managerial regimes at FCI and CPT simultaneously increase the case for union membership and the risks associated with organizing. Thus, union tactics have to be considered alongside employer strategies in relation to organizing. Employer responses influence union activities in different ways. At IBM, a sophisticated management was better able to maintain the integrity of corporate "voice" mechanisms, a factor which is reflected in the relative failure of the AEEU to significantly expand their membership. At CPT management stalling, rather than directly confronting the union, may prove successful, particularly in the context a threat of closure. At FCI, management's acceptance of formal bargaining does not in itself provide any depth of representation. Given the centrality of tight, arbitrary supervisory control to FCI, unionization was a fundamental challenge to managerial authority and to profitability. There have been few indications so far that senior management has been willing to meet the stewards part way, and FCI has not sat idly back as the union has struggled to establish itself. Indeed, FCI has continued to contest recognition elsewhere in the company, notably at the Ayrshire plants, even in the face of (automatic) statutory recognition of the ISTC in 2001.

Union strategies

In each case basic inadequacies in union support mechanisms undermined recruitment activity, in terms of maintaining membership and subscription records, creativity in planning recruitment events, and providing information needed to make convincing arguments for unionization. Union caution at IBM and CPT has severely constrained the potential of the activist group. Implicit within the organizing model is the view that recruitment campaigns will generate competent and committed activists, who will in turn undertake further recruitment and representational roles with limited calls on union resources. In practice, effective recruitment campaigns generate heightened expectations and additional calls on union resources, particularly where employers are hostile and union activists are inexperienced:

> Nearly all my companies are newly organized. Can I tell you something? I'm doing a shop steward's job in most of them. Not an official's job, a shop steward's job.
>
> (AEEU officer B, 2001)

It is clear that even the limited version of the ISTC's organizing at FCI is problematic. Steward organization remains reliant on a handful of activists who, in turn, depend on local FTO support. Aside from the implications of this for officers themselves, such heavy dependence is not sustainable in the longer term, which is acknowledged yet under-appreciated in discussions of organizing. In addition, the ISTC's proactive approach is not uncontroversial within the union itself, where considerable reservations are expressed over some of the organizing tactics adopted. As one officer notes, "ISTC's history is more partnership than confrontation" (ISTC officer C, 1999). Moreover, the union's internal structures are not well suited to its wider approach to recruitment, and new members are not easily assimilated into its organization. That the FCI membership now accounts for approximately 30 percent of the Scottish district yet has no real voice inside the union raises profound questions for the union's democratic processes.

Conclusion

While union recruitment has impacted little on the major corporate employers in Silicon Glen, there have been significant, if patchy, gains in supply companies. This was likely, since few positive incentives supporting non-unionism are present in companies like FCI. Beneath their shared commitment to organizing, ISTC and AEEU exhibit significant differences in strategies. The ISTC have attempted to translate the principles of grassroots campaigning into practice while the AEEU's recruitment activities continue to be cautious in confronting hostile employers, whilst aspiring towards more co-operative relationships with companies. Yet, this seems forlorn in newly organized sites in Silicon Glen. Where shop steward leadership is inexperienced, shop-floor union organization has shallow roots, *and* there is determined management opposition, the potential for co-operative relationships is severely constrained (cf. Kelly 1998). Indeed, any hint of such relationships may be counter-productive as stewards and officials are seen as complicit in sustaining aspects of a despised managerial regime. Equally, however, adversarialism must be tempered by the practical necessity of developing stable bargaining relationships in the workplace and in negotiations. Walking the tightrope between each of these scenarios will continue to challenge union officers, stewards, and shadow stewards.

Acknowledgments

We gratefully acknowledge ESRC support for this project and give thanks to the union officials and, particularly, to the members and shop stewards for co-operating.

8 Organizing in transport and travel

Learning lessons from TSSA's Seacat campaign

Jane Wills

Introduction

In the mid 1990s, the TUC began to promote a new agenda amongst its affiliates, that of putting greater resources into organizing new groups of workers and revitalizing existing workplace organization (Heery 1998, Heery *et al.* 2000b, 2001). As part of this, the TUC established the Organising Academy to train a new generation of specialist organizers, new courses in organizing theory and practice have been established for FTOs and lay members, and annual conferences have been held to address the issue of organizing. The organizing model or agenda is widely understood to mean a focus on generating sustainable self-activity by union members at the workplace, rather than relying on FTOs and union services from the top down, as well as the creation of strong workplace unionism amongst new and established workplaces. In the context of securing new recognition agreements, organizing is focused on finding workplace union activists to recruit their colleagues and build up support from within.

A number of unions have put significant resources into this type of activity. Prime amongst these are the GPMU, which employs a large number of specialist organizers at branch level, the ISTC which now calls itself the "community union" and is organizing in former steel communities, Connect, and TSSA, which employs a large number of specialist organizers across transport and travel. If they are to survive as independent unions, these smaller unions face an imperative to find new sources of membership and have seen organizing as a method of growth.

This chapter focuses on the activities of one team of organizers working for TSSA. In what follows, the profile union is outlined and current efforts to organize the travel trade in general and the work of the Greenfield Site Team (GFS) in particular are examined in more detail. Using the lens of mobilization theory, the first organizing campaign undertaken by the GFS at Seacat during the summer of 2000 is recounted and evaluated. The data was collected through attendance at GFS project planning meetings as well as interviews with the Deputy General Secretary (DGS) of TSSA, the organizers employed in the GFS, and the Seacat lay activists, holding two focus groups with TSSA staff involved in the campaign, and attending various organizing committee meetings. These methods were deployed six months before the campaign "went live" and for more than a year after. The chapter concludes by exploring the key lessons of the Seacat campaign for unions in Britain.

From transport to travel: an overview of TSSA

The National Association of General Railway Clerks was established in Sheffield on 9 May 1897, winning collective bargaining rights in 1921 for its white-collar membership. Over time, the union recruited other office-based staff working for the railways and other modes of transportation, and in 1950, delegates changed the name of their organization to TSSA (Wallace 1996). The union now represents about 30,000 non-manual workers in railway, docks, road haulage, freight-forwarding, bus, canal, shipping, and travel companies throughout Britain and Ireland. After 1945, the union became almost exclusively based in the public sector until privatization of the docks, buses, and railways in the 1980s and 1990s. TSSA has faced a triple challenge of privatization and the multiplication of negotiations, employment decline in their core sector, and employer resistance to unionization. Recognizing the long-term implications of such change for its own survival, the union has embarked on an ambitious program to refocus the energies of the union: it has sought to develop a culture of organizing and start to increase recruitment and build new workplace organization in the growing travel trade. As the union's DGS put it, "We had an imperative. The imperative was did we want to exist. It was stark and clear and nobody could walk away from it" (interview, 14 March 2000).

While TSSA has its core membership on the railways where union density is reasonably high amongst white-collar staff and there are limited possibilities for expansion, there are large numbers of potential members in the travel trade. It thus makes sense for the union to maintain its core but to also organize workers in the travel trade. Travel trade companies include those that provide holidays (tour operators) and the travel agents that sell holidays to the public, such as Thomson/Lunn Poly, Airtours/Going Places, First Choice, Thomas Cook, and the Carlson Leisure Group/AT Mays. These companies have more than 2,000 retail outlets between them, and they control a growing share of the holiday market. At least 100,000 people are employed in the travel trade industry in the UK, the majority of them women, working in small shops and call centers. The industry is characterized by low pay, poor human resources management, high staff turnover and limited training for employees (LRD 1997, Cranfield School of Management 1999). In many ways, the travel trade is typical of much employment in the private services sector. The work is largely performed by women, in non-unionized firms, working in small workplaces, and involving a lot of contact with customers and more senior staff. Indeed, the union's DGS pointed out that in many ways, this organizing challenge is emblematic of all that the British trade union movement has to face if it is to survive for the future:

> This is a real test about whether the unions actually have any relevance for the future. If we try to be as intelligent as we can about organizing, and put serious investment into it, but we still can't organize this sector then I think we've got to rethink whether unions are the right way to look after workers' interests. I think it is as fundamental as that. Now I believe we can do it but we need to be much more intelligent about the way we operate and we need to ask people to shed a lot of the traditional frameworks with which they see the world. They have to step outside the paradigm as it were. Then I think we can unionize the travel trade sector.
>
> (Interview, 14 March 2000)

Since taking the decision to become an organizing union in the late 1990s, TSSA has taken a systematic approach to its reorganization that is probably unparalleled in the rest of the trade union movement. The union has used its attempts to secure Investors in People (IiP) as a mechanism to rethink every task in the organization with a view to meeting its goals. The demand for a clear mission statement, strategy, and planning highlighted the importance of organizing for the union's future, not least because relying on FTOs to service a membership spread across hundreds of workplaces, not to mention organizing greenfield sites in the transport industry and the travel trade, was neither practically nor economically feasible. Unless workplace activists could be identified, trained, and mobilized, the union would be stretched far too thinly to reach all possible sites.

To provide valued services, a strong body of workplace representatives, effective workplace organization, and influence with employers and policy-makers, the union recognized its dependence on well-trained, highly motivated FTOs to spread the message and practice of organizing. TSSA has thus clarified the role of each member of staff and introduced job descriptions that reflect these expectations. Union officials are expected to produce their own plans and targets for the year ahead, to evaluate their own performance, and to develop their role as much as they can. As part of this process, the union has recognized the way in which the management of union officers has to be changed, as the union's DGS explained:

> We have had to recognize the complexity of what trade union officials are asked to do and I think we have seriously underestimated that in the past . . . But it's also about not being blown around in the wind anymore . . . and that's been the biggest cultural change that we've come across. We have to get officers away from a focus on individual

problems to look at the big picture. They need to step back and think of the way they teach and lead others.

(Interview, 14 March 2000)

To demonstrate this new way of working, and to start to hone the organizing skills of the union, TSSA has appointed a large number of new organizers since early 2000. By early 2002, the union had four organizers to work with each of the four negotiating teams of the union in the UK, a three-person GFS and an eight-person Travel Trade Team that has five dedicated organizers, and a public relations expert. Organizers now make up well over 10 percent of union staff and account for an increasing amount of union expenditure. The union have set membership targets that they hope organizers, in conjunction with a team of paid recruiters, will reach across a range of companies in both transport and travel. The GFS is designed to lead organizing at small and medium-sized non-union firms across the transport and travel industries. It was set up to work by prioritizing planning and strategy from the outset. The team has developed a set of criteria from which to assess the relative merits of potential targets when selecting their new organizing campaigns, including the nature of collective grievances, access to staff, the number and views of existing members, management attitudes, campaign timing, having a relatively small number of sites, and the absence of inter-union rivalry. Once a potential target is selected, the team use project planning techniques to research the company and map out the campaign as much as is possible, while preliminary activity takes place. Such research involves exploring the company, the workforce, their issues, and the logistics of any campaign before coming up with a clear set of objectives and plans. In an effort to improve the way in which the union learns, the team also complete an evaluation after every organizing campaign.

To date, the GFS has undertaken six major organizing campaigns (see Table 8.1), with these initiatives covering both transport and travel and some being more successful than others. Three have resulted in recognition, two were ongoing at the time of writing, and one was withdrawn. Seacat, B2S, and Momentum have been successful, Airmiles and Vertex are ongoing, long-running campaigns, and TV Travel Shop was abandoned after several months of the campaign.

The remainder of this chapter looks at the first organizing campaign undertaken by the GFS at Seacat. Even though their first campaign was in a traditional transport company, some of the characteristics of the workers involved are similar to those found across the travel trade, these being young men and women workers, the common use of seasonal contracts, and workers being organized for the first time. Subsequent sections of the chapter introduce the campaign, consider the extent to which mobilization theory is a useful lens from which to view the activity that took place, and outline some of the wider lessons that might be learnt from organizing at Seacat.

Table 8.1 TSSA's Greenfield Site Team campaigns, 2000–2001: summary

Firm	Economic activity	Bargaining unit	Staff characteristics	Dates of union activity	Outcome of campaign	Reasons for the outcome
Seacat, Belfast	Ferry services from Belfast to Scotland and Northern England	Troon terminal: 12, Belfast terminal: 26, Belfast call center: 40, *Seacat Scotland* (boat): 39, *Superseacat* (boat): 50. Total: 167	Majority under 30, 60% female, some staff on seasonal contracts	TSSA recruitment activity in 1999. Intensive organizing from April to July 2000	Recognition for shore-based staff (including Belfast call center and Liverpool terminal) and RMT for sea-going staff in August 2000	Real grievances and willingness to join the TSSA. Fast rise in union density and support for industrial action. Strong relationships with TSSA organizers. Good local leadership doing recruitment and organizing, co-ordinated by representative organizing committee. Staff had evidence of working alongside unionized deck-hands on the boats
B2S, Tonbridge, Kent	Customer service and call center for Connex South Eastern and Govia	22 letter writers, 26 phone staff and back office staff in two different offices. Total: 57 including part-time staff	12 older staff in 50s and early 60s were TUPE protected from Connex, others tend to be younger (<35), women the majority in call center	TUPE protected staff stayed in the TSSA but not active. Re-ignited by arrival of new MD and attempts to impose a bonus scheme. Union organizing activity from autumn 2001	Recognition December 2001. More than 70% staff in membership, active organizing committee of 5 or 6, and well-attended membership meetings	Small workplace made it easier to organize: people know each other and they are keen to defend the "old culture." Two union activists had long experience of trade unionism and were prepared to take a lead. High levels of participation (2 ballots and a petition) closely tied to key workplace issues (pay and bonus scheme)

Table 8.1 (Continued)

Firm	Economic activity	Bargaining unit	Staff characteristics	Dates of union activity	Outcome of campaign	Reasons for the outcome
Momentum, London, UK	Onboard catering for Eurostar	Ground-based staff, clerical, admin. and management: 40	60% female, fairly young, considerable number from continental Europe, few with union experience	TSSA took servicing approach 1998–2000 with sporadic recruiting. The 250 on-board staff (pursers and cabin crew) became a more -active target in June 2001	Recognition January 2002. Late 2001, one workplace activist approached the T&G and took others with him, so GFS withdrew to allow successful recognition campaign. TSSA then involved in signing recognition deal alongside T&G, but for ground-based staff only	"Old" railway culture with strong traditions of union organization. Keeping membership long-term. Working alongside the T&G for recognition
TV Travel Shop, Bromley Kent	Selling holidays advertised on cable TV channel	Call center agents and team leaders: 425	60% female, range of ages and races but mainly young white staff	November 2000– April 2001	Dropped campaign. Recruited 30 workers including some activists and started well but due to turnover and loss of key issue, only had 19 members by April 2001. No sign of upward trend	Turnover very high, particularly of those with grievances who joined TSSA. Activists not recruiting colleagues or leading at work. TSSA organizers taking on case work rather than leading organizing campaign

| Vertex, Scotland | Train bookings with other customer service work. | Edinburgh call center: 200, Dingwall (near Inverness) call center: 200. Total: approx. 400 | 60% female, range of ages and backgrounds (esp. in Dingwall), but mainly young white staff | TSSA recruitment activity for 4 years in Edinburgh and 3 years in Dingwall. Had 3 week "blitz" on membership in winter 2000. Intense organizing activity from May 2001 | By January 2002 had 100 members and agreed timetable for voluntary ballot for union recognition | People have tended to join for personal representation, tying up organizers in meetings although by 2002 case-work largely dealt with by local reps. In Dingwall, Vertex is a good employer so people do not want to rock the boat and in Edinburgh, people can get jobs elsewhere, so progress is slow. See increase in lay recruitment over time |
| Airmiles, UK | Managing airmiles. | Two sites in Warrington: 200, call center in Crawley: 47 and HQ staff: 40. Total: 287 | Mainly female, sales and customer services staff in call centers. All part-time in Crawley | Sporadic activity started in June 2001, focused on Warrington. Reactivated at both places due to grievances in January 2002 | Ongoing. Small membership but growing | Grievances are helping to increase interest and activity |

Sources: Participation at GFS team meetings, interviews with organizers and case study work at Seacat and TV Travel Shop.

Ferrying trade unionism back and forth across the Irish Sea: TSSA's Seacat campaign

Stena and Seacat are the companies that provide ferry transportation between Northern Ireland, England, and Scotland. Seacat is a subsidiary of the multi-national company Sea Containers that has a large portfolio of transport, leisure, and hospitality activities across the world. Sea Containers Ferries Scotland Ltd (known as Seacat) is just one small part of this empire, running high-speed vessels between Scotland (Troon), Northern England (Heysham), and Northern Ireland (Belfast), and between Liverpool and Dublin (see Figure 8.1). The vessels between Belfast and Troon carry up to 80 vehicles and 450 passengers, and a vessel with space for twice this number runs back and forth to Heysham during the summer. The journey from Belfast to Troon takes $2\frac{1}{2}$ hours each way and that to Heysham takes 4 hours each way. Most of the vessel staff are employed by Seacat Scotland Guernsey Ltd which is registered in the Channel Islands, making it difficult to get information about the company and raising questions about the extent to which the company meets its social obligations (such registration exempts the company from paying National Insurance contributions for staff). The company has its head office in Belfast where it also has a small call center for reservations and enquiries.

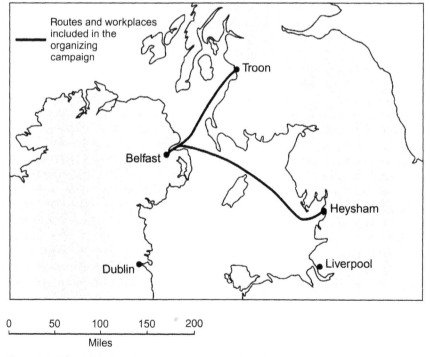

Figure 8.1 The Irish Sea ferry services operated by Seacat.

In April 2000, the GFS, in consultation with three senior TSSA staff, selected Seacat as their first target. The union already had a small group of members there (around 30 percent of staff) as a result of TSSA recruiters visiting during 1999 and others joining of their own initiative. Crucially, unofficial industrial action had indicated that staff had a collective sense of grievance that could be used as a basis for more sustained workplace union organization. During the last week in March 2000, at the start of the holiday season, a number of union members on the Belfast–Troon route led their colleagues in an unofficial walkout in protest at shift patterns and working hours. These workers were expected to do two return trips from Belfast to Troon every day for four days. In effect, staff were doing four consecutive 13-hour days before getting any time off, and then they often started back less than 48 hours later on the night shift. Up to thirty staff walked out after loading the boat with passengers one morning in March 2000 and in response, managers agreed a cut in working hours ensuring that staff did one long day (including two return trips) followed by one shorter day (with only one return trip), reinforcing the message that collective action could resolve collective concerns. Although it was short-lived, this collective action indicated the strength of feeling among sea-going customer services staff. Moreover, two members of the GFS had been employed as TSSA recruiters during 1999, and it was these individuals who had made contact with staff at Seacat, providing a good foundation of personal relationships from which to conduct a campaign. After some preliminary investigations into the structure of the company, the workplaces involved, and the concerns of the staff, the GFS made plans for the forthcoming campaign.

The team agreed five key objectives for the Seacat campaign. First, to organize the customer services workforce by securing density of at least 70 percent, creating an organizing committee, identifying union representatives in each workplace, establishing a communication system, and getting union representatives trained. Second, to secure genuine improvements in working conditions by ending breaches in health and safety legislation, and making improvements to pay, hours, and holidays. Third, to secure recognition by the end of December 2000, establishing bargaining machinery and facility time for representatives. Fourth, to develop a working relationship with management that involved genuine movement by the employer. And fifth, to ensure a successful exit strategy, handing over to a TSSA negotiating team based in Dublin, in a smooth and effective manner.

Concentrating on the customer services staff on the boats, and in the terminals and the call center gave TSSA a bargaining unit of 167, which later excluded the call center as the union organizers got very little response from the staff that worked there. Staff in the bargaining unit were spread between Troon (12 staff) and Belfast (26 staff) terminals, the Belfast call center (40 staff), *Seacat Scotland* (a boat with 39 customer services staff over 3 crews, working alongside 8 unionized bridge and deck staff), and *Superseacat* (a boat with fifty staff over three crews, working alongside nine unionized bridge and deck staff). The small bargaining unit thus included five different workplaces (two of which were afloat) and shift working also meant that customer services staff were never all in the same place at the same time. In addition, a union survey indicated that this was a young workforce (the majority were aged less than 30), women made up about 60 percent of staff, and very few had any prior knowledge or experience of trade unionism. At least 30 percent of the staff on the boats were on seasonal contracts (running from March 20 to October 31) putting pressure on the organizers to secure recognition before these workers lost their jobs for the winter.

In the light of such challenges, the GFS made significant progress in organizing these workers. In the first few weeks, the organizers conducted a staff survey to further explore the issues highlighted by union activists in the workforce. The survey, entitled "Your Voice at Work," asked workers about the length of the working week, the longest hours they worked in a day, the length of rest periods between shifts, rostering arrangements, annual leave entitlement, and union recognition. Compiling the results of this survey gave the organizers and activists confidence about the issues around which they could mobilize. Working hours, inadequate breaks, inconsistencies in the holiday entitlement, and the management of seasonal contracts thus became the key issues on which the GFS then focused the campaign, demanding union recognition as a means of solving concerns.

Existing TSSA members were encouraged to recruit their colleagues and the GFS organizers made regular trips back and forth across the Irish Sea, talking to workers and getting them to sign up. In round-the-clock organizing, GFS staff met Seacat workers on the boats, at the terminals, in bars, clubs, and homes. As one of the organizers later explained: "It was immediately clear that the moment was right. People were coming forward to talk to us and every week we were being introduced to new faces" (group interview, 12 September 2000). GFS organizers soon realized that union interest was greatest amongst customer services staff on the boats. These workers had the strongest grievances arising from their long hours of work, inadequate breaks, and resulting exhaustion. There were fewer problems facing the terminal staff although annual leave entitlement was a grievance, and membership did increase here. A few weeks into the campaign, however, the GFS decided to exclude the Belfast call center from the campaign, having had no success in recruiting these staff. Whereas they had identified a set of issues around which to campaign on the boats and in the terminals, the GFS got no response amongst staff in the call center. Throughout the campaign, the union retained only one member from forty staff in the call center, and this individual had transferred from the boats. The GFS organizers thus decided to focus the campaign solely on customer services staff working on the boats and at the terminals.

On the boats, the campaign worked as the organizing model might suggest (see Heery *et al.* 2001). The union clarified the key grievances, built up membership, developed the skills of activists, co-ordinated a representative organizing committee, and established the union as the voice of staff. Even though managers threatened their staff with disciplinary action for getting involved, and TSSA organizers with arrest for approaching staff on the boats, union membership quickly rose to more than 50 percent. The union was seen as a potential means to transform working conditions, and the strong social ties between workers helped to raise membership fast. The GFS were able to involve around seventeen workers in an embryonic organizing committee, and to get them involved in leading the campaign. As one of the GFS organizers explained:

> Organizing is not just about reps, it's about getting an organizing committee up and running. This structure is key, getting some kind of group, you know, not just a rep here and a rep there. We wanted to bring those individuals together so they weren't atomized, so they are actually able to share their experiences and take a lead . . . It's not just a nice way of working, or a way to recruit people, it is absolutely fundamental if you're going to be successful in what you do.
>
> (Group interview, 12 September 2000)

This accords with Kelly's (1998) mobilization theory. These Seacat workers had a clear sense of injustice, strong social ties that allowed them to trust one another, colleagues they regarded as leaders, and through the experience of the campaign, these workers developed a shared belief that TSSA was a means to solving their outstanding concerns. Thus as Kelly (1998: 29) puts it "It is not enough for employees to feel aggrieved: they must also feel entitled to their demands and feel that there is some chance that their situation can be changed by 'collective agency.'"

The GFS organizers were able to reinforce the arguments of workforce activists that the union provided a route for winning a collective resolution to their collective concerns. Management threats over union involvement helped to polarize opinion because it was seen that management was taking the union seriously by these actions, demonstrating the influence of the union. In early July, Seacat management agreed to meet TSSA representatives. The union claimed density of 70 percent overall and 80 percent on the boats but the company disputed this and refused to recognize the union for sea-going staff. This only served to heightened members' senses of injustice and thus their resolve to continue the campaign.

In response to pressure from members, TSSA sanctioned a ballot for industrial action, asking members on boats and in terminals to secure improvements in working conditions and recognition of TSSA. Although only 31 of the 90 members returned their ballot paper on time, reflecting, at least in part, the short deadline given to return ballot papers, all but one voted for strike action. Despite this low turnout, the organizers and organizing committee were confident enough to push ahead with a strike because

"We knew we'd made a mistake with the short turnaround of the ballot, but we also knew how strongly our members felt about the issues. We knew we could win on those issues and could not let our activists down" (GFS organizer, group interview, 20 September 2000).

During July 2000, the GFS moved closer to the campaign site, finding temporary accommodation with the TGWU, some seven minutes walk from the terminal in Belfast. The three GFS organizers were fully devoted to the campaign and they could draw on the support of other organizers and officials from within TSSA. Following consultation with the fledgling organizing committee, the strike was set to start at 6 a.m. on 3 August 2000, led by the best-organized crew and designed to hit the holiday traffic at a peak time of the year. TSSA promised £100 weekly strike pay and the GFS organizers put out regular circulars and held frequent meetings to counter the management threats of redundancy in the event of a strike. With the threat of strike action, the company entered into talks at the Labour Relations Agency (of Northern Ireland) but twelve hours before the strike was due to begin, Seacat won an injunction against TSSA, making the proposed strike "illegal." In court, the company argued that an ex-member of staff on the boats had received a ballot paper and that there was no legitimate trade dispute over the terminal staff. Managers declared that they had offered to talk about recognition for shore-based staff on 3 July and that they were prepared to recognize the RMT for sea-going staff. The judge upheld these complaints on both counts, arguing that the strike was unlawful and unnecessary. Legal advice to the union was that, although it had a good chance of winning an appeal over the ballot for boat staff, the imminent introduction of the ERA union recognition provisions (which removed the legal requirement to supply a list of all workers balloted) meant that appeal judges would be less inclined to overturn their colleagues' decision given that such a harsh precedent would not stand for long. Moreover, Seacat, drawing on its international resources, had flown in forty strike-breakers from Estonia, the Isle of Man, and Liverpool to Belfast to run the boats if need be. The legal decision allowed the balance of power to swing back towards management, and the time-scales involved made it impossible to re-ballot staff before the end of the high season and the resultant loss of industrial muscle.

On the morning of the intended strike, the GFS met with TSSA senior officers in Belfast to decide how to resolve the dispute. In light of the willingness to recognize TSSA for shore-based staff and the RMT for sea-going staff, and that recognition could secure significant gains for both groups of employees, union staff felt they had to accept. The GFS had secured a bargaining unit of about 100 shore-based workers in Troon, Belfast (including the call center), and Liverpool (as the terminal had been included in the offer from management), and a similar number of sea-going staff to transfer to the RMT. The proposed recognition agreement allowed for two representatives at each workplace and guarantees of talks to resolve long-standing concerns. Although disappointed that they had not secured recognition for staff on the boats, not least because it was here that the union had greatest strength and had found most of their activists, the deal was signed in the belief that this benefited the labor movement as a whole.

The organizing campaign and threatened dispute demonstrated that in this case TSSA could organize a partially greenfield site with a hostile management culture, that the young, female, and seasonal workers were not inherently anti-union, and that it was possible to develop active workplace trade unionism. These workers had experienced the potential power of collective organization. But there was also a sense that it felt like a defeat because the campaign had not secured TSSA's right to recognition for its target unit and the key demands – that working hours be reduced and shift patterns changed – had failed. As Kelly's mobilization theory makes clear, Seacat workers wanted change, and had joined the union in such large numbers because they came to believe in it as a vehicle for change. Nonetheless, recognition had been achieved and sea-going TSSA members were encouraged and assisted to join the RMT. The TSSA won recognition for staff in the Belfast, Troon, and Liverpool terminals and the call center in Belfast and their action did change the balance of power in Seacat. As this activist on the boats explained when interviewed eighteen months later:

> Conditions have definitely improved. Added to which there is always the fear in the company's mind that we can pull together if the will is strong enough . . . We put fear into the management about what we can do. Trade unions have the power to strike fear into the heart of the company and there is real strength in numbers.
>
> (Interview, 3 January 2002)

The campaign also reinforced an important message about the union's new focus on organizing, as a TSSA Executive Committee member commented:

> TSSA demonstrated that it has the ability, the will and the resources to see a campaign through to the end and that it is serious about organizing and gaining recognition in new areas and difficult circumstances. In this respect, the campaign was inspiring not just to the members directly involved but also to other members who became aware of TSSA's actions.
>
> (Email correspondence, 6 November 2000)

The GFS organizers felt supported in taking risks and doing all that was necessary to win the campaign:

> We felt that people were backing us in what we were doing, and that was reflected in the involvement of very senior officials from the union.

That gave us a boost of confidence and we knew that we were not going to be hung out to dry if things went pear-shaped. We were taking risks and got all the support that we needed to do it.

(Group interview, 20 September 2000)

The Seacat campaign thus underlined and supported the shift towards organizing underway in TSSA.

Learning lessons from the Seacat campaign

The Seacat campaign raises a number of important issues for the wider union movement as organizers seek to unionize non-union sites. These are the resource intensive nature of organizing activity, the complexity of organizing work, variations in the propensity to unionize that exist between workers in different sectors of the economy, and the need to re-scale trade union activity, building connections beyond the workplace.

The resource intensive nature of organizing

As Kelly (1998) indicates, organizing critically depends upon finding workers who are able and willing to become active in organizing their colleagues around issues of collective concern. Where the GFS could not find activists or interest, as in the Belfast call center, they were not able to sustain a campaign. However, even when activists were mobilized at Seacat, TSSA had to devote considerable staff time and money to supporting the campaign. GFS organizers spent a lot of time in face-to-face meetings with staff, in mapping the workforce and their grievances, in producing circulars to respond to managers, in developing the organizing committee, and in managing the proposed strike. Thus, new union members at Seacat cost a lot to recruit. For four months between April and early August 2000, the three organizers were working full-time on Seacat, drawing on the support of other organizers and recruiters from the union and various senior staff such as the DGS. The inexperienced nature of many of the new members increased this cost.

Establishing strong personal relationships between the union and the workforce was important to the Seacat campaign but this in itself accentuated the difficulty of GFS organizers moving on to their next target and left the members with the task of forming relationships with new FTOs. If TSSA had had an office of organizers and officers in Belfast, members might have developed relationships with these local FTOs and thus felt less abandoned at the end of the campaign. Moreover, the campaign might have been less expensive, as it could draw on local staff, office space, and support. Larger unions with larger networks of local offices might thus be better able to sustain strong local relationships for the long term. Following recognition, TSSA faced the additional difficulty of losing its "best"

members to the RMT while having to develop those workplaces which were
the smallest and had the weakest union presence – indeed, the Belfast call
center and the Liverpool terminal had not even been part of the campaign.
This task was given to the Irish TSSA office in Dublin. More than twelve
months later, the relevant FTO had not managed to meet management to
discuss outstanding concerns, the potential shop steward in the Belfast
terminal had not been trained, and there was no active workplace representation in Troon. These problems illustrate the importance of a coherent
exit strategy and demonstrate that British unions, even self-consciously
organizing unions, are still struggling with this aspect of managing a
campaign (interviews, various).

Organizing thus needs to be supported in the longer term, and in this
case, the union did not ensure that the GFS's work was sustained. Although
the Dublin TSSA organizer did visit the call center and Liverpool terminal
on a number of occasions, identifying new representatives and recruiting
new members in Liverpool, negotiations on grievances did not take place.
It would appear the union did not prioritize this work and the Dublin
office did not have the time or resources to continue working on Seacat.
Moreover, activists on the boats report that there has also been very little
RMT activity, there has been no attempt to create union representation
structures, nor has there been any ongoing union recruitment or activity
since the organizing campaign. It can thus be argued that neither union
has done a great deal to sustain and augment a union presence since
recognition.

The challenges of managing organizing in practice

Mounting an organizing and recognition campaign at Seacat was a considerable challenge by virtue of its different sites, staff being employed by
two different companies (some of whom were on seasonal contracts), and
the hostile response from the employer (using the law and playing "divide
and rule" between TSSA and the RMT). The case illustrates how difficult it
can be to anticipate developments and plan a campaign. As one of the GFS
organizers pointed out:

> Our efforts to plan things and think strategically were a very serious
> attempt to move away from the traditional trade union reactive and
> scattergun approach. But we were guinea pigs for a new approach and
> sometimes we *didn't* think things through as well as we might. We had
> so much to handle at each point of the campaign.
>
> (Group interview, 20 September 2000)

For example, TSSA met management on 3 July 2000 when the company
offered to start talking about recognition for shore-based but not sea-going
staff. Yet because the GFS had set its sights on recognition for sea-going

staff, and most of their activists and members were sea-going staff, they did not reflect on the implications of this offer. In retrospect, talks over recognition for part of the bargaining unit might have provided an opportunity to work with the RMT, or at least win recognition for part of the staff body in the first instance. With hindsight, the GFS senior organizer believed that tension between the two unions was the most serious weakness of their work at Seacat, and was something to avoid in any future campaigns:

> I think the biggest mistake we made, with hindsight, is that we *didn't* try to build cordial relations with the RMT at an earlier stage because we *didn't* look at an inter-union solution to the problems that were facing us. Because we already had members there on the boats, we went on recruiting more members, not least because the RMT *didn't* have any members at all. But when you look at what happened in the end, in the high court, the employers were able to use the RMT as the reasonable party and we looked like a bunch of nutters, just interested in causing trouble. That influenced the high court judge.
>
> (Group interview, 20 September 2000)

Likewise, it is arguable that more thought should have gone into the industrial action ballot in terms of gaining a higher turnout rate. The low turnout undermined the campaign's credibility and arguably made the company more confident to apply for an injunction. In the circumstances, the union organizers should have spent more time getting people to return their ballot forms quickly, perhaps visiting workers in their homes as part of the campaign.

During TSSA's subsequent internal evaluation, senior officials also highlighted issues of communication as a problem during the campaign. Arguably, TSSA needed a daily forum where organizers, activists, and members could meet together, share experiences, and reflect on the campaign, even if they had to do it via telephone or video conferencing. In this way, it would have been easier to manage the campaign as it developed and rebut management statements. Moreover, TSSA needed to find a more effective way to involve the organizing committee in decision-making. Although the GFS recognized the need to "empower" the activists to develop their own collective capacity and leadership skills, when it came to the critical decisions of the campaign, the representatives were not fully involved. For one of the organizers, this represented a significant failing:

> The model of the organizing union is all about getting activists to take the lead in their workplace and making sure that workers feel they are the union, not us. In practice though, it is very hard to do and in Seacat our activists didn't have facility time, they couldn't come to meetings except after work and we had to respond to things when they came up. I know we should have found a way of consulting but on that final day

we had to make decisions without getting the organizing committee involved. I don't know what else we could do.

(Group interview, 20 September 2000)

This weakness is perhaps reflected in the absence of any of the lay activists, of either union, acting as trained union representatives more than a year after the campaign.

The problems of organizing call center staff

The GFS found it problematic to find activists and support amongst the call center workforce by comparison to the sea-going staff. Illustrating Kelly's (1998) arguments about union mobilization, the latter had a clear set of shared grievances with respected indigenous leadership and viewed the union and strike action as a means to improve their working conditions. Thus, the GFS was pushing at an "open door," finding a group of workers who were already thinking and acting collectively and who were willing to join the union and take action to resolve their concerns. In contrast, the call center staff did not articulate any shared grievances, they showed little interest in the union, and produced no workplace activists or leaders. Even though call center workers have been successfully unionized elsewhere in Britain (see Taylor and Bain 1999, 2001a), the forty Seacat staff in Belfast proved resistant to TSSA. This again compares starkly with the results of the efforts to recruit the thirty Liverpool terminal workers. Four visits produced nine members and the TSSA organizer identified two members prepared to be union representatives, both of whom have been on a union summer school and have plans to recruit their colleagues.

The Seacat campaign thus highlights variations in workers' propensity to unionize. The labor process, work experiences, and expectations of current and previous work (often reflected through the lenses of age, gender, and so on), the prevalence of grievances, and identification with the union were found to vary across the company. Whereas the call center workers had a similar age, gender, and educational profile to those working on the boats and in the terminals, the sea-going and terminal staff had stronger collective grievances and personal ties, and they worked in close proximity to other unionized workers. In this context, it was easier to develop a strong sense of collective injustice and a willingness to get involved in the union. Being employed alongside unionized seafarers may have given these workers greater insight into the role and benefits of union organization. Seacat's sea-going workers were very conscious of their inferior terms and conditions compared to the unionized deck-hands and bridge staff who had recognized skills. As one activist explained:

Our pay could be better for what we do. we're on about £11,500 for looking after customers, serving them food and drink, and cleaning up sick, not to mention handling an emergency. The deck crew get paid 4 or 5 grand more than us for sitting in the mess room playing cards and the bridge crew get a lot more for holding a steering wheel!

(Interview, 3 January 2002)

A growing body of evidence now indicates that unions in Britain have had greater success in organizing workers in those sectors of the economy that have traditionally been unionized (such as manufacturing, transport, and public services) suggesting that while these workers may have stronger reasons to unionize, union traditions and experience remain an important factor shaping the propensity for unionization (IRS 2000, Gall and McKay 2000, Wills 2001a).

Towards a comprehensive organizing approach

The GFS tackled Seacat as a workplace organizing campaign but even though the GFS carefully planned their campaign, the *scale* of their thinking was quite *narrow* in practice. Seacat was tackled as a set of work-places more or less in isolation from the rest of the corporation of which it is part and from the rest of the wider community of which the workers are part. Experience in North America, however, illustrates the leverage that can be gained from taking a more comprehensive, and scale-sensitive, approach to organizing that

> [o]n the one hand emphasizes bottom-up worker participation and militance and on the other hand uses top-down tactics to confront employers on an industry-wide basis, as opposed to individual shops. These top-down strategies include corporate campaigns . . .
>
> (Zabin 2000: 151)

In this regard, Sea Containers, the multi-national parent company, has an international reach and a large numbers of other subsidiaries in the UK. TSSA has members in at least one of these, Great North Eastern Railways (GNER), but these workers were never involved in the campaign. By taking a broader view in the planning stages of this campaign, TSSA might have been able to find additional avenues to add weight to their case. GNER workers could have been asked to raise the Seacat campaign within their own bargaining channels, other unions and the International Transport Federation who have contacts with Sea Containers and its affiliates could have been contacted early on in the campaign, shareholders of the company and the AGM could have been targeted and so on. These initiatives would have helped create additional pressure on Sea Containers and Seacat senior managers to recognize TSSA and to resolve outstanding concerns. By widen-ing the scale of the campaign and fostering new alliances, Seacat workers would have witnessed the potential power of TSSA and the wider trade union movement to work together for change.

During the campaign, Seacat workplaces were largely viewed in isolation from the local communities of which they were part. The TSSA Belfast branch meeting was keen to give support but was not called upon to do so. Such a local network would have provided the opportunity to allow the new Seacat members to build relationships with other trade unionists in the area, fostering support for the long term. This local dimension would have also allowed the campaign to enter the consciousness of people in the communities of Belfast, affecting ticket sales and so helping to put pressure on the company to concede. The North American experience indicates that where strong local coalitions of community groups and union branches exist, they can be called upon to support demonstrations, to mobilize important local figures such as politicians and clergy, and to influence the local press (Brecher and Costello 1990, Fine 2000/1, Wills 2001b, Wills and Simms 2001). Such tactics could have broadened the scope and scale of the campaign at Seacat.

Concluding remarks

The Seacat campaign highlights a number of important issues for TSSA and trade unions in Britain. The first is the resource intensity of organizing work and the need to provide resources and support for workplace unionism in the long term. Organizing young workers with no experience of trade unionism, in small and isolated workplaces, with hostile employers, is labor intensive. The Seacat campaign demonstrated that organizing *can* work in such circumstances, even though it is difficult and expensive. Organizers successfully identified issues and found activists around which to mobilize others, developed one-to-one relationships with staff, and built up collective organization. As such, the campaign reinforces Kelly's (1998) argument that the development of workplace unionism depends on shared grievances, locating attribution, demanding justice, and leaders who can mobilize around these concerns.

Second, the Seacat campaign also demonstrates the practical complexities of organizing. Organizers had to grapple with a wide range of tasks and demands, making it difficult to step back and reflect on strategy. On reflection, the TSSA GFS might have done more to avoid being divided from the RMT and to involve workplace union activists in key decisions during the campaign. Moreover, there may have been scope for using additional levers of power to effect change, rather than relying solely on membership strength and industrial action. Indeed, one of the issues arising from the Seacat campaign is that unions need to think *beyond* the workplace in planning and implementing organizing campaigns. The networks of capital to which Seacat is connected might have proved useful additional terrain on which to fight the campaign and thus gain further support (through links with other workers, trade unionists, shareholders, and customers), just as connections to the local community might have been mobilized to build support for unionizing the staff.

Following the Seacat campaign, the GFS has moved on to new targets and the larger travel trade team is now making plans to tackle a retail chain in the sector in early 2002. Such organizing activity will raise many unanticipated challenges, but finding and developing a new generation of trade unionists and activists remains a critical task ahead of both TSSA and the union movement in Britain.

Acknowledgment

I am grateful to the ESRC for the financial support needed to undertake this research (fellowship award number R000271020) and to staff and activists from TSSA.

9 Call center organizing in adversity

From Excell to Vertex

Phil Taylor and Peter Bain

Introduction

Emerging research on trade unions in UK call centers has concentrated on developments in the unionized financial sector (Bain and Taylor 2001a, 2002, Taylor and Bain 2001a) and collectivization across unionized and non-unionized call centers (Gall *et al.* 2001). Published studies explicitly engaging with union organizing campaigns have been limited to the Communication Workers' Union (CWU) campaign at TypeTalk (Heery *et al.* 2000a). This case study aims to contribute to our knowledge by analyzing the experience of workplace organizing at an outsourced telecommunications call center, Excell Multimedia, in Glasgow. Excell qualifies as a significant case study not simply because, in circumstances of extreme employer hostility, a union-free environment was transformed into a workplace with a substantial CWU membership. Widespread media coverage and public interest not only reflected events but helped frame them, influencing intermittent episodes of worker–management conflict, which culminated in the dismissal of two leading activists in February 2000. Media exposure (e.g. *Channel 4 News*, 14 December 1999, *Guardian*, 9 September 2000, *Independent*, 9 February 2000, *Mirror*, 21 July 2000) of Excell's working practices, their treatment of the workforce, and, particularly, allegations of malpractice in relation to customer service, provided a sporadic and high-profile backdrop to the unionization campaign. Concerns regarding conditions at Excell also prompted political intervention in both the Scottish Parliament and at Westminster (*Hansard*, 2 December 1998) and attracted the close attention of the trade union movement. Ultimately, these sackings further damaged the company's reputation, contributing to a decision by Excell's main client to terminate their contract and replace Excell with an alternative outsourcer, Vertex.

This chapter aims to make a distinctive contribution in several areas. First, despite valuable work on non-union enterprises (e.g. McLoughlin and Gourlay 1994, Scott 1994) and evidence of the effects of employer hostility on unions (e.g. Gallie 1996), Kelly's assessment that it "still remains unclear how unionism ever gets started up in a workplace" (1998: 44) is valid. While the TypeTalk call center studies (Simms *et al.* 1999, Heery *et al.* 2000a) usefully analyze the application of the "organizing model" and its associated techniques, they do not relate these to a detailed exploration of the processes of interest formation amongst the workers involved. One exception to the relative neglect of the internal dynamics involved in the unionization of previously union-free workplaces is Fantasia's (1988: 121–79) case study of organizing amongst hospital workers in Springfield, Vermont, US. However, the Springfield events are now twenty years old, and while it is still possible to generalize from Fantasia's "cultures of solidarity" thesis, we know virtually nothing about the early stages of union formation in non-union workplaces in contemporary Britain.

Second, Darlington (1994, 1998, 2001), Kelly (1998), and Greene *et al.* (2000) have emphasized recently that leadership is central to the processes by which individual workers are transformed into collective actors. While the importance of shop stewards and worker leaders in building and sustaining collective organization, and in leading action against employers, has been long acknowledged (Batstone *et al.* 1977), as Darlington (2001: 3) and several others (e.g. Gall 1999, McIlroy and Campbell 1999) have stressed, the significance of left-wing leadership in union activity and mobilization has been underestimated. Understandably, given this focus on organized union groupings and factions, studies of leadership have concentrated on unionized environments.

Whilst concurring with the re-emphasis on the importance of leadership, the Excell case study adds value by examining the crucial contribution made in a non-union workplace by worker leaders. Further, although Darlington (2001: 3) usefully includes "independent non-party industrial militants who share class/socialist politics" in his definition of left-wing leaders, this categorization barely encompasses the initial orientations and characteristics of the Excell leaders, who *came* to express solidaristic values and develop leadership attributes in the course of a struggle against an employer increasingly seen as unjust. This is not an account of a pre-conceived campaign to organize an unorganized workplace, involving left-wing activists, but one where leadership emerged organically.

Third, a further advantage of the Excell case lies in the methodologies employed. One reason for the paucity of evidence on how unions get started in non-union workplaces is the difficulty in pre-selecting non-union locations likely to become the locus of internally generated unionizing efforts. Problems of access and data collection present further obstacles, particularly for researchers wishing to chart workers' attitudes and activities during the prolonged and hidden "gestation" periods, which frequently characterize the unionization of such environments. It is often only when these cases are publicized by unions, or become the subject of media interest, that they attract the attention of academics. Consequently, data on the formative periods of interest definition and mobilization, areas where we are weak (Kelly 1998: 27), is rarely gathered at the time these processes are occurring. Even Fantasia (1988) appears to rely on retrospective interviewing to reconstruct events. In contrast, the authors gained direct access to meetings of Excell workers over many months, beginning in the early stages of their organizing campaign. Recording these meetings provided a first-hand and *contemporaneous* account of organizing efforts.

Throughout this analysis of the growth of collective organization, reference is made to the key tenets of mobilization theory. Drawing on the work of several authors (Kelly 1998, Gamson 1992, McAdam 1988, Tilly 1978), mobilization theory provides a conceptual framework in which the interests, motivations, and actions of these Excell workers can be given meaning. In addition to giving prominence to worker leadership (Kelly 1998: 44) and the formative process of interest definition within mobilization theory, this chapter emphasizes McAdam's (1988: 134–5) "micromobilization context," defined as "that small group setting in which processes of collective attribution are combined with rudimentary forms of organization to produce mobilization for collective action." Before examining mobilization at Excell, it is necessary both to explicate the research methodologies and to profile the "micromobilization context."

Methodology

Research commenced into the call center sector in Scotland in 1996 with a survey, which included a profile of Excell. Closer attention followed an interview with a former student, known to the authors, then working at Excell. Following this serendipitous contact, the authors were invited to attend out-of-work, evening meetings of a group of Excell workers, who gathered to discuss how to campaign against their employer, and to organize a union. Between November 1998 and February 1999 twenty-seven meetings, lasting from two to four hours, were documented. In effect, these transcriptions are the proceedings of a loosely structured, informal committee of between four and twelve workers, whose debates and decisions were recorded against a background of conflict with Excell management. Attendance at additional meetings, during 1999 and 2000, provided insights into later stages of the campaign.

The meetings afforded opportunities for parallel interviews with workers, enabling detailed inquiry into the labor process and employee relations. Further valuable data was derived from ten retrospective interviews, conducted in late 1999 and 2000, in which key participants in the organizing drive reflected upon the significance of earlier and current developments. Finally, a lengthy interview with the national officer of the CWU with overall responsibility for Excell delivered important insights into his and the national union's perspectives. Together, these data sets allow us to reconstruct the mobilization process, combining vibrant contemporary accounts with participants' later reflections.

Excell, work organization and trade unionism

Excell opened its Glasgow call center in April 1995 and, by late 1998, employed 350 agents on seven separate "24×7" services including directory inquiries and 999 emergency services. As call volume expanded, a second facility opened and by spring 2000, 800 were employed in total, with an additional 400 at a sister center in Birmingham. As an outsourcer, Excell operated customer services for cable and mobile phone companies, including their major client, Cable and Wireless. Excell Global Services, the parent company, is a transnational outsourcer providing "call handling solutions," mainly in telecommunications. Founded in 1994, its growth from its Arizona base was spectacular, having exploited deregulation in the global telecommunications industry (Pitt *et al.* 1997) and the profit-generating opportunities created by outsourcing. The attraction of Excell to clients, and the source of its profits, lay in the ability to minimize operating, particularly labor, costs. It is the severity with which Excell implemented its cost-reduction strategy, and the consequences for work content, which profoundly influenced the micromobilization context.

How work was experienced at Excell should be considered against the background of recent studies of call center work organization (Bain and Taylor 2000, 2001b, 2002, Batt 2000, Callaghan and Thompson 2001, Frenkel *et al.* 1999, Taylor and Bain 1999, 2001a, Taylor *et al.* 2002). Despite commonalities in the integration of computer and telephonic technologies, call centers are not uniform. In short, differences in work organization can be identified, reflecting the relative emphases management place upon quantity and quality. Call center operations at Excell stood at the quantitative extreme of a quality/quantity spectrum (Taylor and Bain 2001: 44–9). The overriding priority was to take maximum numbers of calls, which subjected agents to strictly imposed and exceptionally detailed measurements and targets. For example, on directory inquiries agents had to answer calls every thirty seconds and call handling times were measured to one-hundredth of a second. Further evidence of task intensity can be seen through agents being obligated to spend 97 percent of each shift on "switch." While it is not suggested that the labor process constituted the sole influence shaping workers' attitudes, the daily experience of repetitive and regimented work was a crucial feature of the "micromobilization context," creating a deep well of discontent.

Equally important was Excell's overt hostility to trade unionism, originating in the attitudinal orientation of the company's founders. For Excell, union recognition was an institutional obstacle in the path of achieving unconstrained labor flexibility and cost reduction, threatening the very advantages of outsourcing. Excell's recent practice includes cases of harassment and dismissal of union members in their Arizona heartland (McGrath 2000) and, in the case of its partnership with Bell Canada, "union busting" (*Montreal Gazette*, 17 May 1999). Integral to its business strategy, Excell's resolute anti-unionism defined its management's attitudes to dissent and collective organization in its call centers in Britain.

From discontent to collective grievance: October 1998 to February 1999

Developments at Excell in this period provide valuable illustrations of the formative stages of mobilization. In concrete terms, a significant, if initially fragile, CWU membership base of approximately fifty was established, in contrast to the near-complete absence of union presence which had prevailed since Excell's start-up. However, these bare facts tell us nothing about the dramatic changes which occurred in the consciousness, activity, and interest identification of a minority of the workforce. What were the principal sources of dissatisfaction expressed by these workers? In what ways did a sense of injustice emerge from the welter of discontents? To what extent did the emergence of union organization have roots in the acquisition of collective grievance? Is the recent prominence accorded to the role of leadership justified?

Discontents

The daily experience of a highly regimented labor process was a principal and inescapable source of dissatisfaction. Several workers provided vivid illustrations of the alienating effects of taking up to 900 calls every shift.

> My flatmates used to laugh at me because I'd shout in my sleep, "Which name please, which town please, thank you, here's your number now" and I'd only been working there for a month.
>
> (Interview, Maddy, 9 February 1999)

Amongst growing numbers, unhappiness with this incessant routine of mentally and physically exhausting toil deepened into a sense that something was quite wrong at Excell. Driven by supervisors to meet unachievable targets, agents made pointed comparisons between their pay, £3.97 to £4.47 per hour, and the profits Excell made from the 50p each thirty-second call cost the customer. The eight-hour day- and twelve-hour nightshifts included only minimal breaks, with no concessions for operators who experienced abusive customers or health problems. One asthma sufferer reported how he was disciplined for being "not ready" when taking shots from his inhaler. To many, the bonus was "*the* massive grievance," as average earnings had halved over two years while productivity had soared (meeting transcript, 22 November 1998). Entire payments would be lost if workers were only five minutes late in a three-month period. This symbolized Excell's punitive management style.

Disciplinaries were perceived as arbitrary, meted out by unpopular supervisors for minor indiscretions. Workers reported many examples of "bullying managers" who picked on those seen as troublesome or, conversely, vulnerable. Dissatisfaction followed management's failure to respond to profound health and safety complaints including an outbreak of scabies, insect infestation, polluted drinking water, and stress leading to employees suffering black-outs. We have only touched here on the diverse discontents, from the material and profound, to the apparently trivial but no less significant as sources of dissatisfaction, which workers expressed by autumn 1998. However, to be discontented does not automatically and necessarily lead workers to interest identification or to a sense of injustice. Indeed, at Excell, many chose to exit after short periods of employment, while others sought to escape pressures through alcohol or drugs.

Injustice and interest identification

Yet, out of this milieu of alienation and widespread dissatisfaction, some workers came to express themselves in collective terms with common objectives. In a classic affirmation of a central tenet of mobilization theory this happened because, initially, a small group of workers coalesced around a sense of injustice and tapped the "veins" of discontent running through the workforce. None of the individuals forming this group were acquainted with each other prior to working at Excell, and although a handful had been union members in previous jobs, none had a history of activism or membership of left-wing political organizations. Two, Dave and Debbie, joined the CWU in 1997 as individuals motivated by a general belief in the legitimacy of trade unions, and neither was aware of the other's membership. This is not so say that the group lacked conviction or strongly held beliefs, for it is clear from the early meetings that, to varying degrees, all were motivated by moral concerns of fairness and justice.

The group was generally representative of a workforce who were mainly in their twenties or early thirties and contained equal numbers of men and women, although men were disproportionately concentrated on the nightshift. However, marginally different characteristics in gender, educational background, and length of service were to be found amongst the individuals who became leaders. Two held degrees in media/cultural studies, and their ability to criticize company communications, to write fluently, to argue effectively with managers, and to use the media undeniably stemmed in part from skills acquired at university. However, this did not mark them out as particularly distinctive, since several Excell workers were graduates and had come to work there to pay off debts or secure a regular income. Others had either a breadth of school qualifications or diverse life backgrounds, factors which may have contributed to their emergence as opponents of Excell:

People who were street smart and had quite a developed intellect and who were thwarted in some ways by their life experience actually wanted to kick over the statues. They were being told what to do in demeaning jobs by people who were their inferiors, intellectually and as human beings.

(Interview, Gary, 12 December 2000)

Some believed that a creative mix of individuals[1] from contrasting backgrounds was more influential than the presence of a well-educated minority. Length of service, though, was significant, for all had worked at Excell for two years or more. They had experienced a deterioration in conditions of work and had "seen through" Excell by autumn 1998. The final difference relates to gender, for in the early stages the leadership group was predominantly male.

However, neither marginal differences in the educational background, length of service, and gender of those who became leaders, nor the widespread discontent amongst the workforce in themselves explain how or why a collective grouping with a common purpose developed. To do this, it is necessary to acknowledge the importance of grievance formation. The retrospective interviews provide invaluable accounts of the processes by which individuals arrived at the conclusion that something had to be done. Kevin perceptively described the process of "cognitive liberation" (see McAdam: 132–4):

I think the trajectory of it was very different for every individual, but I think everybody who was involved thought, in a moment of epiphany, "Right, no more."

(Interview, 12 December 2000)

For Gary, health and safety issues provoked critical analysis:

. . . once the light had been shined in my eyes, as it were, the whole working environment really opened up to intense scrutiny and from that point I was asking a series of questions. Where were all the promises that had been made about bonuses . . . of extra holidays, increased wages, decreased workload? And it would be particular things that really annoyed me like the attempt to foist an American business culture and corporate world view . . . there seemed to be a kind of ideological struggle going on behind the scenes, which was really about hearts and minds rather than voices and hands . . . this I found particularly repellent.

(Interview, 9 March 1999)

Sammy's breaking point followed "maybe the third or fourth" meeting where a manager had bullied him over sickness absence. Colin saw intimidation of older workers as important: "People were being robbed of their dignity . . . Something had to be done" (interview, 15 June 2000). For Dave, who became the key leader, the inhumane treatment, work intensity, poor pay, and understaffing were not accidental but were caused by Excell's business priorities:

> A new contract had been signed with Cable and Wireless, which led to a huge change in culture and management. It was after this that call-handling times were introduced and work pressure was stepped up.
> (Interview, 20 February 2000)

All these individuals drew the conclusion that the company was to blame for the problems workers faced. In essence, this was the first stage in the attribution process (Kelly 1998: 30, 46) and what fueled the conviction that action was urgently required was a sense of injustice, not individualistic instrumentalism. Before October 1998, perceptions of injustice were still individually held, but the motivation for change was most often borne out of a concern for fellow workers. The union was built by individuals who, in the formation of their attitudes, had defied Olsonian logic (Kelly 1998: 79).

A sense of collective injustice

To answer the neglected question of how workplace unions "get started," we must analyze concretely how leadership groups emerge and forge common micro-world views. At Excell, first, these individuals became aware of each other through acts of resistance; for example, Dave's willingness to represent fellow workers in disciplinaries, or through raising thorny issues in company forums. Second, more prosaically, was the accidental circumstance that most were smokers, and came to know each other's views through frank discussions in the smoking room: "a fertile ground for people who defined themselves in a certain way" (interview, Gary, 9 March 1999). Third, they became friends, meeting in pubs to ridicule Excell and its managers, but also to discuss seriously what could be done to change things. The protagonists concede that the emerging group had a "laddish" character which, while initially a source of clannish strength, had later to be overcome for the union to grow deeper roots. Fourth, management, by dubbing these individuals the "bad boys," gave them a collective persona and unwittingly contributed to group cohesion. Colin reflected, "it was kind of like 'them and us,' only instead of the workers causing it, it was management" (interview, 22 June 2000).

That the group saw a union as the appropriate vehicle for achieving change was due to the initiative of Dave, who contacted the CWU in October 1998. One early recruit recalled that conditions were favorable, as many workers were "union-minded and waiting for the chance to join."

The initial base was in Dave's 999 nightshift team, where as in Fantasia's study (1988: 152), greater social space assisted the emergence of oppositional attitudes and organization:

> Team 7 was an easy recruiting ground and within a short period of time we had fifteen of the twenty people into the union. We would just say, "Look, I have joined the union and we think it is a good thing because things are going downhill with Excell, and I think we should try and protect ourselves" and bit by bit there was a sense of trust.
>
> (Interview, Dave, 8 March 2000)

Although this group was honing widespread dissatisfaction with pay, conditions, health and safety, work intensity, and intimidatory management into a sense of injustice, the catalyst for broadening union recruitment was company malpractice over service delivery. For several months, management had ignored workers' concerns over errors in customer databases, maintained by Excell for their clients. The problem was potentially life-threatening on emergency services where, because the on-screen records of "many customers were displaying the wrong details, we were sending fire engines, police, and ambulances to the wrong addresses" (meeting, 29 November 1998). Many 999 operators took pride in the valuable public service they provided, but management negligence eroded their sense of worth in the job. Moreover, the consequences could be profoundly stressful:

> If you can imagine the effect of listening to a woman being beaten up in her home and dragged from the phone, then consider how you would feel if you were exposed to this kind of thing every night. The emergency authorities need those addresses urgently and we can't supply them. How do think we feel? We've complained 'til we are sick to the back teeth; now we want something done.
>
> (Meeting, 1 December 1998)

Monitoring the system's malfunctioning, gathering evidence of incorrect addresses and misdirected emergency vehicles, should be regarded as the group's first collective activity. Staggered by the scale of the problem caused by the company's failure to update records, and frustrated at the futility of seeking remedy through Excell's "Open Book Management" communication structures, they embarked on a course of action in which they forged a genuine collective identity. The protagonists' motivation again confounds simplistic notions of individualistic cost-benefit calculations as they consciously saw themselves engaged in a "moral crusade." Through the persistent refusal to admit responsibility, management lost legitimacy in their eyes. Following unsuccessful appeals to Oftel, the Consumer Association, and the Department of Trade and Industry to try to force Excell into remedial action, the activists initiated media and political campaigns to highlight the system's failures. Extensive public disclosure ensued, including an Early Day Motion in Parliament (*Hansard*, 2 December 1998) signed by thirty Members of Parliament. This ushered in a period of intense conflict, provoked by management's strenuous efforts to identify, isolate, and expel the whistleblowers.

What sharpened management's hostility, creating profound shopfloor tension, was their awareness that the individuals responsible for damning news reports were simultaneously using the revelations to persuade colleagues to join the CWU. Excell responded with a memo stating that "anybody found discussing union matters would be reported to management and the disciplinary procedure invoked" (interview, Debbie, 9 March 1999). As the emergency services campaign established the prestige, legitimacy, and authority of the activists, by now clearly identified with the CWU, management's standing correspondingly declined. In short, the processes of cognitive liberation and collective interest identification spread ever wider.

Leadership and organization

The culminating event was precipitated by a press conference organized, on behalf of Excell workers, by the STUC, emergency services unions, and the local MP, which highlighted the 999 issue and working conditions. In retaliation, Excell suspended, apparently intending to dismiss, Gary who had been present at the conference, but who had taken no part. Management's subsequent failure to sack this popular worker, because of a robustly conducted defense, in which the union "came out" and stood up to management, represented a major turning point in mobilization. More than anything, it built confidence by demonstrating that collective action could win. The widespread support for Gary exemplifies the quasi-collective action, which Kelly (1998: 50) suggests may occur in non-union environments. Here, a demonstrative show of strength contributed to union victory. Dave, who represented Gary, recalled the mood surrounding his disciplinary meeting:

> We walked into Gary's disciplinary and the boys started clapping . . . that's as bold as you like. The bad boys clapping. That sent out a signal to people, we don't have anything to fear, we don't care what management thinks.
>
> (Interview, 20 December 2000)

The importance mobilization theory ascribes to small numbers of leaders is supported by these developments, as is the recognition that individuals with particular qualities make a critical difference during decisive periods. After all, it was one individual, Dave, who initially contacted the CWU, seeing the union as the vehicle which could give expression to his, and others' growing sense of injustice. His ability to pull together a core of activists, to facilitate the formation of a commonly held micro-world view, and to articulate shared objectives proved decisive. Equally important was his understanding that a group of leaders could act like a small cog, which could turn the larger cog of a wider circle, which, in turn, could influence layers of workers. Acknowledging the particular contribution of one individual, however, does not devalue the significance of the leadership group. Collectively, they performed all the roles required of effective leaders – highlighting grievances, attributing blame to management, giving fellow workers confidence, "framing" issues, and responding to counter-mobilization.

Their close relationship with fellow workers confirms the importance of further aspects of leadership, participatory style, and collectivist outlook (Darlington 1994, Greene *et al.* 2000). The leaders helped create "cultures of solidarity" similar to those analyzed, albeit incompletely, by Fantasia. During intense periods, meetings were held every evening in Dave's flat, where open discussion was encouraged because "everybody's input was seen as valuable" (interview, 3 March 2000). These meetings were important for defining leadership roles, allocating responsibilities, and for creating a collective organization, as distinct from an identification of common interests. The fluidity of the organizing committee compares with that in Fantasia's (1988: 132) Springfield study. Yet, similarly, an organizational purpose always followed debates as appropriate tactics were planned in response to, or anticipation of, management actions. One example will suffice. Recognizing that union members remained a minority on 999 services, the group initiated a petition aimed at winning non-members to their campaign. Several newer members were invited to a meeting, where the wording of the petition, calling on management to rectify the problems, was agreed and its circulation planned in detail. A successful response depended on the boldness of these new recruits, who were given the confidence to approach fellow workers to secure signatures. As a result almost all 999 agents signed and management "was forced onto the back foot." For the leaders this was but one step in the organization drive. At the next meeting, the newly involved members were encouraged to approach the signatories with CWU membership forms, a tactic which delivered several recruits. Success depended on the linkages between the leaders, new members, and the wider workforce.

Extrapolated from its context, the successful circulation of this petition might seem a minor achievement. Set in the micromobilization context, it demonstrates the sophistication of a leadership, who discovered in the course of engagement that collective action was the only means by which the "moral crusade" could be won. It also tells us much about the willingness of previously passive individuals to act, when given a lead, even in circumstances where the threat of dismissal was real.

Mobilization and organization – February 1999 to February 2000

> The 999 issue was double-sided . . . it gave the initial group the impetus to join the union, to move together and work collectively. But the problem we had with the 999 issue was obviously that it is a small part of the service and most people weren't involved . . . we had to expand trade union involvement and broaden the issues.
>
> (Interview, Dave, 20 February 2000)

The character of mobilization after February 1999 contrasts with that of the preceding period. After the frenetic campaigning, and partial victory around the 999 issue, the leaders' priority shifted to the longer-term objective of establishing the union on a firmer footing. Necessarily, this involved sustained recruitment activity and the creation of formalized structures. The leadership group, in framing an agenda composed of more "traditional" trade union issues, succeeded in tapping into the interests of greater numbers of workers. Until this point what the union was *for*, as opposed to what it had been *against*, had been relatively unclear, so the formulation of specific demands marks a big step forward, by giving organizational form to collective interests. The vague appeal that "being in a union makes a difference" could develop organization only so far. Concrete demands were specified in a leaflet distributed, in March 1999, outside Excell by sympathetic local trade unionists.

Demands over pay, particularly parity with the higher rates in the Birmingham center, and those relating to deep-seated concerns over health and safety, the sick pay scheme, holidays, and disciplinaries were prominent. Significantly, calls on Excell to recognize the CWU and permit representation in individual cases were made for the first time. The preparation and distribution of this recruitment leaflet is evidence of a growing maturity in the leadership's organizing abilities. The demands were consciously designed to appear fair, were widely supported and, in the parity issue, the leadership highlighted a discriminatory practice, seized on by the Scottish press (*Daily Record*, 23 June 1999). Of course, there was no expectation that Excell would meet these demands. Rather, the purposes were to legitimize the union's right to express such demands, to raise workers' expectations, and to increase recruitment. Consequently, non-members increasingly brought their problems to the union, whose response was consistent with their participatory and representative leadership styles.

> We won't say to them, "Go away, because you are not a trade unionist." What we say is, "We will look into this problem for you, get the information and try to help. But it would be helpful to all of us in the workplace if you joined."
>
> (Interview, Dave, 9 March 1999)

When the leadership became aware of the potential impact of the ERA, recruitment activities were accorded an even higher priority. Although the precise detail was not known, the ERA proved a tremendous incentive, because ". . . all of a sudden you could see the winning post. That changed things and gave us a longer-term view (interview, Dave, 8 March 2000).

Using "organizing model" techniques, learnt by the CWU from the Communication Workers of America (Heery *et al.* 2000a) and passed to Excell's unionists by a national organizer, union members assessed the recruitability of colleagues on a scale of 1 to 5. If scores were favorable, workers were asked to join. This method led to membership growth, to which management unwittingly contributed. Keen to dissolve concentrations of suspected members, individuals were moved to "safe" teams, but, "rather than isolating cliques of union activists it spread activity throughout the center" (interview, Gary, 9 March 1999). The results of this recruitment drive were impressive. By autumn 1999 membership had quadrupled to 200 workers (about a quarter of the multi-shift workforce), the "laddishness" diluted as many women joined, and an embyonic reps structure created. Increased recruitment generated a confidence which saw the union fully emerge in late 1999, when a leaflet naming six representatives was distributed by workplace unionists themselves: "People thought Excell would come down with a hatchet and cut us away and when they didn't the confidence we had just grew" (interview, Dave, 8 March 2000).

Effective leadership involved integrating this "raw" membership into the union. Structures were improvised at workplace level, with combinations of experienced and newer members acting as team/shift representatives. Over time, Excell members became involved in local CWU bodies, although the process was far from straightforward. Initially, they were obliged to join the engineering branch, rather than the more appropriate clerical branch, which included British Telecom (BT) call center workers.

> So there was a kind of cultural gap between us. At first, we didn't understand their problems as BT engineers. And they hadn't really experienced the kind of things we faced in a call center. I think the branch felt we were fly-by-night and they were going to have to spend lots of time and energy helping what they saw was a handful of us.
>
> (Interview, Dave, 30 April 2000)

Through persistent explanation of their problems, and by demonstrating commitment through high levels of attendance at meetings, the Excell members persuaded the CWU to establish a sub-branch of non-BT call center workers. The successful integration of Excell's membership with CWU structures demonstrated that leadership meant more than developing workplace organization. Establishing enduring trade unionism required the Excell leaders to influence, negotiate with, and draw upon the resources of external bodies. Principally this meant the CWU, and the adoption of certain organizing techniques – union mapping, one-to-one recruitment, communications with the workforce, petitions (cf. Heery *et al.* 2000a).

External resources also included, at various times, local media, networks of trade unionists, academics, politicians, and advice organizations. However, despite organizational successes, the Excell leaders came to believe that the CWU's resources were not being fully marshaled behind their efforts.

Frustration followed the union's refusal to endorse certain initiatives. The roots of this refusal lay in the CWU's national priorities. Cable and Wireless (C&W), Excell's client firm, was a major, non-union telecommunications company employing 6,000, and a prime recognition target. Negotiations with C&W had been underway for some months and the union was optimistic that "some kind of quasi-recognition" was achievable (interview, national officer, 24 January 2001). Because "the union had a strategic interest in improving [their] position with C&W" (interview, national officer, 24 January 2001), the CWU nationally was reluctant to be associated with adversarial activity. The logic of the CWU's position was that recognition at C&W, in the form of a "partnership" agreement, could be achieved only through a process of persuasion during which the union convinced the company of its "reasonable" approach. Put bluntly, the mobilizing activities at Excell could be interpreted by *both* C&W and the CWU as threatening their respective interests. On the one hand, media exposure of the emergency service problems and working conditions implicated C&W as Excell's main client. On the other hand, the perceived militancy of CWU activity at Excell could call into question the union's claims to be "responsible" and threaten to jeopardize the high road to recognition at C&W.

Mobilization at Excell was increasingly characterized by the frequent clash of competing priorities, as the national officer's desire for moderation collided with the "bottom-up," and unavoidably adversarial, approach of the workplace membership. Excell activists soon concluded that the reason they were instructed not to contact the media, or distribute leaflets, lay in the national officer's perception of the realpolitik of the situation:

> On his side, he was trying to set up a good relationship with C&W and, on the other, he had these few punters who were working for a place that was outsourced to it and who were prepared to go to the national press, the television and be utterly critical. This was not a good situation. So basically his whole project was about containment. If the CWU gains recognition at C&W it's thousands of members . . . We had handfuls by comparison.
>
> (Interview, Dave, 30 April 2000)

The national strategy of moderation was reinforced by a mistaken assessment of Excell's preparedness to grant union recognition voluntarily, which fundamentally contradicted the workplace perspective:

It seemed to us that the national officer was more benign to Excell than he needed to be, and that's putting it mildly. We found out that Excell were anti-union and anti-worker throughout the world and should be shamed in front of the telecommunications industry.

(Interview, Dave, 30 April 2000)

The workplace union advocated a high profile and sustained campaign against Excell, with maximum support given to recruitment and organiz-ation activities, in the belief that the company would only grant recognition if compelled to. Because of their experience and understanding of Excell's profound anti-unionism, the activists consciously developed an alternative course of action – to campaign for the company's removal and to secure continuity of employment with another outsourcer, who might be more amenable to trade unionism. In contrast, the national officer encouraged a "softly softly" approach believing Excell would ultimately grant recognition if the union was "reasonable." Evidence of this strategy can be seen in an interview in the union magazine with Excell's HR manager (CWU 2000). That the workplace activists' assessment was correct was confirmed by later events, and by admission of the national officer:

With the benefit of hindsight we should have been harder . . . I was genuinely trying to put forward a platform where those with common ground could try and discuss the problems. I was probably looking at it from an optimistic point of view. Their [Excell unionists'] position was actually quite different . . . [Excell] were absolute cowboys and should be driven out the UK. They were correct, absolutely, no way would I disagree with that.

(Interview, 24 January 2001)

Unfortunately, belated recognition of Excell's ruthless anti-unionism did not alter this strategy. That, in sixteen months, the activists had built a solid membership of 30 percent of the workforce across the two sites by February 2000 was no small achievement. However, it is difficult to escape the conclusion that recruitment would have been even greater had the national union fully supported initiatives proposed by the Excell unionists, including leafleting, the continued exposure of working conditions, and a preparedness to openly confront Excell. For example, the national officer forbade raising the parity demand, although it seemed fair, achievable, was immensely popular amongst members and non-members alike, and, indeed, attracted many to the union. Mobilization at Excell was sacrificed in favor of pursuing a partnership strategy with C&W. Whenever a head of steam for change and action developed amongst the workforce, national intervention ensured that the momentum was restrained. It is in this sense that we refer to the concept of dissipated mobilization.

Counter-mobilization, dissipated mobilization and postscript: March 2000 onwards

Excell embarked on a course of repression, dismissing Dave and another leading member for gross misconduct, following a television report exposing working conditions. The character and timing of this retributive action suggests a corporate-level decision to move against the union. Yet, although re-instatement efforts failed, Excell's counter-mobilization did not immediately lead to membership loss and disorganization, demonstrating that the union's roots were deeper than the company believed them to be. The adverse publicity generated by the dismissals finally persuaded C&W to revoke their contract with Excell, transferring operations to an alternative outsourcer, Vertex, on 31 March 2000. The workplace activists saw Excell's departure as creating highly advantageous conditions for securing union recognition. With 30 percent membership and a functioning union structure, a solid platform was already in place. It seemed likely that Vertex, pragmatic towards trade unions, would be receptive to approaches from the CWU for recognition, notably because the union had been instrumental in precipitating Excell's departure. Only four months previously, following an overwhelming ballot result, Vertex had conceded recognition to Unison in their Bolton call center, having previously derecognized the union. Self-evidently, Vertex would be keen to demonstrate they were not another Excell, by addressing grievances, and possibly conceding recognition.

Yet, for two years after Excell's departure, the CWU remained unrecognized. This can be explained by reference to several factors. First, Vertex adopted a sophisticated strategy towards the CWU, permitting leaflets and notice boards, but denying recognition, whilst simultaneously and successfully attempting to incorporate workplace unionists through "employee consultation" forums. Second, the workplace union had lost two capable leaders, who would have undoubtedly responded more effectively to Vertex's twin-track strategy of incorporation and delay. Third, several experienced union builders had departed for better jobs or higher education. Thus, the union was deprived of important ideological and organizational resources, at a time when effective leadership was needed in a more complex situation. Fourth, the orientation of the national officer continued to be a decisive factor, as the strategy of moderating demands, for fear of alienating C&W, persisted. Shortly after Vertex's arrival, workplace unionists were prevented from distributing a recruitment leaflet, repeating key demands, on the grounds that the climate of trust being cultivated with Vertex would be undermined. The strategy agreed by the national officer with Vertex was based on partnership principles, where trust would be established through joint company/CWU training initiatives. Only after the completion of "milestones" to Vertex's satisfaction, would permission for a recognition ballot be granted. The outcome, however, was delay, which may appear a minor irritation from the perspective of the national organization pursuing a partnership approach. However, from the standpoint of those building workplace organization, where expectations had been raised following Excell's departure, it proved more damaging. The momentum for continued recruitment since April 2000 was lost and membership levels fell. However, the fact that membership stabilized at around 20 percent was largely due to the legacy of the previous organizing activities in circumstances of employer hostility. Paradoxically, membership attrition occurred under an apparently less adversarial managerial regime, where the pursuit of partnership succeeded in restraining workplace activity and dissipating mobilization. One of the new generation of union reps reflected on the effects of the cautious approach adopted by the CWU nationally.

> We were sort of emasculated because the union was having this compromising period of dialog – we did not have access to people within the building, we could not campaign, we could not distribute leaflets even in our own break times, and we could not say anything that was derogatory or even critical of the company.
>
> (Interview, Shona, 25 February 2002)

In early 2002, Vertex agreed to a recognition ballot, whereupon 99.4 percent of workers across both Glasgow sites and the Birmingham call center voted for recognition in a 63.4 percent turnout. Such an overwhelming majority in favor can be explained by several factors. First, Glasgow workplace union activists were re-energized by the ballot, launching a vigorous recruitment campaign propagating the advantages of union membership. That 240 joined the CWU in four weeks created widespread identification with the union prior to the ballot. Second, many of the widely held grievances that had underlain earlier mobilization efforts remained powerful. For many, working conditions appeared to have deteriorated under Vertex; for example, target call times had been reduced to 27.5 seconds and call blending introduced, leading to greater work intensity. Third, workplace activists had begun to regain confidence following their prior disorientation. Finally, although union membership declined following Vertex's arrival, it remained at around 20 percent of the Glasgow workforce, providing a substantial basis from which to rebuild membership and organization.

However, according to the workplace leadership, past and present, the ultimate success in achieving recognition did not justify the national union strategy. They remain convinced that had a determined approach to Vertex been made within weeks of Excell's departure, and had the union demonstrated to the company its preparedness to pursue the statutory route, Vertex would have granted recognition. In this perspective, recognition had been delayed unnecessarily. While the detail of the partnership agreement between the CWU and Vertex has yet to be decided, the workplace leaders are concerned that the union's willingness to make concessions will lead to a weak agreement which will constrain their ability to resolve the deep-seated grievances held by their members, suggesting mobilization and organization will remain in conflict with partnership.

Conclusion

Discontent at Excell, however widespread, was a necessary but insufficient condition for the emergence of interest identification and a sense of injustice. The very character of interest definition is inexplicable without taking account of how the experience of work led many to profound disillusionment with their employer. Excell's business priorities, management style, and employment relations further contributed to a deep well of often unfocused discontent, fueling a sense that "something had to be done." Mobilization theory informed the examination of how discontent led to a sense of injustice and then to collective interest identification, organization, and action. At Excell, this process began with the "cognitive liberation" of several individuals who possessed an acute sense of right and wrong and who came to see the workplace regime as illegitimate. In the detail of how they formed a group, developed a cohesive micro-world view and embarked on a course of collective action to remedy what they saw as unjust, core concepts of mobilization theory – injustice, attribution, and identity – are richly illustrated. Excell management assisted group formation by defining these individuals as an outgroup (Kelly 1998: 30). "Them" and "us" was, initially, as much a product of managerial action as the efforts of the "bad boys" themselves, and the "regular skirmishing between workers and formal authority" (Fantasia 1988: 171) helped define and maintain the group's internal coherence.

The leap forward in consciousness and collective organization came with the 999 issue which, in its consequences, provides a clear case of a ruling group losing legitimacy through a profound violation of accepted moral norms. The sense of injustice sprang not from the more conventional abuse of job rules, but less typically, through the feeling of "moral outrage" created by Excell's willful disregard for public safety. From the processes of collective interest definition and attribution, there arose "the desire for unionism, a particular form of collective representation" (Kelly 1998: 51). In the development of collective organization, leadership proved decisive. Perhaps the most telling contribution made by the key actor, Dave, was in acting as a fulcrum for a leadership group, who collectively were central to the organizing success. Dave provided sure tactical direction, ensuring that the vital ingredient of confidence permeated wider layers of workers, creating "an emergent culture of solidarity" (Fantasia 1998: 174). Perhaps most significantly, given Darlington's recent work (1994, 2001), none of the leaders had a history of socialist or trade union activism, but through their experience of engagement, *came* to display attributes and express ideas associated with left-wing leaders.

The union was built through "bottom-up" mobilizing activities that were necessarily adversarial and bore similarities with the "organizing model" (Bronfenbrenner *et al.* 1998). Although workplace unionists received some guidance from their national union, the originality and creativity of many methods and tactics devised by the Excell activists is more striking.[2] The scale of recruitment, the integration of workplace organization into CWU structures, and Excell's removal represented considerable achievements in the face of well-resourced employer counter-mobilization. However, despite successes it must be acknowledged that 70 percent of the workforce remained non-members, even at the high point of recruitment. Clearly fears of reprisal, a fatalistic view that the union would not be able to force fundamental changes, and an expectation that employment at Excell was merely a stop-gap until alternative employment opportunities presented themselves were factors influencing the choice of many not to join the union. Yet, sympathy towards the union was widespread amongst non-members and, according to the workplace activists, many were ready to join following Excell's departure, believing that an immediate improvement of working conditions was now possible. This was the specific window of opportunity for achieving a clear majority membership as the union's credibility was at its highest and the arrival of Vertex promised change. The rapid de-escalation of organization activities through national union intervention must be regarded as the principal reason for the failure to capitalize on this particularly advantageous conjuncture.

Mobilization theory can accommodate trajectories which are not always "upwards." Counter-mobilization encompasses employers' strategies of repression, and pre-emptory acts such as dismissals can halt or reverse the forward momentum of worker mobilization. Excell's purge of leading activists deprived the workplace union of arguably their greatest resource. But, on balance, the commitment of the national officer to a partnership strategy with C&W, and later Vertex, exercised a greater influence in stymieing the mobilization momentum. It explains, more than anything, the failure to realize the potential evident at Excell's departure, and more generally, questions the TUC's perspective that the "organizing model" can co-exist with partnership without the emergence of profound contradictions. Mobilization theory contributes to our understanding of why and under what conditions a union was established in this non-union workplace. However, the Excell case suggests that fuller recognition needs to be taken of the ways in which strategies adopted by unions at national level can conflict with, and stifle, organizing activities generated in the workplace, leading to the phenomenon of dissipated mobilization.

Notes

1 One long-standing agent exemplified the wealth of creative talent amongst the workforce by winning a Scottish writing prize for his short story based on his Excell working experiences. It illustrates the alienating effects of call handling and Excell shopfloor regime (Mahon 2000).
2 For evidence of their use of humor and other creative forms of subversion, see Taylor and Bain (2001b).

10 Comparisons and prospects

Industrial relations and trade unions in North America and Britain

Brian Towers

Introduction

The British Labour government, elected in 1997 after eighteen years out of office, had some debts to the unions, though fewer than in earlier elections. The older industrial relations terrain had been "transformed," in particular by a major decline in union membership and a corresponding contraction in collective bargaining (Cully *et al.* 1999, Millward 2000 *et al.*, Hawes 2000). Such a seriously weakened union movement was a situation not previously encountered by an incoming government since 1945. The 1997 government, partly in consequence, had also earlier shed much of old Labour's pro-union ideology in favor of the interests of business; although there was some even-handedness, not least in the commitment to a statutory recognition procedure. This drew, in its design, upon the lessons of the earlier failure as well as, in both in their similarities and contrasts, the experience of Canada and the US.

The unions were not, however, relying solely upon the government. For some years they had been looking abroad for strategies to stem their membership losses. EU legislation and institutions were attracting increasing attention, especially from the mid-1980s as membership decline showed no sign of abating. But, most of all, the TUC and the unions came increasingly under the spell of the organizing strategies of the American Federation of Labor-Congress of Industrial Organizations (AFL-CIO) and certain of its pioneering affiliates. Yet, although in the US the vigorous promotion of new methods of member recruitment and retention have led to some success, progress remains limited to a few unions (Rose and Chaison 2001) and, overall, both private sector membership and density have continued to decline.

This raises the question as to how far the US case is an appropriate example for the organizing strategies of British unions (Towers 1999b). Assessments of these strategies are found elsewhere in this volume. This chapter has a wider, comparative remit, seeking answers to two related questions. First, to what extent do the North American industrial relations systems of the US and Canada – individually and collectively – provide useful comparators for British industrial relations reform? Second, how far should British unions rely upon the North American experience to return to a sustained revival in membership? This chapter provides the background to finding answers to these questions, describing and explaining the still growing divergence in union membership levels between the US and Canada, and drawing the general lessons of this experience for Britain and its unions. It then discusses and assesses the prospects for British unions, under Labour, including the extent to which statutory recognition and their own efforts can revive membership growth. The conclusions return briefly to the still continuing importance for British unions of their relationship with a viable party of government and British membership of the EU.

The North American experience

The data of divergence

Canadian trade union density began to overtake the US in the early to mid-1960s as the American continued the long decline which had begun ten years earlier. The outcome is that though Canadian unions have made major gains, they have been unable to maintain no more than a degree of stability. However, this has proved superior to the steep, unremitting decline experienced by the US unions (see Figure 10.1).

Although US membership held up reasonably well for many years and, by 1975 exceeded 22m, it fell well behind growth in the labor force so that density continued to fall rapidly and, by the early 1980s, both membership and density were falling together. Losses on this scale were soon translated

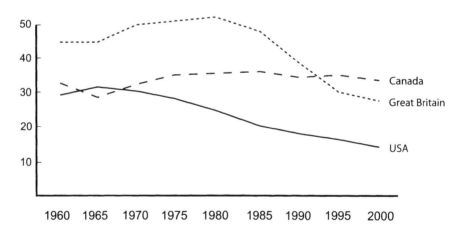

Figure 10.1 Trade union membership density in the USA, Canada, and Great Britain, 1960–2000.

Source: Bain and Price (1983); Rose and Chaison (2001); Sneade (2001).

into diminishing political significance, even when the Democrats controlled the presidency and both houses of Congress in the late 1970s and early 1990s. This was seen in the fate of the modestly ambitious, and substantially amended, 1977 *Labor Law Reform Act* that narrowly failed to pass the Senate under the Carter administration. This setback was followed by further decline and, despite high hopes, the Clinton presidency's failure to redress the pro-employer policies of the Reagan and Bush years (Towers 1997: Ch. 7). Yet, American unions and the AFL-CIO, with no political alternatives, continued to use membership of the Democratic "coalition," as well as their funds and personnel in elections, to press for political advantage. But in legislative terms they have nothing to show for this and, under Clinton, failed to dilute Clinton's support for the North American Free Trade Agreement (NAFTA) despite vigorous, sustained, and expensive campaigning.

Inevitably, political failure forced US unions to put even more energy into self-reliance, the other prong of their revival strategy. Their campaigning and organizing efforts have been strenuous, innovative, and expensive. New-style organizing campaigns at AFL-CIO and affiliate union levels have been complemented by promoting alliances with local community, often non-union, groups. At the same time, some unions have been successful in campaigning to compel employers to recognize unions outside the delays, and *de facto* employer-biased, of the National Labor Relations Board (NLRB) procedures. Yet despite some organizing and campaigning successes and the continuing growth of some unions – notably in education and health– the overall outcomes remain the same: recent membership increases have been both minimal and transient and density continues to fall. The scale of the challenge facing US unions is revealed by calculating that, for the period 1996–2000, more than 12m additional members (allowing for high attrition rates) would have been required to increase private sector density from 11 percent to 18 percent when total private sector membership in 1996 was only 9m (Masters 1997). However, few unions have organizing programs or have increased their resources for organizing, which, on AFL-CIO estimates, need to be 30 percent of total budgets to increase membership at 3–4 percent per annum (Cohn 1997).

The only consistently good news for US unions is that public sector density (federal, state, and local) remains relatively high, and stable, at about 37 percent. Thus, as private sector unionization continues to decline, public sector unions will soon constitute more than half of all US union members. This reveals the continuing parlous state of private sector unions in an economy largely defined and driven by the private sector.

Canada has for long offered an intriguing contrast to its southern neighbor. Its 1944 wartime legislation was modeled on the US National Labor Relations Act (NLRA) of 1935. Both systems were designed to support the growth of collective bargaining within an economic context of extensive corporate links and Canadian unions commonly forming subsidiaries of US

176   *Brian Towers*

"international" unions. Observers were not, therefore, surprised that membership and density initially grew strongly in both countries. From 1945 to 1953, Canadian membership almost doubled to 1.2m, with the US membership increasing from 12.3m to 16.3m. By 1953 both countries' densities were at 35.5 percent (Kumar 1993: 12) with every prospect of continuing, parallel growth. This looked even more likely in 1955 when the old schism in the US labor movement ended with the absorption of the Congress of Industrial Organizations (CIO) into the American Federation of Labor (AFL), forming the AFL-CIO. Yet from 1953, US density began its long decline, except for a brief recovery in the early 1960s. In contrast, except for a brief decline in the early 1960s, Canadian density grew until 1985, reaching a peak of 36.4 percent, twice that of the US, a ratio which has since been maintained. Though both have fallen since 1985 (Figure 10.1), Canadian density at 32.5 percent can be described as "relatively stable."

Although Canadian unions have more reason for optimism, "relative stability" is not revival. The Canadian political environment is now less favorable to the unions than it was previously and there is evidence of rising employer resistance – albeit much short of that in the US (Rose and Chaison 2001). Canadian union organizers are, in consequence, encountering major difficulties in the "harder to organize" sectors, notably private services, small and medium businesses, and within the rapidly expanding "knowledge economy" (Finlayson and McEwan 1998). These are the critical areas where organizing gains are required if Canadian unions are to achieve more than stability, a situation not dissimilar to that currently facing British unions where decline now seems to have "bottomed out" but significant revival remains problematic.

Explaining divergence

Attempting to explain the initial convergence and much longer, later divergence between US and Canadian unions' fortunes is an interesting, though daunting, exercise, as Lipset (1990) suggests. In particular, it cannot be assumed that the divergence between the two union movements will last. Canadian organizers are facing difficulties maintaining growth and the prognoses of academics are generally pessimistic (Kumar 1993, Rose and Chaison 2001). Nor can improved prospects for US unions be necessarily ruled out. There have been some successful campaigns and the longer view suggests that union growth and decline may be cyclical, and closely associated with "long wave theory" (Kelly 1998). The US's experience, especially the revival in union membership in the 1930s and the formation of the AFL-CIO, provides some support for Kelly's argument. This wider, more optimistic assessment will be returned to later in the chapter. Here the comparative experience of divergence between Canada and the US is considered, not only for its own intrinsic interest but also for its practical lessons for British unions. The factors accounting for this divergence fall into four broad groups: differences in economic and employment structures; difference in political contexts; small, though ultimately significant differences in labor law; and the extent to which these differences influence the organizing strategies of unions.

Economic and employment structures

Differences in economic and employment structures between the USA and Canada include the greater openness of the US economy and the impact this has on employment stability. Additionally, the Canadian public sector is almost twice as large as the American (Rose and Chaison 2001). Troy (2000) is closely associated with the view that lower levels of unionization in the US, relative to Canada, can be explained by differences, not least the benefits to Canadian union recruitment, flowing from the country's much bigger public sector. Public sector management tends to have more favorable attitudes towards unionization, including even in the US where public sector density is four times greater than private and public sector unions have a much higher win-rate in certification elections (Bronfenbrenner and Juravich 1995). However, the public sector effect is difficult to establish conclusively. Though Canada's public sector is bigger than that in the US, almost all Canadian private sector industry has higher unionization levels than in the US (Robinson 1994). Hence, although differences in structure of employment and the relative sizes of public sector employment have *some* influence on union density, it may not be as sizable as some maintain. One estimate, for the early 1990s, suggested the differences in structure explained no more than 15 percent of the US–Canadian unionization difference (Riddell 1993).

Political contexts

Political systems in which collectivist and class-based values are strong will tend to have both relatively high levels of union density and continuing electoral success for left-wing parties. This has been well demonstrated for Western European countries, especially where institutional links have developed between trade unions and "labor" parties (Visser 1988). The US has not been entirely immune from these political processes. A working-class perspective was an important characteristic of its labor movement and electoral politics in the late nineteenth and early twentieth centuries with strong support for state intervention, income redistribution, and social welfare, ideas often propagated by European immigrants. Some also brought with them anarcho-syndicalist and communist ideologies and tactics, although the Socialist Party refused to compromise with the pragmatism of the AFL-CIO under Samuel Gompers. Yet the unions did come close to forming their own political party in the early 1900s, much like contemporary developments in Britain, discounting the widespread acceptance of US "sociological exceptionalism" (Forbath 1992). Despite this, what has been termed a "social democratic tinge" (Lubell 1941) remained an important influence upon politics from Roosevelt's first administration to Johnson's "Great Society" program forty years later.

By then, the enduring benefits of full employment and prosperity were returning Americans to their deeply rooted individualistic and meritocratic values (Lipset 1990). The unions, having purged communist influence in the 1950s, consistently avoided any serious temptation to form their own party under a system that, in any case, strongly inhibited such ambitions. They retained their role within the Democratic "coalition" as their political leverage fell with the absolute decline in the union vote and the weakening of union members' attachment to Democratic candidates. American unions, whatever the historical and sociological explanations, remain seriously handicapped by the absence of a functioning, electable political party of their own. This, in turn, is an important part of the explanation for the continuing weakness of the "labor movement," a term which, in the US, refers solely to unions.

Canadian unions, despite many originating as affiliates of US "internationals," have followed a different political path, eased by major differences in outlook, conditions, and circumstances. Historically, the conservative and socialist traditions in Canada shared a similar statist outlook, in contrast with the widespread suspicion of government in the US, including union activists and leaders from both left and right. The strong Tory presence in Canada also encouraged a socialist, class-based reaction which viewed politics, elections, and the capture of the state as complementary to collective bargaining in advancing workers' interests. This strategy was espoused by both socialists and non-socialists in the labor movement from as early as 1900. Their support for the socialist Co-operative Commonwealth Federation, founded in 1933, eventually translated into the formation of the social democratic New Democratic Party (NDP) in the 1960s following the merger of the craft and industrial wings of Canadian labor in the 1950s (Lipset 1990: 167–8, Lipset and Marks 2000: 19). Although the NDP's electoral strength has declined since its formation, it remains a significant minority in most provinces and at federal level, and an important means by which the unions can promote favorable policies and legislation at all levels of the political system (Bruce 1989, Rose and Chaison 2001).

The continuing influence of social democratic traditions and union influence is also maximized by the nature of the Canadian decentralized political system. Each province can pass its own labor legislation – in contrast to the US where derogation is limited. The relationship between social democracy, union strength, and the special features of the Canadian political system is well illustrated by Quebec. Quebec, controlled by the social democratic as well as the separatist Parti Quebecois, has the highest level of union density in Canada at 40 percent (81 percent public sector, 27 percent private sector). Dubinsky (2000) has thus concluded that the political climate in Quebec, its labor laws, and the relatively accepting attitudes of its employers towards unions, make the province the best North American comparator for British unions seeking to restore their fortunes.

The impact of labor law

Political and ideological climates favorable to unions are positively associated with laws which will be at least neutral with regard to union recognition and organizing as well as seeking to limit employer anti-union activity. In its origins, the NLRA (Wagner Act) was intended to encourage unionization and *voluntary* collective bargaining under a beneficent NLRB. For a few years, the intentions were realized under conditions favoring union organizing. The political contexts remained supportive and traditional employer hostility became less overt, especially when the needs of wartime production, from 1942, required a more positive approach towards labor relations. Voluntary recognition, via card counts rather than ballots, became the norm. The aggressive enthusiasm of the CIO unions was rewarded, in such a favorable climate, with rapidly rising membership. The climate also strongly favored the craft unions of the AFL who had much longer organizing experience than the CIO and their greater conservatism was more attractive to employers. Between 1936 and 1941, the Machinists' union membership grew from 90,000 to 285,000 and the Teamsters from 150,000 to 530,000 (Galenson 1986: 55). Yet, even before the war ended, the employers began to revert to type. Under strong employer pressure, the NLRB gradually abandoned card counts in favor of ballots, a practice which was to become mandatory under the 1947 Taft-Hartley Act.

   The mandating of ballots did not, at first, seriously affect the union win-rate: private sector union success of 75 percent in the 1940s fell to only 72 percent ten years later. But employer pressure consistently increased as union confidence declined. The union win-rate fell steadily and has not risen over 50 percent for the last twenty years. The number of elections has also declined, reflecting a union policy of only fighting elections where there is a strong chance of winning (Gould 1994, Towers 1997). Research confirms the important advantage offered to US employers by mandatory balloting (Friedman *et al.* 1994), and this has been increased by case law prohibiting union campaigning on employer premises prior to ballots or even *de facto* "public," though privately owned, locations such as shopping malls. Even where unions do overcome their serious handicaps, they do so mainly in small companies. For example, in 1997 the union win-rate in bargaining units of under fifty employees was 54.4 percent (1,131 elections). In units of more than 500 employees the win-rate was 32.1 percent (eighteen elections) (BNA 1998). Not surprisingly, in recent years some unions have sought to win recognition by voluntary agreements or ballots, conducted outside the NLRB procedures. Recent research has shown the value of such a strategy (Eaton and Kriesky 2001) but only one union, the Service Employees International Union, has had significant voluntary successes.

Canadian labor law was modeled on the NLRA and strongly supported by the unions, impressed by US growth in membership – 4m in 1935 to 16m in 1948. The Canadian legislative framework, established in 1944, does, however, operate in a different constitutional context. The Canadian federal government has the usual set of residual powers not reserved to the provinces but the ten Canadian provinces have greater autonomy than the US states. This autonomy has been expanded, by case law, since the 1967 Constitution Act. In the case of labor law, each province determines its own legislation with the federal authority's powers limited to the regulation of labor relations in the inter-provincial sectors of rail, air, and road transportation, and telecommunications. This level of provincial autonomy has resulted in wide variations between provinces. In particular, it allows scope for pro-labor public policy and legislation administered by provincial labor boards. In the US, federal policy and legislation is much less supportive and allows for much less derogation. Where it has done so, it tends to encourage anti-union policies and laws. The prime example is the outlawing of the closed shop under the Taft-Hartley Act which also allowed each state, should it wish, to legislate against all other forms of union security, a provision dubiously labelled as a "right to work."

The differential impact of Canadian provincial autonomy in labor law is especially seen in the case of recognition. Under the federal jurisdiction, and in six provinces, certification is granted where evidence is shown, on cards, that a majority of employees in the bargaining unit wish to be represented by the applicant union. Where a ballot is required (Alberta, Nova Scotia, Newfoundland, and Ontario), the legislation sets short time limits between petition and ballot (Logan 2001), so that the average time between petition and ballot is seven weeks, although delays of up to two years are not uncommon. In the case of unfair labor practices adjudication, a study comparing the NLRB and Ontario Labour Relations Board found that the average time from filing to decision was 658 and 137 days respectively (Bruce 1989). The NLRB has also been sharply criticized by a former chair for unacceptable delays (Gould 2000), although this can be partly explained by the wider scope of the NLRB's federal adjudication function, compared to the narrower provincial jurisdiction under Canada's boards. NLRB appointments are, however, prone to political patronage, notably evident under Reagan. Overall, these differences have an important influence upon the outcomes: US unions over a long period have won just under half of all elections while Canadian unions, between the 1950s and 1990s, were consistently successful in 70 percent of their applications (Logan 2001). Moreover, US employers are adept at avoiding the post-certification duty to bargain in good faith. One-third of ballots won by unions do not result in a first contract as employers exploit the capacity for procedural delay. Under the Canadian federal jurisdiction, and in some provinces, undue delay in contract negotiations can be remedied by the availability of first contract arbitration.

It is clear that US labor law has consistently failed to achieve its original objectives. Furthermore, the Canadian system – modeled upon that of the US – has paradoxically become the model for the reform of the American. It is also of some note that the UK government, in the design of its third statutory procedure, seems to have learned from the differences between the two North American systems. It has drawn upon some of the positive features of the Canadian whilst avoiding the negative features of the American. The most notable examples are the availability of an "automatic" (i.e. without ballot) route to union recognition and union access (though limited) to workplaces during election campaigns (Wood and Goddard 1999).

Union organizing strategies

The differences in the political and legal contexts offer important parts of a comprehensive explanation for the greater relative success of Canadian unions compared to those in the US. Favorable political and legal contexts are also likely to increase the effectiveness of organizing strategies and favor the extension of collective bargaining. Organizing becomes easier under union-friendly regimes and as membership and density rise, employer resistance, in the face of government exhortation and the availability of effective routes to recognition, becomes weaker. Further advances in membership and density will then strengthen union influence within government, as rising membership income makes it easier to fund expensive organizing campaigns as well as to service both existing and new members. Growing recognition and rising membership will also be reflected in the extension of collective bargaining and improvements in pay, benefits, and conditions, making union membership more attractive to non-unionists as well as limiting and discouraging free-riding. This "virtuous circle" process or "a symbiotic relationship between density and effectiveness" (Rose and Chaison 1996: 38) enabled the Canadian unions to grow in the difficult 1980s and, since then, to maintain a degree of stability. The American movement, in contrast, has experienced a long-running "vicious circle" of declining density, followed by absolute falls in membership, in a context of political and legal emasculation. Membership losses have also limited the funds available for organizing whilst collective bargaining concessions have diminished the unions' influence, prestige, and attraction to non-members. In polls taken between 1977 and 1986 ". . . large and increasing majorities of non-union American workers . . . [said they] would vote against a union in their company in a representation election" (Lipset 1990: 169).

It is of some note, however, that this period was one of special difficulty for US unions. The defeat of the Carter Labor Law Reform Bill, on which the unions had pinned their hopes in an expensive campaign, was followed by the Reagan administration's anti-union policies in the federal sector and its encouragement of similar tactics by private sector employers. Recent evidence also suggests that the "demand" for union membership by the unorganized would be much greater if employees were not so afraid of employer retribution. That fear is much less in Canada ". . . because unions represent a significantly higher proportion of the workforce, are a potent political force, and enjoy a more favourable labor law environment that constrains employers' anti-union behaviour" (Kochan *et al.* 1991: 110). Ten years after this assessment and some union setbacks in Canada, it still holds true that despite the common legislative principles underlying the two systems, and their not dissimilar features, their governments have ". . . fundamentally different approaches to . . . recognition . . ." and ". . . most American employers [have] never fully accepted the legitimacy of collective bargaining" (Logan 2001: 92, 102). Even this is an understatement. The virulent anti-union ideology and tactics of US employers is indeed "exceptional" as a recent, authoritative report confirms (Compa 2000).

Yet although the Canadian labor movement remains in much better shape, this judgment is relative and may not necessarily endure. Rose and Chaison (2001: 56–7), referring to both countries, point to the growing sophistication of anti-union tactics by employers; the pressures of globalization and the regional impact of NAFTA; the growth of occupations without collective bargaining traditions or prospects; and the preference of employees for advancing individual rights through the law rather than using their collective strength. They (ibid.: 40) also note the decline in certifications in Canada and the numbers of new recruits organized falling behind the growth in the labor force. The political context is also becoming less favorable. The NDP, faced with electoral decline and a strong challenge from the Tories, has become less supportive of pro-union legislation, especially at provincial level; and at federal level it has offered greater support to business interests. This political shift makes it even more difficult for Canadian unions to deliver major organizing successes which are essential to a "virtuous circle" revival. But it remains far more difficult for American unions. Rose and Chaison's (2001: 39) ingredients for union revival in the US are indeed daunting: ". . . the causes of low density rates, . . . , are the very issues that must be addressed in proposals for union revival – increasing organizing, regaining bargaining power, and changing labor laws to enable the first two to happen."

Some general lessons for British industrial relations reform

The primacy attached by Rose and Chaison, and others (e.g. Friedman *et al.* 1994), to "changing labor laws" reflects the great significance which North American analysts give to the role of law in the day-to-day regulation of the employment relationship. Yet in the case of labor law, it is widely held that the New Deal legislation has not only failed to achieve its objectives but has even subverted them, and for a long time (Gould 1994). The importance of supportive law is emphasized by the different experience of Canadian unions and the significance attached, by analysts, to the Canadian model in their proposals for reform. US unions have also looked to changes in the law to achieve their aims although earlier union leaders feared state intervention in labor relations. Both the left and the right, before and during the New Deal, thought it would undermine self-reliance, and what the state gave it could take away. Furthermore, changing labor laws requires a high level of political influence. That has rarely been available to US unions and any influence has been within a shifting coalition of political interests, some of which are not sensitive to unions. The contrast with Canada is again evident, where the unions have gained much from their association with the NDP. But even that has proved much less durable as the NDP's political strength has declined. In both cases, therefore, unions have been required to give priority to organizing. US unions have found it far more difficult given the absence of meaningful political advantages, the law's perversity, and the intent and capacity of employers to exploit increasing union weakness. Successful US union campaigns have encouraged activists, but they remain rare and have not dented union density decline. Nor have Canadian efforts yet revealed convincing evidence of a return to the successes of the 1960s and 1970s despite starting from a much better position *vis-à-vis* the US.

The consequences of this minimal and declining political influence provide an important lesson for British labor: the continuing importance of its association with a party of government that supports an acceptable platform of individual and collective employment rights. The downside is the older union fear of over-reliance on any political party, even one with friendly intentions seeking a wide base of support. Labour was out of office between 1979 and 1997. Its return to office lay partly in its discovery of the electoral case for supporting business as well as its union friends. Yet despite political hazards, British unions have undoubtedly gained from their association with Labour. The value of that association is more clearly seen in the comparison with North America. US unions' problems may be largely explained by the presence of well-resourced, hostile employers, and the unions' political friends, when in office, are unable or unwilling to use the law to achieve even moderate reform. The Democratic Party is the party of labor, but it is not a labor party. In contrast, Canadian labor, even allowing for concerns over its weakening political base, remains in much better shape. This again is explained by fundamental factors beyond the application of the law. Canada's similarities with Britain are instructive:

> The United States has much to learn from Canada in the labor law arena. Contrary to what some writers assume, the differences between the United States and Canada cannot simply be dismissed as differences between legal approaches; much more is involved than that. To begin

with, there is Canada's history and culture; it has a tradition that shares more characteristics with Britain than the United States.

(Gould 1994: 233–4)

The prospects for British unions

British unions' prospects have been substantially changed, although not yet transformed, since 1997. "New" Labour has moved in ideology and policies from the Wilson–Callaghan governments but it is still very different from the Conservatives of 1979–7. It has delivered on the two major pledges sought by the unions: a national minimum wage and a statutory recognition procedure, and provided for, under the ERA, access for union officials to accompany members in grievances and disciplinaries where there is no recognition, giving unions some potential to extend their influence and membership into non-union organizations. Other advances in employment rights include the extension of legislation to cover workers under part-time, temporary, and fixed-term contracts. Health and safety legislation has been strengthened; paid holidays were increased; and controls were imposed on the length of the working week – although subject to numerous exceptions and derogations. Unions could not claim any credit for these gains since all arose from EU Directives which even the Conservatives would have found it difficult to resist. The Government did, however, go with the tide of EU legislation which fitted well enough with its "family friendly" policies. It only seriously opposed, along with British and German employers, the extension of information and consultation rights. In the end, compromises with other member states allowed for agreement on phased implementation by 2005 and exclusions for small companies.

Exemptions for small organizations (under twenty-one employees) were also a feature of Labour's statutory recognition procedure. This provision was opposed by unions as was the requirement, in recognition ballots, to secure 40 percent of those entitled to vote in the bargaining unit as well as a majority of those actually voting. Both were introduced under strong employer pressure and demonstrated the extent to which "new" Labour had moved from its "old" Labour past. But it remains that Labour's election was the only available route to a statutory recognition procedure, whatever its limitations. Even with this, unions still had high hopes for the new procedure. This suggests two questions. First, given its intended limitations, could it be made to work and work fairly? Second, even if it did, how far could it contribute to the revival of union membership growth?

The influence of the statutory recognition procedure

British unions, in the words of the TUC general secretary, sought "fairness not favors" from Labour. The government, in the design of the new procedure, clearly saw it as both workable and fair, as well as contributing to its economic objectives: "... a procedure which will work, which will improve fairness and which will enhance competitiveness, prosperity and growth" (DTI 1998: 24). The inclusion of the economic objectives precluded a government commitment to extending recognition and collective bargaining, unlike before (see Introduction). In practice, this required a compromise which employers found acceptable, given that most of them preferred the voluntary system which had been restored in 1980. The unions' traditional attachment to a voluntary procedure had been abandoned as membership fell from 1980 and employers were increasingly able to deny recognition, limit its scope, or withdraw it. Voluntary recognition worked well for the unions when their membership was high and growing and government favored unionization and the extension of collective bargaining. Those conditions had not been available after 1979 and Labour was not planning for their return. It did, however, favor the encouragement of voluntary recognition because there was some fear of polarization and confrontation under a statutory procedure as was the case in the US. Voluntarism was also seen as complementary to the revived vogue for partnership. The intention was that the availability of a statutory procedure, i.e. the "shadow of the law," would be seen as a last, imposed resort and much less acceptable than voluntary deals which could help to promote partnership, productivity, and competitiveness.

The implicit dangers of a statutory procedure for unions and their members, as well as other employees' representation rights, have been well documented, especially in North American contexts (Gould 1994, Adams 1995, Towers 1997). But these dangers can be at least minimized, if not entirely avoided, by a number of conditions, suggested, again, by the contrasting experience of Canada and the US. These concern the design of the procedure; the ability of the procedure to be improved as circumstances and experience dictate; the requirement of the application of the law to be at least neutral in the adjudication of recognition issues and disputes; employers to be pragmatic towards unions and unionization; and lastly, and most importantly, since it can decisively influence the other conditions, government willingness to indicate its commitment to the success of the procedure.

The presence of these conditions to an extent distinguishes both Canada and Britain from the US. The design of the US procedure has been essentially the same as it was under the Taft-Hartley 1947 amendments of the Wagner Act and its application has been no more than neutral towards unionization and collective bargaining. The NLRB has also frequently been subject to undue political influence, especially under Reagan, and attempts at constructive, though modest reform of the procedure have been frustrated by the power and resources of employers. Canadian political contexts, in contrast to those of the US, offer a more favorable climate for unionization and collective bargaining and the law has been amended on many occasions towards this end, including the availability of first contract arbitration at federal level and in four of the ten provinces (Kumar 1993: 127). In the US, first contract arbitration was last recommended by the US Dunlop Commission in 1995. This, and all the Commission's recommendations, were opposed or ignored.

The design of the British procedure was clearly influenced by the experience of both North American countries, perhaps most clearly in the availability, as in Canada, of an "automatic," card-count style route to recognition. The government has also indicated its intention to monitor, consult, and, if necessary, reform the procedure. Unions are pressing for reforms to extend access for unions prior to ballots, remove the exclusion of organizations with fewer than twenty-one employees and lower the numerical thresholds.

On the early evidence, the government's belief that the availability of a statutory procedure would encourage voluntary agreement seems to be being realized. These were even growing well before the procedure came into force in June 2000 and even before the 1997 election as employers began to anticipate the intentions of Labour and sought the advantages of agreement over compulsion (Gall and McKay 2001, see Introduction). The impetus to voluntarism has also been strengthened by the roles and traditions of the CAC and ACAS. Although activity at the CAC was modest during the first year of its recognition responsibilities, of the fifty-seven applications to 31 March 2001, ten were withdrawn at different stages because the parties had concluded voluntary agreements (CAC 2001). These outcomes are strengthened by the power of the CAC to reject an application if the parties refuse to use ACAS to assist towards a negotiated agreement. There is also ACAS's own voluntary alternative to the CAC. In the year to 31 March 2001 ACAS received 384 requests for assistance with recognition compared to the CAC's 57 applications. Of the 384 requests, 264 proceeded as cases compared to the CAC's 27 acceptances. ACAS's recognition work currently accounts for 20 percent of its collective case load and between 1998 and 2001 the number of cases increased from 125 to 264 (ACAS 2001).

There does, therefore, seem to be little doubt that the law is indeed casting its shadow. Some employers are also accepting, and even proposing, partnership agreements alongside recognition. Partnership initiatives from unions are also endorsed by the TUC and some of its larger affiliates. But employers and unions can also be influenced by events, not least high-profile defeats or victories in CAC ballots. Such events can have lasting effects as US history has frequently demonstrated. Reagan's decertification of the air traffic controllers' union (PATCO) in 1981 encouraged private sector employers to step-up their anti-union tactics. Eight years later, the United Auto Workers at Nissan's Tennessee plant, after an expensive seventeen-month, well-fought campaign – and the security of a 50 percent affirmative card count – lost the election by a margin of 2 to 1. In contrast, in December 2001 at Honda's Swindon plant in Britain, the AEEU won a convincing victory. On a turnout of 77.1 percent, 72.8 percent voted for recognition, securing collective bargaining rights for 4,000 workers. The AEEU also has long-standing, sole recognition agreements with Nissan and Toyota in Britain.

But even spectacular recognition victories do not automatically translate into union membership revival. They need to be widespread and sustained; across all economic sectors and occupations (especially those growing in employment and minimally unionized); covering younger workers as well as old; and taking place in large and medium-sized organizations as well as smaller ones. In the end it is, of course, a numbers game. Recognition, together with partnership, may demonstrate to employers that unions can "add value" to their businesses and, with employers' help, transform their prospects for recruiting new members. Yet, so far the official membership figures are only recording small increases, after losses averaging 2.9 percent per annum from 1990 to 1997 when the total loss was 1.5 million members. For the two years 1999 and 2000 the net increase was 169,000. This two-year increase will need to be sustained every year for the next nine for membership to reach the level of 1990.

Recent membership gains are partly explained by the surge in voluntary recognition itself encouraged by the presence of a statutory alternative. There is also recent, though limited, survey evidence of a significant relationship between the pursuit of recognition and the "propensity to organize" (Wood *et al.* 2002). But recognition drives can only do so much and are likely to achieve less, over time, as organizers tackle the hard core combining strong employee resistance and intransigent hostility from employers. There is also the possibility, even perhaps the probability, of a future government abolishing the statutory procedure. British unions, with all the difficulties, may largely have to shift for themselves, as do their American counterparts. The difference is that though the British have been strongly influenced by the American organizing example. In the still very different British context that gives them much better prospects.

Can British unions save themselves?

Some grounds for union optimism, at least in the longer term, have recently been provided by Kelly (1998: 130) in his attempt to advance the claims of mobilization theory:

> . . . on all past experience and in the light of mobilization theory, we would predict that the long period of employer and state counter-mobilization and of labor weakness will not last. As the next long economic upswing gathers momentum then so too should the organiz-ation and mobilization of workers across the capitalist world.

Kelly's long view reflects the well-documented cycles of alternating growth and decline in labor movements in industrialized countries and the periods of transformation which can be both short and sudden at the top and bottom of the cycles, perhaps especially in Britain and the US. Mobilization theory does seem to be useful in explaining cycles of growth and decline in the US labor movement – witness the extraordinary rise of the CIO before 1935 and without the NLRA. The CIO provided the "organizational means" for the large numbers of local activists, many of whom were communists, to be the important catalysts of mobilization, inheriting the role of the earlier anarcho-syndicalists. The CIO's collectivism was able to draw upon the widespread sense of injustice and distrust of employers arising from un-precedented mass unemployment, and employers' attacks upon the unions, Roosevelt, and the New Deal legislation, culminating in the waves of resistance and sit-down strikes. The inevitable employer and Republican counter-attack was largely postponed until after the war. But Taft-Hartley was perhaps less important than the CIO's loss of identity under its merger with the AFL and the purge of the communist union leadership during the decade when union membership peaked and began its long, historic decline. As the labor movement weakened and its political influence fell, the employers pressed home their advantage – especially in the 1980s when Republican anti-unionism was at its highest.

In present conditions, mobilization theory also has some explanatory value. A few unions, notably the SEIU and HERE (Hotel and Restaurant Employees), have revived their campaigning activism in response to serious workplace injustice and violations of the law by employers. But these successes are limited, with, as yet, no evidence of a nationwide surge in local activism, and few union locals are responding to national calls to spend more on organizing. By 2001, only 7 or 8 unions out of 66 had met the AFL-CIO's target of spending 30 percent of their resources on organiz-ing (Labor Notes 2002). At the same time, US employers do, of course, remain unsparing in their opposition to unionization and the resources devoted to it including, significantly, the substantial and rapidly growing use of "union-busting" consulting law firms (Logan 2002).

Mobilization theory offers fewer insights in the British case. The strong growth in density in the 1960s and 1970s can be associated with the "challenge from below" but it was concentrated in only a few sectors and largely without the support of the national leadership. Union growth was perhaps better explained, in this period, by the support of the TUC, the employers, and government for "responsible" trade unionism within a framework of orderly, strike-free, collective bargaining. This support fragmented towards the end of the 1970s, and after 1979 the unions were left largely alone to face a hostile government and the growing strength of employers. However, it was not anticipated, in 1979, that it would be twenty years before Labour would be able to legislate to restore some collective redress for the unions, in the form of the ERA. This is an important part of the unions' revival strategy. There are two others: the promotion of partnership, much-favored by "new" Labour, and influential pressure groups such as the long-established Involvement and Participation Association with its backing from politicians, employers, unions, and academics. The third arm of the revival strategy is a strong emphasis on organizing using centrally trained but locally deployed activists on the American model.

British academic industrial relations debate has recently focused upon assessing the relative contributions of partnership and organizing towards union revival, for example, the work of Heery (2002). Traditional union pragmatism does not, however, recognize any conflict between partnership and organizing. Heery's and other recent union surveys confirm this approach, reporting that the signing of a partnership agreement need not mean that a union is less committed to organizing. Other research evidence even suggests a symbiotic relationship between campaigns for recognition and successes in recruiting and organizing new members, even in non-union workplaces (Wood *et al.* 2002).

Guarded optimism for British unions is, therefore, appropriate. But, on the evidence of current density levels, it is going to be a long haul and significant advances need to be achieved in service sector occupations, in the strategically important South East and, most importantly, among young workers. In 2000, only 6 percent of those under 20 were unionized compared with 38 percent of those aged 40 to 49 and 35 percent for those 50 and over (Sneade 2001: 437). One possible lifeline is the addiction of the young to information technology which could yet provide a breakthrough for organizers, allowing direct, collective communication with actual and potential members. It is also already reported to be proving itself as an important instrument of dissidence for union members disaffected with the performance of their elected representatives. "Mobilization theory" may need to incorporate this new development.

Conclusions

Despite the case for some optimism in terms of organizing, this does not seem to be a time for discarding other strategic advantages. British unions are, unlike their US counterparts, closer to the Canadian in retaining a still significant political leverage with a credible party of government. Britain is also a prominent member of the EU with all that membership entails for exercising influence and being influenced by it. The relationship between Labour and the unions has always, perhaps inevitably, been strained; but it serves them both. For the unions, when Labour is in government, it has delivered many "favors" and continues to do so, even if now described as "fairness." For Labour, unions still deliver organization, money, and votes at elections, even though union members increasingly vote for other parties. Labour may also gain from the union relationship in keeping it in touch with the wider world of work and the lives of ordinary working people, as Minkin (1992) has argued. Overall, the presence of a viable

Labour party and its continuing, though "contentious alliance" with the unions, remains the single most important distinguishing feature of British industrial relations.

British unions' conversion to the EU has been late but, as late converts often do, they have proven to be exceptionally zealous, not least the TUC's present general secretary. Individual employees, whether union members or not, have gained new, or extended employment rights from EU membership. Unions, too, have benefited as institutions. Two ways may be briefly noted. First, union movements in EU countries are fully integrated both into the institutional structures of individual member states and those of the EU as a whole. In that context, it has extended their influence beyond national boundaries within treaty initiatives such as Social Dialogue. This "social partner" status has also prevented hostile governments – such as the British from 1979 to 1997 – from ignoring union interests. Second, the EU has made it possible to promote and implement, at EU level, information and consultation institutions developed in member states. The European Works Council is the prime example to be followed, despite opposition from some EU governments (including the British Labour government), by common information and consultation arrangements in all member states. These national "works councils" do not, in themselves, amount to a significant advance of collective rights. But they may yet prove to be the "Trojan horse," promoting the revival and growth of unions as the principal instrument in the advance of democratic rights at work and in the wider society. Kelly's longer view may yet provide the more optimistic, and more accurate, prognosis.

11 Union organizing in the United States

Jack Fiorito

Introduction

This chapter assesses US union organizing.[1] After describing the legal and institutional environment, a conceptual model for individual unionization decisions is presented. Next, the organizing process is summarized. Following this, various data are examined, with particular emphasis on organizing since the 1980s. This period encompasses important developments in the US labor movement, including a change in top AFL-CIO leadership with the new Sweeney administration campaigning for greater organizing effort. Data for US national unions indicate a diversity of effort and results. Recent change toward a commitment to organizing is as yet more in words than deeds, although the direction of change is consistent with rhetoric. Reasons for the slow pace of change are considered, and prospects for future change and learning about union organizing are reviewed.

Historical background

Among the first records of US union activity are accounts of worker trials for illegal conspiracies in restraint of trade (Commons 1909). It was not until 1842 that judges began to accept that unions were not illegal *per se*. Despite beginnings of acceptance then, following decades included numerous bloody battles as workers organized to advance their interests and block employers', and sometimes government-led, attempts to destroy their unions. It took until 1902 for the federal government to intervene as a neutral, rather than employer ally, in a labor dispute. Even as government, employers, and society began to accept the moderate pro-capitalism craft unions of the AFL, intolerance and repression of "radical" unions (e.g. Industrial Workers of the World) continued. One should not overlook the heavy hand of employer, vigilante, and government repression as a formative influence (Fusfeld 1985).

By the 1920s, moderate craft unionism emerged as the "mainstream" form, claiming roughly 10–20 percent membership. Even this was unpalatable to many employers, and campaigns (e.g. the "American Plan" and "Mohawk Valley Formula") were launched to establish rival company-controlled unions and marginalize independent unions. Union density declined steadily throughout the 1920s, accelerating with the Great Depression when unemployment reached roughly 25 percent.

Two key forces came together to shape unions in the 1930s. First, within labor, calls grew for industrial unionism as a structure suited to growing masses of unorganized unskilled and semi-skilled workers. Conservative leaders within the AFL persisted in their belief that only craft unions provided the power base necessary to survive. The mineworkers' president led the "radicals" to secede (in 1935) and form the rival Congress of Industrial Organizations (CIO) to pursue industry-based organizing. The CIO created the UAW, the USWA, and other giant industrial unions. Meanwhile, AFL unions maintained nominal allegiance to craft unionism while often organizing opportunistically. Beyond structural principles, the rival federations and their affiliates differed in philosophy, and in rhetoric. CIO unions enlisted communist organizers who saw industrial unionism as part of a larger, Marxist transformation. Communist leaders secured control of some CIO unions. Even the CIO's more conservative leaders favored an active social role for unions as compared to the more economistic "business unionism" of AFL affiliates. Often, employers who bitterly fought AFL unions earlier now worked closely with the perceived lesser evil of AFL unions to avoid the "radical" CIO.

The second key force was broader social and legal change of the 1930s. The severe hardship of the Great Depression shook Americans' faith in capitalism, changing values dramatically, although temporarily, toward a more collectivist orientation (Lipset 1986). Even the Republican Congress and President in 1932 produced legislation declaring collective bargaining to be favored policy (Norris-LaGuardia Act 1932). Still, the legislation's main focus was to reduce judicial intervention for employers in labor disputes. "*Laissez-faire*" was not enough for the public, and in 1932 voters elected a Democratic President and Congress that launched a "New Deal," consisting of various interventions intended to restore economic stability and growth. Most notable was the National Labor Relations Act 1935 (NLRA). It codified most private sector workers' rights to join or form unions, banned certain employer "unfair labor practices" (ULPs) that interfered with those rights, established election procedures for union representation, and created the NLRB to conduct elections and resolve ULP charges. This and developments within labor combined to produce the most spectacular sustained union growth in American history. Both AFL and CIO unions grew rapidly, and by 1945 union density stood at over 30 percent. At the end of World War II, industrial *and* craft unionism seemed firmly institutionalized.

Some felt that the New Deal had gone too far, however, and in late 1946, the year of highest US strike activity, voters gave control of Congress to

Republicans. In 1947, Congress passed (over Truman's veto) the Labor Management Relations Act (LMRA or Taft-Hartley) amending the NLRA. The amendments established rights to refrain from union activity, specified union ULPs, and created an election process whereby workers could oust unions (derecognition). Also enacted were the so-called "employer free speech" clause that essentially says that expressing an opinion is not an employer ULP, the redefinition of "employee" to exclude supervisors (hence removing legal protection), and a provision allowing states to ban "union" or "closed shop" agreements. Twenty-two states, mostly in the south, plains, and western mountain regions, have passed such laws.

The anti-union LMRA amendments, along with changes in AFL and CIO leadership, purges of communist leaders by CIO unions, purges of corrupt elements by some AFL unions, and perceptions of diminishing returns to raiding were among the main factors spurring AFL-CIO merger in 1955. The merger decreased private sector union competition, with its new constitution including provisions to resolve jurisdictional rivalries. The merger's timing corresponds roughly to peak private sector and overall union density at about 35 percent.

Private sector union density fell steadily afterward. In contrast, public sector unionization soared in the 1960s and 1970s, exceeding and remaining at over 35 percent density since 1975. The federal government and most states passed laws to regulate union–management relations and union recognition procedures for government workers during this time. Generally, these laws followed the amended NLRA model, although most ban strikes. But by the late 1970s, several factors combined to accelerate *private* sector union decline. Foreign and non-union competition emerged as significant forces. Deregulation raised new competitive threats to union strongholds in trucking, airlines, and telecommunications as new firms opened and typically remained non-union.

Reagan's election weakened labor influence in Congress, and severe recession in the early 1980s produced talk of a "crisis" and brought matters into sharper focus. "Denial" about their decline, or complacency about retaining millions of members and substantial power in certain sectors, was wearing thin. Unions had been failing for almost three decades to organize sufficient numbers to match employment growth and membership attrition through closings and layoffs. Unions were simply not organizing enough. Indeed, NLRB statistics suggest that the union response to the deepening crisis and hostile government of the early 1980s was to slash organizing efforts (Chaison and Dhavale 1990). Employers increased union avoidance efforts and learned to use and abuse their LMRA rights. Reagan's 1981 firing of 12,000 air traffic controllers signaled employers that vigorous union opposition was acceptable. Further, Reagan appointed officials who were openly hostile to unions to the NLRB and Department of Labor. In conjunction with high unemployment and an ample supply of would-be striker replacements, union decline accelerated.

By the mid-1980s, unions realized they could not wait for favorable change. A 1985 AFL-CIO report was hailed widely as a blueprint for the future. It suggested mergers to establish more viable unions, direct benefits to strengthen member–union bonds, and new membership forms independent of bargaining relationships to enroll members effectively excluded by traditional arrangements (AFL-CIO 1985). The AFL-CIO and many affiliates also adopted strategic planning techniques to take a more proactive approach to their futures. The AFL-CIO created a department dedicated to organizing (as opposed to the predecessor Department of Organization and Field Services) and an Organising Institute to train organizers.

Still, unions tended to focus on external factors: hostile employers and government, adverse worker attitudes, cheap imports, illegal immigration, and unhelpful laws. Nonetheless, some unions devoted substantial effort to developing organizing techniques that bypassed NLRB procedures through union authorization "card checks" (rather than contentious election campaigns) and employer-neutrality agreements (whereby employers would not campaign against unions). New organizing techniques such as "salting" (encouraging union supporters to seek non-union employment and organize there) and "one-on-one" approaches were tried. Unions continued to press for legislative reform through electoral politics and lobbying. With Democrat control of the Presidency and Congress, unions had high hopes from Clinton's Presidential Commission on the Future of Worker Management Relations (the Dunlop Commission) for labor law reform. Those were dashed when Republicans regained control of Congress in 1994. An AFL-CIO (1994) report announced that unions were willing to work more co-operatively with employers by promoting "partnership," partly in the hope of reducing employer opposition to organizing.

Thus, US unions began to confront decline by the late 1980s. Research suggested structural change, innovation, and perhaps the "organizing model" (OM) in particular could help reverse union fortunes (Bronfenbrenner, 1997, Fiorito *et al*. 1995), even without favorable change in the external environment. But when John Sweeney, then leader of SEIU (one of the few unions that grew in the 1980s), challenged AFL-CIO leadership, many union leaders felt the incumbent Kirkland-Donahue leadership was offering too little too late. To oversimplify Sweeney's challenge, it was "Organize!" Sweeney's successful 1995 campaign included other elements such as more confrontational tactics, renewed emphasis on alliances with religious and community groups, and more prominence in electoral politics. But the centerpiece was a pledge to increase organizing, challenging unions to spend 30 percent of their budgets on organizing by 2000. It is unclear how much unions were then spending on organizing but estimates of 3 percent have been offered.

Just how this shift was to be accomplished is not entirely clear. Unquestionably, Sweeney was counting on the "OM." The resources freed from servicing could further organizing. New IT was also envisioned as part of the solution to free up resources (Mountjoy 1997). Sweeney was not simply calling for the AFL-CIO to redirect its own efforts. There are roughly seventy affiliated national unions. Therein lay a problem – in national unions being sovereign bodies and power centers of American labor. Union dues flows underscore this, with the AFL-CIO receiving only about 50 cents of approximately $30 each member pays for monthly dues. National union autonomy has long been a fundamental principle among US unions, a principle reflected in the AFL-CIO's relatively limited powers and financing.

Contemporary organizing environments

The legal environment

Understanding US organizing requires recognition of varied legal environments unions face. The amended NLRA is the principal private sector law. The NLRB has operationalized "affecting interstate commerce" (i.e. the US Constitution basis for federal regulation) via sales volume and similar standards. (There is no explicit minimum employment size, but since the NLRA protects "concerted" activity, the minimum is two employees.) This leaves some smaller firms outside its jurisdiction. Taken together with other major exclusions (i.e. rail, airlines, government, agricultural, and self-employed workers), it is estimated that the NLRA covers 40–50 percent of the workforce. The Railway Labor Act (RLA) applies to railroads and airlines. Although generally similar to the NLRA, one notable difference is the RLA's encouragement of "systemwide" bargaining units. In airlines, unions often must mount campaigns at facilities scattered across thousands of miles.

State and local government workers are subject to different laws or common law rulings in different states. The state-level statutes tend to mirror NLRA provisions with the general exception of strike prohibitions noted earlier. Most establish a Public Employee Relations Commission (or Board) to administer their provisions. Federal workers are covered by the federal Civil Service Reform Act 1978 that bans strikes but otherwise also tends to mirror NLRA provisions. A Federal Labor Relations Authority administers its provisions on elections and ULPs. The postal service, however, is under NLRA jurisdiction. Although its workers can not strike, they have recourse to an arbitration procedure. Agriculture is the only private sector industry specifically excluded from NLRA coverage that is not covered by the RLA. California is the only major site of hired agricultural employment with state-level legislation extending NLRA-like provisions to agricultural workers. Some other states have NLRA-like laws that extend to certain private sector workers not covered by the NLRA, i.e. small private employers.

An implication of this legislative diversity is that unions face varying rules depending on their organizing target. For example, Iowa City, Iowa has three major hospitals: one run by a private organization (the Sisters of Mercy), one by the federal Veterans Administration, and the third by the state's University of Iowa. Three different statutes apply.

Employer attitudes and opposition

More important than differences in rules are varying norms of management conduct. None of the hospitals cited above is a for-profit venture but health care organizations are often "big business" in the US. Some for-profit health care providers have been the staunchest opponents of union organizing and persistent labor law violators. Bronfenbrenner and Juravich (1995) found that union success rates were typically around 80 percent in public sector representation elections, as compared to 50 percent in NLRB elections. The critical difference appears to be intense private sector employer opposition, versus acquiescence typical among public sector employers. Observers elsewhere sometimes have difficulty appreciating the intensity of union opposition among US private sector employers. The "union mark up" is estimated at upwards of 10 percent (Freeman and Medoff 1984). Even if we ignore other union effects or allow that union cost impacts may be partly offset by positive productivity effects, there are substantial financial implications associated with unionization. As representatives of owner or shareholder interests, managers almost instinctively respond unfavorably to organizing efforts. Beyond the economics, managerial opposition to unions may stem from union threats to managerial control within an ideological environment that strongly supports private property rights.

Employer emphasis on union avoidance is strongest among less unionized firms, but even moderately unionized firms assign substantial importance to keeping their companies as non-union as possible relative to getting the best union contract possible (Freedman 1985). A 1983 poll reported that 73 percent of employers with 25–50 percent unionization emphasized union avoidance, as did 39 percent of those with 51–75 percent unionization. Comparison to a 1978 poll shows growing opposition. This accords with data showing employer ULPs rising fourfold between 1960 and 1980 while organizing activity remained roughly constant (Freeman and Medoff 1984). Two employer philosophical approaches are sometimes distinguished. In what Fossum (1999) calls a "doctrinaire" approach, union avoidance is an end itself. In contrast, Fossum's "philosophy-laden" approach suggests that union avoidance is merely a by-product of good HRM where providing good wages and benefits, dispute resolution procedures, respect for workers, etc., are goals for profit reasons and/or because of corporate values. Distinctions between two union avoidance strategies are also commonly drawn (e.g. Katz and Kochan 2000), namely between union suppression (e.g. victimizing union supporters) and union substitution (e.g. offering good compensation and fairness).

Not surprisingly, most workers who have experienced organizing campaigns report management opposed the union, and most non-union workers favoring union representation cite management opposition as the main obstacle (Freeman and Rogers 1999). The vast majority of managers prefer to deal with workers individually, a majority would oppose unionization efforts, and a substantial minority, one-third, feel that their promotion chances would be harmed by successful organizing (Freeman and Rogers 1999). Evidence on the impact of union substitution or good HRM on worker support for unions is limited but suggests the expected effects (Fiorito 2001). There is substantial evidence on particular aspects of union suppression – ULPs under the NLRA occur at a rate of roughly one per election and illegal firings for union activity occur in 25 to 33 percent of elections, with roughly one in twenty union supporters fired (Freeman and Medoff 1984). Obviously, the risks are much higher for outspoken activists. Data suggest that employers spend about $300 million annually on "union-busting" consultants, that most require supervisors to meet one-on-one with workers to convey the employer's opposition during organizing campaigns, and that 50 percent of employers use illegal threats to close facilities (Freeman and Rogers 1999). Moreover, even when unions win representation rights, it is estimated that 25 to 33 percent of those victories fail to result in a union contract. Derecognition often follows such failures.

The intense employer opposition stressed here is fairly typical of the private sector, and rare among public sector employers. The contrast in nominal and effective legal-organizing environments is suggested by a recent report stressing worker rights abuses by US private sector employers:

> The reality of NLRA enforcement falls far short of its goals. Many workers who try to form and join trade unions to bargain with their employers are spied on, harassed, pressured, threatened, suspended, fired, deported, or otherwize victimized in reprisal for their exercise of the right to freedom of association. Private employers are the main agents of abuse . . . [L]abor law enforcement efforts often fail to deter unlawful conduct.
>
> (Compa 2000: 9)

A similar description is provided in a rather unexpected forum:

> All's not fair in labor wars . . . there is a disturbing trend of management coercion that inhibits workers. . . . The U.S. wouldn't tolerate companies that intimidated employees who supported a politician management disliked. The standard of fairness should be no less democratic for workplace elections.
>
> (Bernstein 1999: 43 in *Business Week*)

Worker attitudes

By law, unionization decisions reflect *worker* preferences. Although preceding discussion suggests important qualifications, worker attitudes are critical (Barling *et al.* 1992, Fiorito and Young 1998). Dissatisfaction with jobs and perceptions of union instrumentality stand out as decisive attitudinal variables with a lesser role for general attitudes to unions. Indeed, much of employer union avoidance activity can be interpreted as efforts to boost job satisfaction (via substitution) or to diminish union instrumentality perceptions (via suppression and substitution). By Kelly's (1998) mobilization framework, substitution could be viewed as seeking to avoid the sense of injustice that mobilizes workers for collective action.

Most workers (70–80 percent) expect employers to use illegal coercive tactics to counter organizing campaigns. Fewer (40–60 percent) think their *own* employer likely to use such tactics (Fiorito and Bozeman 1996–7) and few expect their employer to resort to threats or violence (perhaps 20 percent; Freeman and Rogers 1999). Although it has been suggested that such coercive tactics may backfire, evidence indicates these tactics generally work. In addition to fear of employer retaliation, organizing is inhibited by fear of employer–union conflict (Cohen and Hurd 1998). Poll results noted earlier show most non-union workers desiring representation cite management opposition as the prime obstacle. Coupled with perceptions of their own employers as relatively benign opponents, the suggestion is that many workers are more fearful of ongoing conflictual relations than of retaliation.

Data consistently show that many non-union workers desire union representation; Freeman and Rogers (1999) reported that in 1994, roughly one-third of non-union workers would vote for union representation if given the opportunity. Roughly twenty years of such data indicate fairly stable results. Recent polls suggest there may be growing attitudinal support for unions, and perhaps especially among younger workers (AFL-CIO 1999, 2001), significant given low union density among young workers. Density is lowest among those 16–24 (5.2 percent), and generally increases up to age 65 (US Bureau of Labor Statistics 2002).

Public opinion polls have consistently shown majority support for unions for decades. In a question of general approval versus disapproval, approvals have consistently outnumbered disapprovals by 2:1, and recent polls show this ratio rising nearer 3:1 (Lester 2001). Why does this support fall dramatically when the question becomes voting for a union at the workplace? (Also, why is the public unmotivated to demand legislation to address the unfairness broadly perceived in employer opposition?) There are a number of explanations. Workers often distrust management and think unions are necessary for fair treatment, but workers think more highly of their own employers than employers generally. Workers also believe that unions improve terms in the abstract (roughly 80 percent think so) but less think that unions can improve terms in their own workplaces (less than 50 percent) (Deshpande and Fiorito 1989). Finally, there is the possibility that workers support unions in principle, but have various objections to specific unions they may choose, perhaps seeing them as too corrupt, undemocratic, counterproductive, or confrontational. Employer campaigns against unions often stress just such elements of union images.

The individual decision to join or form unions

Figure 11.1 presents a simple conceptual model of the individual psychology of unionization decisions. Whilst emphasizing the individual's perspective, the model parallels in several regards Kelly's (1998) mobilization theory perspective stressing the progression from individual grievances or dissatisfactions to collective action. Although the decision to join an existing union can differ importantly from the decision to form a union anew, the basic elements are similar. This process will be stressed in examining the model.

At the core of the model is a sequence of psychological concepts: knowledge, beliefs, attitudes, intentions, and behavior. The general causal flow is indicated. That is, knowledge (e.g. workers at a similar unionized firm are paid more) informs beliefs (e.g. we are treated unjustly; unions raise pay) that underlie attitudes (e.g. "unions enhance collective efficacy"). Attributions and ideology clearly influence these beliefs and attitudes (Kelly 1998).

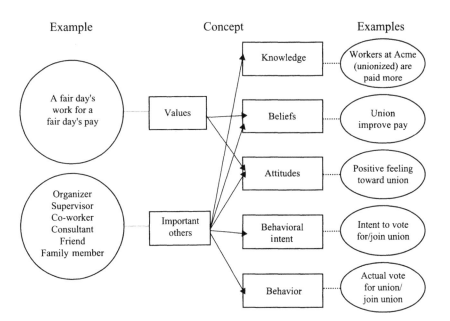

Figure 11.1 Simplified psychological model for union organizing.

In turn, attitudes condition intentions (e.g. plans to contact a union) and intentions influence behavior (e.g. attending organizing committee meetings; volunteering to recruit others). Examples for each concept are shown to the right in the figure. Values and referents (important others including co-workers, supervisors, family, friends) influence various components in the causal sequence, as illustrated in the figure. In Kelly's (1998) terms, referents are important sources of interactions that transform individual perceptions of injustice into collective perceptions and a sense of collective efficacy. This is similar to the "union instrumentality" concept in much US literature on worker attitudes to unions, although the latter term suggests the union as "a thing apart," an instrument, rather than being "of and by us."

In a sense, the model depicts the battleground on which union organizing campaigns are fought for the hearts, minds, votes, and membership of workers. Many points discussed earlier can be related to specific model components. For example, a key battle is fought over beliefs about union effects. Organizers attempt to persuade workers that workers can improve terms through collective action. Knowledge of terms in union contracts elsewhere is transmitted in flyers, meetings, and perhaps member testimonials. Many important nuances are necessarily omitted. For example, information sources vary in credibility. Some unions' emphases on one-on-one testimonials from like workers and organizers reflect beliefs that these messengers are most credible. Similarly, employers and union-busting consultants rely heavily on first-level supervisors as credible messengers for management (Levitt with Conrow 1993).

The organizing process

The NLRA and similar statutes lay out steps for union recognition. In response to expressed interest or a union's strategic decision, organizing campaigns begin with assessment of potential union support. If warranted, the union proceeds to build support toward the goal of winning a representation election or securing voluntary employer recognition upon alternative demonstration of majority support. For example, signed union authorization cards indicating workers desire union representation may be submitted to a neutral party (a "card check"). Typically employers reject efforts at voluntary recognition, due to genuine doubt about the union's support or because they desire to campaign for a "no union" victory. The union can force an election by demonstrating substantial worker interest in representation, via petition or similar evidence (e.g. authorization cards) signed by 30 percent plus of workers in a proposed bargaining unit. Anticipating defections due to employer campaigns, unions typically will not file petitions or proceed to elections with less than majority or substantial majority (say 65 percent) support. Although the union may attempt to campaign secretly early on, the request for voluntary recognition or petition filing marks the point where campaigns necessarily "go public."

In addition to establishing interest in union representation, the election petition defines the proposed bargaining unit. Although the immediate question is really the definition of the electorate, statutes call for a unit appropriate for collective bargaining, and include specific criteria (e.g. similarity of work, common supervision) and exclusions (supervisors, confidential employees). These guidelines leave considerable room for genuine disagreement and strategic maneuvers aimed at delay and defining the electorate to one's advantage, so unions and management devote significant effort to this. For example, a union might file a petition to represent workers at one store, only to have the employer challenge the unit, saying that all stores in its chain should be included. Apart from the unit determination implications *per se*, challenging the unit is one of many ways that employers can delay the organizing process and erode workers' union instrumentality perceptions. Consistent with other indicators of growing opposition, employer acceptance of proposed units ("consent elections") has declined dramatically.

Campaign tactics are many and varied. Unions use buttons, logo- or slogan-bearing clothing, printed flyers, one-on-one and group meetings, house calls, media advertising, endorsements by community leaders, comparisons of employment terms with union-represented workers, and similar to persuade workers that it is supported by other workers and will be effective in advancing their workplace interests (Bronfenbrenner 1997, Diamond 1992, Gagala 1983). Secondary emphases may include political representation (particularly for government workers) and social justice. Increasingly, unions rely upon electronic media such as e-mail and web sites (Fiorito *et al.* 2000, Shostak 1999). Anticipating vigorous opposition, unions typically devote considerable effort to "inoculating" workers against expected employer arguments. As part of the "OM," increasing stress is laid on what workers can do for themselves through the union rather than what the union as an outside third party can do for workers.

Employers use some of the same tactics and others to persuade workers that they have little to gain and much to lose through unionization. Union dues are attacked as unneeded expenses. Unions are vilified as corrupt, undemocratic, conflictual, and counterproductive "outsiders" that jeopardize personal employer–worker relations, favorable employment terms, and employment security. Failed strikes and associated earnings losses and union constitutional provisions for disciplining members are prominently cited to undermine union instrumentality perceptions and incite fears of adverse unionization consequences. "Vote No" worker committees are encouraged if not tangibly supported by employers and allied business interests. Direct correspondence to worker homes, mandatory group meetings, and one-on-one meetings between first-level supervisors and subordinates are commonly the media for the employer's message. Many employers hire specialist "union-buster" consultants to gain and display expertise, but such consultants often emphasize direct employer worker communication and particularly the immediate supervisor's role. In effect, consultants tend to specialize in analysis, strategy, and message, but prefer employer and supervisor messengers. Details on many "darker elements" of employer anti-union campaigns are provided in Compa (2000), Hurd (1994), and Levitt and Conrow (1993).

Despite some controversy arising from observation that most workers made up their minds early in campaigns (Getman *et al.* 1976), most analysts recognize that employer campaigns are important (Fossum 1999). Unions' efforts to secure "neutrality agreements" whereby employers will not campaign against them, and to avoid long and bitter election campaigns via voluntary recognition, illustrate union *modus operandi* (see Eaton and Kriesky 2001). Bronfenbrenner (1997) showed that union organizing tactics also matter, perhaps more than employer tactics. Bronfenbrenner and others (Fiorito *et al.* 1995, Maranto and Fiorito 1987) have shown that union structures, strategies, and tactics are influential. Given this, and the key role of highly autonomous national unions, attention now turns to organizing efforts and results of national unions.

National union organizing efforts and results

Organizing-related data for large unions are presented in Table 11.1. These 25 unions are the largest of approximately 100 national unions. Union size is shown in thousands of members. Collectively, these unions claim about 13.7 million members, or roughly 85 percent of US membership. The next three columns provide percentage growth rates. First, growth is shown for 1989–97 and is based on the size figures shown. Growth is also shown for 1989–91 and 1995–7.

Changes in membership levels reflect many factors, including mergers, retirements, quits, closures, downsizing, and organizing. While growth is a "bottom line," it is by no means a clear indicator of organizing activity or success. It is but one piece of evidence (Fiorito *et al.* 2001a). That said, this evidence indicates substantial variation across unions and time. Unions are about evenly divided between growth and shrinkage in any of the three periods. The average growth rate for the unions shown was 0.4 percent in 1989–91, −0.5 percent in 1995–7 (0.2 percent each period for all unions).[2] Only about half show consistent growth or shrinkage over all three periods, and even among these, variation in rates is sometimes dramatic – the SEIU grew more than ten times faster in 1989–91 than in 1995–7. Still, the correlation between growth rates for these two periods is 0.48 (p<0.05), indicating some temporal consistency (but r=0.03, NS, for all unions). Again, caution is advised in attaching too much meaning to any particular figure. For example, the rapid SEIU or IBT growth of 1989–91 may indicate new affiliations or change in per capita payment basis rather than organizing.

The next four columns provide percentage win rates in NLRB elections and union officials' self-ratings (four-point Likert scale) of their union's organizing effectiveness in the late 1980s and mid-late 1990s. Note that organizing by some unions (e.g. NEA and AFT) takes place mainly outside NLRB jurisdiction. In addition, several unions have made conscious efforts to avoid NLRB election processes because they perceive them as prone to employer manipulation. Nonetheless, NLRB success rates provide partial indication of organizing effectiveness and show some consistency over time. The correlation for the NLRB win rates shown is 0.46 (p<0.10) (0.43, p<0.05, for all unions). There appear to be persistent union-specific differences. For example, the IBT has relatively low win rates and the SEIU has relatively high rates in both periods. These may indicate different organizing strategies – the IBT casting a broad net and accepting low success rates, the SEIU focusing efforts more narrowly with greater success (see Fiorito *et al.* 1995). Six of the eighteen unions shown with win rates for both years show changes of 10 *percentage points* or greater, with five of these showing increased success. This seems to indicate improved efficiency in winning, or more focused efforts. For the eighteen unions together, the success rate improved from 51 percent to 53 percent (from 49 percent to 52 percent for all unions).

There is less temporal consistency for the unions shown in organizing effectiveness self-rating (r=0.09, NS) (but r=0.41, p<0.01 for all unions). For the unions shown, the average rating dropped from 3.3 to 3.1. For all unions, the drop was from 2.9 to 2.5. The correlation between NLRB win rates and self-rated organizing effectiveness for unions shown is 0.75 (p<0.01) for 1990, but only 0.18 (NS) for 1997 (r=0.50, p<0.01, for 1990 and r=0.28, NS in 1997 for all unions). Thus, NLRB win rates seem to enter leader assessments of organizing effectiveness, although less clearly so recently, possibly reflecting greater emphasis on "NLRB-avoidance" or organizing *effort* in effectiveness assessments. The membership growth rate for 1989–91 correlates insignificantly with 1986–90 NLRB win rate (r=0.26, NS) and the 1990 self-rating (r=0.33, NS), while the 1995–7 membership growth rate correlates significantly with the 1996–8 NLRB win rate (r=0.47, p<0.10), but not with the 1997 self-rating (r=0.27, NS). (For all unions the respective relations for the earlier period are r=0.12, NS and r=0.04, NS; and for the later period, r=0.43, p<0.05 and r=0.21, NS.)

All told, the three indicators (membership growth, NLRB win rate, effectiveness self-rating) show some, but not always strong, consistency over time and across measures. Each indicates organizing effectiveness, but none is clearly sufficient and reliable. But in sum, they show membership growth is low and little changed over the last fifteen years, NLRB win rates are up slightly, and self-assessed organizing effectiveness is down slightly.

The next four columns of figures relate more clearly to organizing *effort* than to effectiveness. The columns labeled "Organising effort" refer to numbers of workers the union has sought NLRB recognition for divided by union membership (in thousands),[3] and thus represents organizing effort relative to resources (proxied by membership size). Twelve of the twenty-

Table 11.1 Selected data for the twenty-five largest US unions in 1997

Union	Size		Growth			NLRB win rate		Organizing rating		Organizing effort		Organizing commitment	Organizing budget	Representational specialization	
	1989	1997	1989–97	1989–91	1995–7	1986–90	1996–8	1990	1997	1986–90	1996–8	1997	1997	1986–90	1996–8
NEA*	2013	2300	14.3	0.0	4.5	.	.	3.8	4.0	.	.	3	.	.	.
IBT	1161	1271	9.5	18.8	−1.2	43.3	42.1	2.9	.	174.7	180.6	.	.	17	20
AFSCME*	1090	1236	13.4	9.3	2.1	57.0	74.7	3.6	.	12.9	22.7	.	.	0	0
SEIU	762	1081	41.8	15.6	0.3	65.5	65.8	3.6	.	63.2	81.0	.	.	51	57
UFCW	999	989	−1.0	−0.2	−2.0	51.2	50.6	3.5	.	53.3	64.5	.	.	23	15
UAW	917	766	−16.5	−8.4	0.8	49.1	58.2	2.9	.	72.2	69.0	4	.	20	35
AFT*	544	694	27.6	5.3	10.0	.	.	3.6	4.0	5.7	8.1	4	.	44	0
IBEW	744	654	−12.1	−1.9	−2.8	48.3	50.0	2.9	3.0	45.5	43.1	3	27	35	28
CWA	492	504	2.3	0.0	2.7	51.8	50.3	3.4	3.0	22.8	33.4	4	.	26	31
USWA	481	499	3.8	−4.6	−3.4	43.6	43.1	2.1	4.0	161.8	133.3	4	15	14	18
IAM	517	431	−16.6	3.3	−0.1	43.9	57.5	3.3	3.0	77.0	69.8	3	32	8	5
CJA	613	324	−47.2	−19.4	−8.6	50.4	39.3	2.9	.	33.9	52.4	.	.	41	47
LIUNA	406	298	−26.7	0.0	−10.0	54.2	46.3	3.0	4.0	29.8	84.9	4	20	40	25
IUOE	330	295	−10.8	0.0	−0.5	57.0	53.8	3.6	1.0	56.8	80.8	2	.	34	21
APWU*	213	279	31.1	7.0	5.1	.	.	3.6	4.0	.	0.1	2	.	.	0

FOP*	217	277	27.5	.	0.0	.	.	3.3	2.0	.	.	3	.	.	.
PACE	210	226	7.5	-3.8	-4.1	41.5	39.4	2.3	1.0	56.4	91.5	2	4	40	27
UNITE	180	225	25.0	-14.4	-8.1	49.3	63.3	3.7	3.0	101.7	87.8	4	.	12	5
HERE	278	225	-19.1	-3.2	-3.1	37.9	49.7	2.5	4.0	77.0	70.1	4	53	38	22
PPF	220	220	-0.1	0.0	0.0	57.9	49.2	3.3	.	19.2	14.8	.	.	70	77
NALC*	201	210	4.5	4.5	0.0	.	.	4.0	3.0	1.1	.	2	1	0	.
ANA	140	205	46.4	5.1	0.0	58.5	84.2	4.0	.	85.8	50.3	.	.	90	92
AFGE*	156	170	8.7	-3.2	7.9	.	.	3.1	.	3.5	7.7	.	.	0	0
IAFF*	142	156	9.9	6.3	3.3	.	.	4.0	4.0	1.0	2.4	3	.	50	0
IUE	171	128	-24.9	-6.4	-5.9	55.7	35.7	3.4	2.0	130.4	112.7	3	18	8	9

Notes: * Traditional jurisdiction is government, railroad, or airline employment and thus NLRB-related data may be misleading.

(1) Union size is defined as membership in 1989 and 1997 for the purpose of per capita payments to the AFL-CIO, if available. If unavailable, size is membership as reported in the 1990 National Union Survey (Delaney *et al.* 1991) and in the 1997 Survey of Union Information Technology (Fiorito *et al.* 1998). If neither is available, size is membership as reported in Gifford's annual *Directory* (e.g. Gifford 2001). Membership estimation is not unproblematic (Fiorito *et al.* 2001a).

(2) For most unions, the 1990 membership figure is actually a 1989 figure – see prior note. For the 1989–91 and 1995–7 growth figures, per capita membership series are used if available; otherwise estimates from Gifford's *Directory* series are used.

(3) Ratings for 1990, on a five-point scale, were converted for comparability. Fractional values for 1990 also reflect that most unions' data are averaged from multiple respondents, whereas the 1997 data are typically based on a single respondent for each union.

(4) Win-rates are shown for each period only for unions participating in 30+ elections in that period. Given the concentration of union membership and NLRB organizing activity, a limitation is relatively few data points for inter-union comparison. Correlations involving NLRB data often appear meaningful in size, but statistically indistinguishable from zero.

five unions show increases in organizing effort, nine show decreases, and four lack comparative data. For the unions shown, the average in the earlier period was 58.4 versus 61.9 for the later period. (For all unions, the respective averages were 66.4 and 63.2 but the comparison is less meaningful due to sample composition change.) It thus appears that a slight increase in relative organizing effort has occurred. Despite some changes, unions tended to maintain their respective effort levels in both periods as indicated by a 0.91 (p<0.01) correlation between the organizing effort figures for the two periods (r=0.68, p<0.01 for all unions). Some of the variance across unions may reflect differing strategies: the IBT and USWA may illustrate extensive but low-intensity organizing as both show high relative effort but low win rates.

In the 1997 survey, unions were questioned on their commitment to organizing (relative to other unions), and budget percentages devoted to organizing. Large unions see themselves as more committed to organizing. Their average score is 3.2, versus 2.8 for all unions. (Two of the four large unions "disagreeing" enjoy very high union density, and organizing may *not* be a high priority.) This expressed commitment is mildly borne out in comparison to the relative organizing effort measure. While the correlation between relative effort and stated organizing commitment is insignificant among the large unions shown (r=0.14), for all unions the correlation is positive (r=0.32, p<0.10).

A problem with the organizing budget data is that many unions did not, perhaps could not, provide estimates. Nonetheless, on average 21.3 percent of budgets was reportedly spent on organizing for the large unions shown, but for all unions the figure was 15 percent.[4] The higher figure for large unions is not echoed in the relative organizing effort data (r=−0.50; r=0.13 for all unions, both NS with samples of only eight and twenty, respectively). The budget figures, however, do align with respondents' expressed organizing commitment (r=0.64, p<0.10; r=0.58, p<0.01 for all unions).

Fiorito *et al.* (1995) noted that indicators of organizing effectiveness and effort tended to form two distinct clusters, and that union leaders saw these as largely distinct. For the NLRB-based effort measure, that observation tends to hold for both periods examined here, with correlations suggesting a negative no relation to all three effectiveness indicators examined earlier. A slightly different picture emerges when comparing effectiveness indicators with the organizing commitment and budget share measures. Relations range from "none" to positive, so assessments of the relation may be sensitive to the effort measure considered.

The final two columns look at "representational specialization" – the percentage of organizing each union undertakes within its traditional industry jurisdiction. Superficially, it may seem many unions have shifted their organizing strategies to "targets of opportunity" based on frequent reports of, for example, miners organizing nurses and auto workers organizing writers.

Yet the data show no real trend. Representational specialization increased and decreased for roughly equal numbers of unions.

It would be foolhardy to assert that this review provides a complete picture. Some of the most critical issues are neglected or barely touched, such as the extent to which unions have adopted the OM and IT use as organizing tools (Fiorito *et al.* 2001b). As Heery *et al.* (2000a) have shown for the UK, one can measure union adoption of OM elements, but ironically there are no systematic US data on OM adoption. The data on organizing commitment are also limited. There has been no published US study systematically linking either OM adoption or organizing commitment to organizing outcomes *pace* Bronfenbrenner (1997), who examined the impact of organizing tactics that can be linked with OM concepts. There is as yet no published study linking union IT use to organizing outcomes, although Fiorito *et al.* (2001a) found mixed evidence supporting the hypothesis that greater IT use improves organizing outcomes and/or membership growth and effect sizes that indicate IT could matter greatly. Despite limitations, it is clear that union organizing efforts and results vary substantially across unions, even in leaders' assessments, where social desirability biases could skew responses.

Concluding remarks

Various US writers have suggested a need to fundamentally rethink union goals, strategies, and structures, in some instances suggesting new models or resurrecting old ones (see Turner *et al.* 2001). There appears to be consensus in some quarters that improving efficiency and enhancing organizing commitment of existing unions will not suffice (although prescriptions then diverge). Heckscher notes: "The focus on organizing by the AFL-CIO in the last few years has clearly not uncapped a powerful wellspring of desire for unionization" (2001: 59). Data reviewed earlier suggest that while the focus is more squarely on organizing, the resource reallocations have not yet matched the rhetoric. It may be premature to conclude that current models cannot meet the challenge.

The evidence on union differences in organizing outcomes and efforts reviewed here and more formal modeling efforts (e.g. Bronfenbrenner 1997, Fiorito *et al.* 1995, 2001a) underscore that union strategies, structures, and tactics matter. As yet our ability to draw strong inferences and policy implications are quite limited. Efforts to model phenomena such as union organizing effort have produced limited explanatory power (e.g. Voos 1987). Even so, it appears clear that US unions that are innovative, advanced in IT use, decentralized, committed to organizing, strategic in selecting targets, and using OM tactics are faring better than others in organizing.

Yet, it is hard not to feel that something more is needed. Even unions that have led the "transforming to organize" movement have failed to score consistently impressive organizing gains. The AFL-CIO has set a goal of organizing one million new members annually (Lazarovici 2001). With expected membership attrition and workforce expansion, this would restore meaningful growth in union density. In 2001, AFL-CIO unions reportedly added almost 500,000 members (AFL-CIO 2002), but Freeman and Rogers (2002) note that over 300,000 of these were already members of independent unions that newly affiliated with AFL-CIO unions. It is not clear that new affiliations represent *organizing* gains. The net gain in US membership was just 17,000, and union density held steady at 13.5 percent (US Bureau of Labor Statistics 2002). Still, the overall numbers may represent improvement over recent years and are more impressive given losses of nearly 200,000 union manufacturing jobs in 2001.

But they also gloss over some conspicuous failures, including large organizing campaigns among Delta flight attendants and Nissan auto assembly workers that resulted in decisive union losses. In both cases, unions may justly cite unfair and/or illegal employer campaign tactics, but this is little solace given the unlikely prospects for reform (e.g. tougher laws or voluntary employer behavior change). The Nissan case is particularly troubling as it was the fourth UAW attempt to organize these workers, and the UAW seems to have made little progress, gaining only one-third of the votes, the same support won in its 1989 organizing drive (Hakim 2001). OM advocates might attribute these failures to insufficient OM adoption. At least in the Nissan case, there is suggestion that the UAW tried a new approach, placing less emphasis on developing inside support and worker-to-worker recruiting, although some elements of its new approach were clearly "OM-compatible."

Bronfenbrenner (2001) asserts that unions already know what they must do, but that getting diverse autonomous national unions to change is the real challenge. Although many are less certain about what is needed to organize and more impressed by the organizing challenge, there is consensus about the difficulty of effecting organizational change (e.g. Fletcher and Hurd 2001). Calls for decentralization and innovation do not always find receptive audiences among central authorities (Craft 1991, Delaney *et al.* 1996). Organizational change can be difficult even in relatively top-down business organizations. Unions' intertwined administrative and representative systems increase the complexity. There is a difficult balance to achieve. Although decentralization has appeal in many regards, the support and expertise of a competent national headquarters operation can be vital (Fiorito *et al.* 1995, Voss and Sherman 2000). This is not to say that there is a "magic formula" for all unions. US unions face diverse challenges in their environments (Katz 2001). Not all members or prospective members find the OM appealing. White-collar or professional workers may prefer a more service-oriented model. Cuts in servicing to pay for organizing may anger members who perceive they are getting less value for their union dues. Workers generally, and perhaps US workers particularly, already feel intense time pressure. Who has time to undertake unpaid work for the union with so many other demands already at hand?

Others have suggested that the OM is not a proper "model," in that it fails to specify a clear path to organizing non-union workers as the objective. In this vein, Hurd (1998) has proposed making the transformation to organizing *unions* (or cultures) the prime objective (also see Fletcher and Hurd 2001). As Fiorito *et al.* (1991) note, however, while organizing deserves special prominence as a strategy to serve virtually all union objectives, it is not a goal itself. More attention is needed to concepts such as Masters and Atkin's (1999) "value-added unionism," which recognizes that there are alternative paths by which unions can add value for workers, employers, and society. In some contexts, adding value may favor direct benefits and services to members or other forms of mutual aid, in others "partnership" with employers, and in still others an emphasis on political action, "community unionism," or workplace activism. Heery *et al.*'s results (this volume) suggest that British unions' organizing outcomes are linked positively with various strategies and not only to OM adoption.

National union autonomy emerged and persists as a central organizational imperative for US labor because workers face highly diverse work environments with different needs and challenges not easily well served via "one big unionism." There are indeed common "transunion" interests that shift ground over time, and inter-union collaborations and central federations address these. But too much emphasis on these at the expense of national union autonomy evokes the folly and frustration of "herding cats." Still, there is much central federations can do to assist affiliates.

We can surely learn more about what works in diverse union environments *and* about what works in particular environments through cross-union studies. Simultaneously, we should recognize limitations of "thinking inside the box." Focusing on existing institutions and their capabilities to represent workers is limiting. In economists' terms, perhaps there is too much emphasis on the supply side. Heckscher's (2001) comment about the apparent failure of the organizing refocus to unleash a "wellspring" of latent unionism is apt. Although there is some indication that refocusing has stimulated further change, new representation forms or new union structures may better tap this potential wellspring. (See Freeman and Rogers 2002 for an interesting essay calling for "open source unionism," for example.) Here, too, central bodies can play a critical role, providing focal points for community unionism or vehicles for experiments such as the TUC project on college graduates, an initiative that might otherwise fall prey to union jurisdictional protectionism. Recall that it took a "radical" CIO to help unleash a torrent of industrial unionism in the face of AFL craft unions' resistance in the 1930s. The CIO was not only about structure; it also entailed a more "social unionism." This torrent was aided by an attitudinal and legal environment uniquely reshaped by the Great Depression. One can see similar, smaller-scale attitude-shifting potential in events such as the Enron scandal or even the 11 September terrorist attacks, but whether and how such shifts occur is unpredictable. It is also difficult to foresee whether current unions (or new worker representation forms) can provide a vision that will inspire workers and turn latent union support into dramatic organizing gains.

Notes

1 The author wishes to thank respondents to the National Union Survey and the Survey of Union Information Technology, and the US Department of Labor and NLRB for providing some of the data used in this chapter. The College of Business Administration, University of Iowa and the Department of Management, College of Business, FSU, provided partial financing for the author's data collection as did the AFL-CIO and the author's frequent collaborators, Delaney and Jarley. Gregor Gall, Ed Heery, and Paul Jarley provided helpful comments on earlier drafts.

2 Throughout this passage, results are reported for the large unions shown in Table 11.1, and separately for all unions for which data are available. Data availability and sample composition varies with time periods due to mergers, nonresponse, etc.

3 The 1986–90 period consists of 54 months ending in June 1990, while the latter consists of the 36 months of the calendar years 1996–8. For comparability, the numerator for the latter period is multiplied by 54/36.

4 The figure for organizing budget percentage in Table 11.1 is actually an average of three responses corresponding to 1996, 1997 (estimated), and 1998 (estimated) figures for the union. The respective averages are 12 percent, 14 percent, and 16 percent, so one could say that respondents were moving in the direction called for by Sweeney, but the trend line would obviously not have reached 30 percent in 2000 based on these figures. The three-year average figure of 15 percent given is only for unions supplying estimates for all three years.

12 Union recognition in Germany

A dual system of industrial relations with two recognition problems

Otto Jacobi

Introduction

The recognition of unions and workers' representative bodies at plant or company level has never been a major problem in post-war Germany. This is because the high degree of institutionalization and juridification of the industrial relations system represents a barrier against the emergence of recognition problems for unions. The German system of industrial relations is marked by its dual nature. Free collective bargaining is one pillar. According to the Act on Collective Agreements, unions and employers have the exclusive right to bargain and to settle agreements on a broad spectrum of issues. In the cases of failure of negotiations and subsequent arbitration procedures, only the social partners have the right to conduct industrial disputes, i.e. strikes and defensive lockouts. The other pillar is the Works Constitution Act (Federal Ministry of Labor and Social Affairs 1998). Workforces have the right to establish works councils at plant, enterprise, company and group levels and to elect the members of these representational bodies. Works councils are legally independent of both the employers and the unions, with the mission to "work together [with the employer] in a spirit of mutual trust and in co-operation with the trade unions and employers' associations for the good of the employees and of the establishment" (§ 2, para. 1 Works Constitution Act 1952, amended in 1972 and 2001). Their most important right is to act as legal entities and conclude works agreements with the employer on all items that are either not covered by collective agreements or were delegated to them by the social partners. While works councils do not have the right to call a strike and to settle collective agreements, they have comprehensive participation rights and monitor whether employers abide by legal and collectively stipulated standards.

These legal provisions guarantee all actors, especially unions and works councils, comprehensive institutional protection. The dual tier structure of the German industrial relations systems is characterized by a high degree of stability. In this, the representatives of workers' interests act as professional interest managers. The high level of institutional protection has generated tendencies towards inertia and, therefore, the system favors policies and practices that support the status quo. The danger that the industrial relations system may lose its capability to adjust in due time to changes in the wider economic and social environment should not be overlooked. Thus, one indication, illustrating the trend towards a creeping erosion of the established system, is the emergence of growing zones of union-free and works council-free employing organizations in large segments of the economy. These trends can be observed particularly in the private service sector and among small and medium-sized enterprises (SMEs). The unions, thus, do not primarily have a legal recognition problem as such but a *de facto* problem in view of their weakened presence and appeal beyond their traditional core of blue-collar workers in large organizations. In addition, but occasionally and limited to a small number, new occupational group and company-centered associations are emerging whose common goals are to receive official recognition as trade unions and achieve entry into the collective bargaining market. A similar phenomenon can be observed with regard to works councils. The workforces of many SMEs have waived the right to select works councilors, by ignoring or not backing union efforts to establish a works council. According to the provisions of the law, the establishment of a works council is a so-called "can" and not a "must" clause; if the workforce is uninterested or does not back the union works councilors will not be elected. The dual system of German industrial relations has therefore come under considerable pressure through these developments, which may in the long run lead to rather more substantial "erosion" than at present. A means towards maintenance of the current industrial relations system is "modernization" of the system and accommodation of bargaining outcomes to the existing problems. Therefore, "erosion" or "modernization" is the underlying theme of this chapter.

Established unions and new entrants

Privileges of established unions

On the workers' side, the unions exclusively can exert the monopoly-like rights to settle collective agreements and to call on strikes. Empowered by these legal pillars, the established unions have become the unquestioned institutions representing workers' interests (Hoffmann 2000, Hoffmann *et al.* 1998, Jacobi and Mueller-Jentsch 1990, Jacobi *et al.* 1998, Silvia 1999). This privileged position is strengthened by the union movement being neither split by political divisions as in Romanic Europe (e.g. Belgium, Italy) nor fragmented into general or industrial or crafts unions as in Britain. Inter-union competition has been traditionally quashed by the principle according to which one union only represents employees in an industry or enterprise ("one industry, one union"). Both the legal privileges and the centralized structure of union representation explain the prevailing position of the DGB-affiliated unions (see Table 12.1).

In West Germany, the DGB-affiliated unions had an aggregate membership of 5.5m workers in 1950. In the subsequent decades, the number of unionized workers rose to 8m and then stagnated during the 1980s. After the reunification and the result of the integration of East German unions, membership rose to 12m but since then unions have suffered from massive losses, largely due to the dramatic de-industrialization of eastern Germany. In western Germany, the unions have experienced a less dramatic loss where the export-oriented traditional industries are still the backbone of the German economy but the tertiary sector is rapidly expanding. Since the mid-1980s, white-collar workers have outnumbered blue-collar workers within the workforce but union membership does not reflect this, with the bulk of union members recruited from the traditional industries and the public sector. Unions' reputation and profile in the private service sector is low, with white-collar service employees being the "Achilles' heel" of the unions. Both these trends (decline in membership, "imbalance" in composition) are mirrored in the union density rates. Across the economy, union penetration is around 25 percent. This is significantly higher in the public sector and in the traditional industries, particularly in big companies and among high-skilled male blue-collar workers. The density rates in the private sector industries are around 10 percent.

Table 12.1 DGB affiliates and memberships 2001

Union	Industries	No. of members
IG Metall (IGM)	Metals, engineering, vehicles	2,750,000
Vereinigte Dienstleistungsgewerkschaft (ver.di)	Public sector, private services, commerce, post, banking, insurance, media	2,830,000
IG Bergbau-Chemie-Energie (BCE)	Chemicals, energy, mining	900,000
IG Bau-Agrar-Umwelt (BAU)	Construction, agriculture, environment	510,000
Transnet	Rail	300,000
Nahrung-Gaststätten-Genuss (NGG)	Food, drink, tobacco	250,000
Erziehung und Wissenschaft (GEW)	Education, science	270,000
Polizei (GdP)	Police	190,000
Deutscher Gewerkschaftsbund (DGB)	Peak organization	8,000,000

Note: The traditional situation of "one industry, one union" is being eroded by union mergers.

Similar to Britain, the peak union federation, the DGB, could be referred to as something of a "paper tiger" because the right to bargain and strike lie with individual unions. Among the individual unions, primarily the IG Metall (IGM) but also ver.di and BCE play the roles of pace-setters in collective bargaining and social pioneers with regard to ground-breaking events like the introduction of the 35-hour week or private, non-work related pension schemes. With around 10,000 FTOs, they have a large full-time apparatus at their disposal. Most are well funded; in 2000, IGM had revenue of approximately DM500 million, almost exclusively from membership fees. But decline in membership fee income, due to membership losses, became the driving force behind an extensive process of amalgamation, which accelerated during the 1990s (Waddington 2000). Eight individual unions have survived from the sixteen in 1950. Two types of amalgamation can be distinguished: takeovers and mergers. For example, IGM has taken over two smaller unions (the textile and clothing union and the plastics union). The creation of ver.di (Unified Service Union) saw five unions (including one that did not belong to the DGB) merge into the new union. It is likely that the drift towards the creation of super unions will continue.

However, two problems with the process of amalgamation have recently become more noticeable and widespread. First, the creation of ver.di has *aggravated* demarcation disputes between the established unions with the context of trade liberalization and restructuring. Despite agreement that the original union will remain the collective bargaining agent and have the exclusive right to recruit members where companies expand from traditional industrial conglomerates to the service sector, ver.di competes with IGM and BCE for members. Rivalry between ver.di and other unions also exists in the sectors of energy, transport, and university/scientific centers. These demarcation disputes can only be resolved if the principle "one industry, one union" is strictly applied, but the prerequisite for this is a new wave of organizational restructuring of individual unions. In the meantime, unions are trying to establish "collective bargaining partnerships" in order to reduce inter-union tensions. Second, the larger the unions, the more heterogeneous the social composition of their members has become, thus making their array of interests wider and more differentiated. The dilemma is to find a balance between egalitarian and differentiated collective bargaining strategies as a single organization attempts to represent the diversified interests. Particular strongly or self-defined occupational groups have responded to this lack of differentiation and representation by establishing worker associations that are independent of the DGB. The question then emerges as to whether these union-like associations will gain recognition as unions.

Recognition problems

The strike by Lufthansa pilots, organized through their association Cockpit, in early 2001 received enormous media attention. Cockpit accused Ver.di, which claimed to represent Lufthansa's entire workforce, of neglecting the pilots' special interests and not exploiting their advantageous labor market position to the full. Consequently, Cockpit entered into independent negotiations with Lufthansa. After failed negotiations and arbitration, Cockpit conducted an effective strike. A second mediation round was successful, with Cockpit and Lufthansa agreeing a collective agreement which gave the pilots a 12 percent wage increase and a rise of 16 percent in profit-related pay scheme (although the profit-related provisions lost their value following the dramatic fall in Lufthansa's profits). Ver.di, having concluded a 5 percent pay rise, accused Cockpit of violating the principle of solidaristic incomes policy through widening of wages differentials as well as accentuating tensions between different sections of the workforce and aggravating the carrier's problems of international competitiveness. The foundation of UFO (Unabhängige Flugbegleiter Organization – Independent Cabin Crew Organization) was predicated on the same tensions between sectionalist and solidaristic bargaining strategies. Following this, various, high-skilled professional groups such as train drivers, hospital physicians and waterways employees announced to their intention of imitating the pilots' example. However, at the moment these remain isolated cases. But, in the longer run the number of professional group associations could expand, endangering the "monopoly" of the established unions. The questions that arise are how these new associations can gain union recognition and what opportunities do the established unions have to ward off these new entrants from the collective bargaining arena (Weiss 1987).

At first, it must be emphasized that a law on union recognition has never been enacted in Germany. All legal provisions are judge-made, based on interpretation of core human rights provided in the country's constitution. The departure point is the civil right to form associations. Based on the freedom of association as well as both the Act on Collective Agreements and the Works Constitution Act, the principles concerning the recognition of unions are as follows. Trade unions are associations of employees and have to fulfill a range of formal prerequisites. They have to be (a) voluntary with members free to join and leave, (b) democratically structured organizations, with leaders elected by members, (c) associations which pursue members' interests independent of both government and employers, (d) strong enough to push forward their demands, both willing and capable to use strikes as a last resort of putting pressure on employers, and (e) not *ad hoc* coalitions in pursuit of short-run goals but have a permanent apparatus in order to regulate labor relations by implementing collective bargaining agreements. Therefore, the requirements for an association to be capable of achieving its goals are independent financial, personnel, and professional resources which allow the organization to prepare for, and conduct, negotiations as well as sign and monitor collective agreements which are legally binding on both signatories. The existence of a collective agreement is considered to be evidence that an association must be recognized as a union, given that the employer has accepted the organization as its counter-part. However, an agreement has to result from the independent and auto-nomous collective bargaining activity of an organization. An association of workers that simply copies or undermines collective agreements of estab-lished unions will not receive recognition as a union.

The judge-made law on recognition of unions is aimed at safeguarding a balance between two processes. The first is the reduce the likelihood of the emergence of so-called "phantom unions" in view of their weaknesses which make them susceptible to employer, i.e. to sign so-called "unbalanced agreements." The second is the desire not to reduce access to the collective bargaining market by creating insurmountable bureaucratic preconditions. Some examples demonstrate these processes. Two Christian workers' associations in the chemical and construction industries were refused recognition as unions as a result of both low membership and insufficient FTO resources. The courts ruled both were too weak to be able to implement independent collective agreements at the national sectoral level. Currently, court proceedings are underway on whether the "Christliche Gewerkschaft Metall" (CGM – Christian Trade Union Metal) can be regarded as a union or not. In reaction to a collective agreement the CGM signed in Saxony, IGM initiated legal proceedings to deny CGM recognition as a collective bargaining partner. Aimed at safeguarding its "monopoly" position, IGM argued that CGM's poor membership performance (less than 100,000 members in total) and its weak resources (around twenty FTOs) made it incapable of pursuing an independent collective bargaining strategy and escaping from employers' diktats in an industry of 3.5m workers. In an interim judgment, IGM's case was vindicated but CGM is appealing, and a final decision will be made by the Federal Labour Court.

Quite different is the case of Cockpit. This association has been recog-nized as a union because the collective bargaining unit is not a multi-employer industry but an individual company that concludes collective agreements with its union counterparts. With a union density rate approach-ing 100 percent, Cockpit is regarded as a powerful association that has the resources at its disposal to push for independent goals for a special group, namely pilots. By contrast, UFO has been recognized as a union by a local labor court, whereupon the established unions initiated legal proceedings arguing that UFO, representing only cabin crews which are relatively low skilled and easily substitutable, is not strong enough to push through an independent collective bargaining strategy. A final court decision has not yet been made. Thus, it can be seen that recognition as a union and con-sequently, the right of access to the collective bargaining arena is not straightforward or trouble free. However, as multi-employer agreements are replaced by single-employer agreements under the decentralization of collective bargaining, more room is opened up for the emergence of smaller specialist unions for professional or occupational staffs. Estab-lished unions are prepared to deploy a broad array of legal means to erect or defend barriers against new entrants to safeguard their positions. Ver.di has developed an alternative and more innovative path to combat the entrance of new competing craft unions in the bargaining market by the creation of a sub-organization, called "connexx," whose aim is to offer special services and incentives to media workers.

Works councils and reform of the Works Constitution Act

The works councils success story

The second pillar of the industrial relations model is the works councils system (see Bertelsmann Stiftung and Hans-Böckler-Stiftung 1998, Leminsky 2000). Workforces have the right to establish works council in plants or enterprises with five or more waged and salaried workers. Works councilors are elected for four-year terms of office by secret ballots of all workers, including foreign workers. In companies with more than one plant, combined works councils can be established. In large conglomerates with more than one company, a group works council can be set up. A chain of works councils ranging from the bottom to the top of enterprises can thus be established. In companies with more than 200 employees, an increasing number of works councilors are released from their work duties and become full-time members of a works council. Employers bear this cost. Generally speaking, the larger the establishment the more the works councilors behave as "professional interest managers" and in multinationals the works councils chairs travel around the world and act as co-managers.

Works councils are not part of the union structure but an independent body representing social interests at plant, company, and group level, and although some works councils try to remain equidistant from managers and unions, the bulk of the works councils orientate themselves towards the unions. The main reason for this is that both works councils and unions represent in, a fairly clear way, the interests of labor. This is cemented by close institutional links between both bodies where works councils, for instance, are obligated to closely co-operate with the union that has settled the collective agreements in their enterprise. Moreover, unions have the right to initiate the establishment of works councils and to nominate candidates for election. And unions offer a broad range of services which are indispensable for works councils: training, economic and legal advice, information exchange, contacts to other works councils, and so on. About 80 percent of all works councilors are union members and almost 100 percent of the works councils have a trade union majority. Further, works councilors usually sustain union organization by recruiting members and in general – despite the legal distinction between the two – function as the arm of the union in the workplace. Works councilors are often influential members of trade union bodies, for instance, elected lay members of local, regional, or central union executive bodies, or are members of the union negotiating bodies Thus, the relationship between unions and works councils is dense, highly developed, and well established.

Specific rights of participation are ascribed to the works councils, ranging from encompassing information rights and the right to be consulted through the right of control and veto, to the most important right of all, the right of co-determination. Information and consultation rights mean that the management has to provide works councils with full information in due time and sufficient detail in order to safeguard their right to comment on the employer's plans, to give advice or to develop alternatives. Control and veto rights are aimed at protecting workers from unfair or illegal measures by the employer in regard to collective agreements, promotion of equal opportunities, the employment of disabled people and elderly workers, and the integration of foreign workers. Co-determination stipulates that the decision-making process is no longer the exclusive prerogative of the management and unilateral decisions are replaced by joint decision-making.

The works council's rights of participation are divided into three areas, covering economic, personnel, and social topics. First, and in regard to economic matters, the works council has no co-determination rights, merely information rights, with information including the company's economic and financial situation, production and investment programs, rationalization projects, closures, relocation, mergers, and other events or planned changes with potentially substantial impact on the workforce. Economic decisions are exclusively within managerial discretion. However, in cases where economic decisions have a substantially deleterious impact on the workforce, management and works council have to negotiate with the aim of reaching a works agreement on reconciliation of interests. Works councils have the co-determination right to enforce a social compensation plan in the event of staff cutbacks. Personnel matters include personnel planning, hiring, transfer or dismissals of workers, vocational training, and further training. Depending on the issue, the works council has information and consultation rights or control or veto power or – in a few cases like training – co-determination rights. In the arena of social matters, works councils enjoy a strong position thanks to their co-determination rights. Thus, employers are only entitled to impose binding rules after agreement has been reached with the works councils. The main topics here are discipline, sickness/absence, working hours arrangements, technological means for monitoring behavior and performance, health and safety, and company benefits.

No other industrial relations institution is in such an unquestioned position as the works council, because of its democratic legitimacy through direct elections and institutional protection and support, where employers are obligated to engage in participation and provide facilities. They are seen to operate a high degree of professional representation of social interests. In larger enterprises, work councils have become social interest managers and in some multinationals they have developed to become co-managers. Most works councils, particularly the chairs in multinationals, have learnt to think strategically and have accepted joint responsibility with management for determining future developments in "their" companies. According to the findings of the Co-determination Commission on the operation of works councils, company restructuring in the 1990s was substantially supported by these worker representatives. Thus, most works councils have adopted a "co-operative modernization" approach. Employers could have restructured without the support of the works councils, for only the social repercussions of these actions are subject to participation, but most managers, acknowledging that works councils are "reliable partners" in easing in change and preventing unrest, involved them at an early stage. Management, thus, has to negotiate a works agreement, which can be a lengthy and costly process (particularly, over compensation in terms of employment security), but in kind it receives "social peace" with far less questioning or disturbance of the implementation process of the restructuring. Thus, the argument runs that works councils have improved German industry's international competitiveness. Nonetheless, there are potential drawbacks.

Resolution of recognition problems via reform of the Works Constitution Act

Currently, around 40,000 works councils are established, comprising almost 300,000 elected councilors. In companies employing more than 300 workers, the coverage of works councils is almost 100 percent. Very few companies pursue a policy of exclusion from these participation rights. Among those that do, the most prominent are American companies like McDonald's or WalMart who try to prevent the creation of works councils. Royle's (2000: 126–7) research shows that McDonald's have used intimidation and cash incentives to overcome employee desire for works councils. In contrast to well-established American firms like Ford, GM subsidiary Opel, IBM, or Citigroup, which have adapted to the German system, these new entrants attempt to establish "American labor relations" and they have had some success, largely because they regularly employ unskilled and often foreign workers who are less willing and able to press for their participation rights. According to the recently published research findings, WalMart is pursuing a paternalistic strategy aimed at avoiding institutionalized and contractual labor relations (Köhnen 2001).

However, the more alarming challenge for both the industrial system and the trade unions is that works councils have not been established in most SMEs. Table 12.2 illustrates the trend towards lower coverage rates, which are mainly the result of the emergence of SMEs. It can be seen that the coverage rate in the private sector of the economy decreased from 50 percent of the workforce to 40 percent. If the public sector is included, the

Table 12.2 Coverage rate of works councils (percentages)

	Private sector		Overall economy inc. public sector	
	1984	1996	1984	1996
Works councils established	49.4	39.5	63.0	55.1
Participation-free zones	50.6	60.5	37.0	44.9

downward trend is less dramatic. A considerable danger exists whereby the continual increase in the number of SMEs, with the majority being "works council-free zones," may undermine the existing system of worker representation. Both employers and employees in these enterprises, especially in the emerging e-economy, fear the costs and influence of works councils and do not recognize the advantages of such representational bodies. In place of works councils, individual and individualized employment relations hold sway. It is unclear whether the phenomenon of new and young SMEs being "works council-free zones" is an interim stage or a permanent one in the development as they move to become more established, "brownfield" sites as well as possibly grow.

Given this trajectory towards "participation-free zones" in SMEs, the unions successfully urged the social democratic–green government to amend the Works Constitution Act. The provisions, which came into force on 1 August 2001, offer the opportunity for existing structures of employee representation to be brought in line with "modern" forms of company organization. There are five key amendments. First, the method of installing a works council in companies with between 5 and 100 employees has been simplified by the election procedure being streamlined and becoming less bureaucratic. This will help unions and workforces create more works councils in SMEs. Second, the new provisions create new types of supplementary works councils in larger companies. Thus, works councils for special product or business units can be established, as can works councils in subsidiaries by the works council of the parent company. In the event of company restructuring through merger, acquisitions or buy-out, the revised law provides the works councils with a transformation mandate in order to set up a works council in the new company. Third, the revised law has lowered the workforce size threshold for a works council to be entitled to a full-time representative from 300 to 200 and lowered the ratio of employees to released works councilors. The conditions of part-time works councilors as well as the works councils' operating facilities have been improved substantially. Fourth, participation rights have been extended in a variety of fields and new issues for participation have also been introduced. Works councils have been empowered to be informed about and involved in all relevant aspects of environmental protection in the enterprise. They have also been given participation rights in setting the rules for group-work projects, as well as a comprehensive initiating right to submit proposals aimed at protecting employment security, such as measures on skill upgrading and further training. Fifth, combating racism and xenophobia, the strengthening of women's representation as well as reconciling family and work life have become pivotal tasks of the works councils. The revised Works Constitution Act is thus a significant step forward to further consolidation of the employees' participation rights and the inclusion of the workforce into corporate governance.

Interplay between the collective bargaining and works council systems

Recognition problems have thus emerged due to the declining reputation and strength of trade unions in the private service sector and because works councils are often not created in SMEs. The present system of worker representation will largely depend on trade unions' and workers' willingness and capability to fuse together more closely both pillars of the industrial relations system within the context of bringing the whole industrial relations system into line with the requirements of increased competition, globalization, flexibilization, and company differentiation. Whether recent trends will lead to the erosion of the system and its replacement by a more Anglo-Saxon type of labor relations or whether the reconstruction via modernization may strengthen the system is an open question.

The collective bargaining system

The following section returns to examine more fully union recognition within the system of collective bargaining. Under the Collective Bargaining Act, the parties to a collective agreement must be unions on the workers' side and single employers or employers' associations on the other. German employers are highly organized in chambers of industry and commerce, in business associations, and with regard to labor relations in employers' associations. Most private enterprises are members of an industry employers' association, representing around 60 percent of the workforce. Foreign-owned companies with a long-standing involvement in the traditional industrial sector and the financial sector are regularly members of employer associations. New foreign entrants, however, do not often join these organizations, or even end the membership of German companies they have acquired. Public service and public companies have their own employers' associations. These associations settle sectoral or industry-wide collective agreements with their corresponding union counterparts at either regional or national level. Though in many cases (such as metalworking and chemicals) sectoral bargaining is formally undertaken at regional level, it is centrally coordinated by the national organizations on each side. So-called "pilot agreements" reached in a regional bargaining unit of the engineering industry often serve as the model for the rest of this sector and exert influence on other industries. This creates a specific German form of pattern bargaining with IGM as pace-setter: agreements in other sectors of the economy are generally within a narrow margin of the pilot agreement. The public sector does not play an autonomous role. Unions in sectors like the finance industry, wholesale or retail, where the density rates are low, benefit from this pattern system. Multi-employer agreements in combination with IGM's leadership explain the relatively high degree of standardization of wages, working time, and other working conditions.

Many SMEs and a few big corporations are not members of employers' association. Most prominent among the latter are Volkswagen and Lufthansa. These companies and a large number of SMEs have independent single-employer agreements with their union bargaining partners. Most foreign companies that have not joined an employer association adapt to the German system insofar as they have collective agreements with their trade union counterparts: British Airways, IBM, Vodafone, or the French multinational, Vivendi, have established contractual relations with the unions. WalMart is an example of a self-confident management pursuing an anti-union strategy – until now it has persuaded its workforce to accept unilaterally the pay levels and working conditions imposed. Most enterprises which have no relationship with unions normally regard the multi-employer agreements in their sector as a guide. In cases of failure of negotiations and ensuing mediation (which is not based on law but on collective agreements), strikes and defensive lockouts are legitimate means of applying pressure in collective bargaining. Once a collective agreement is signed, a peace obligation during the currency of the contract prevents both signatories from taking industrial action. Collective agreements are legally binding on both unions and employers. In the case of a dispute over implementation, labor courts ultimately decide whether the employer has correctly transposed the collective agreement or not.

Collective agreements cover a broad spectrum of labor relations issues, ranging from wages through working time to a variety of other topics. Given the law-based priority of collective agreements over works agreements, company managers and works councils cannot undermine collectively settled provisions. Table 12.3 presents a brief overview of the main topics of collective agreements and works agreements.

Multi-employer agreements tend to generate uniform and standardized working conditions. International comparisons regularly reveal that labor relations in Germany have a more egalitarian approach than in most other industrialized countries (especially Britain and the US). Although there is a wide diversity of wages by industry, region, and skill level, wage differentials are less developed than in most other countries, with the same being true for working time issues (Bispinck 2001). But a characteristic "deficiency" of multi-employer agreements is the difficulty of accommodating the increasing variety of divergent business situations of individual enterprises within

Table 12.3 Range of collective agreements and works agreements

	Trade unions	Works councils
Employers' associations	*Collective agreements* Around 30,000 sectoral multi-employer agreements exist at regional or nation-wide level, covering a broad spectrum of issues: *Wages*: Wage differentials between categories of workers according to vocational training and skill levels; pay levels and increases in wages. *Bonuses*: overtime, shift, holiday work; vacation pay; performance-related and/or profit-related pay schemes. *Working time*: daily, weekly annual time schedules; vacation; flexibilization. *Miscellaneous*: vocational training, further training, pension funds, arbitration procedures	
Individual employers	*Collective agreements* Around 15,000 single-employer agreements on a similar broad range of topics	*Works agreements* Around 300,000 works agreements on everyday company-related issues and on topics not covered by collective agreements. Surveillance of the correct transposition of collective agreements. Due to options and opening clauses provided in collective agreements, enlarged leeway for the fine-tuning of collectively settled provisions with regard to flexibility, differentiation, and the business situation of the company.

uniform provisions. Resolving this dilemma without dismantling the whole collective bargaining system is the aim of both unions and employers associations. Two clear trends can be observed in the attempt to do this.

Decentralization

The increasing number of single-employer agreements is one indicator of the trend towards decentralization. Large corporations like VW or Lufthansa and the appropriate unions often pursue an autonomous collective-bargaining strategy. Two examples illustrate this kind of innovation. First, in 1994, VW suffered a severe crisis. Part of the restructuring package was a collective agreement that reduced by 20 percent weekly working time (to 28.8 hours) and cut annual wages by 10 percent in exchange for employment security. This contract, imitated by other companies, was regarded as a solidaristic response to avoid the threat of 30,000 redundancies. Second, in 2001, the social partners at VW signed an agreement called "5,000 × 5,000." The contract was closely related to the company's decision to produce the new mini-van in Germany, instead of at competing locations in Central and Eastern Europe, on the condition that IGM was willing to offer concessions. Thus, VW will hire 5,000 unemployed workers and offer special training courses but the monthly wage amounts to DM5,000 (€2,500), which is less than regular VW workers earn. The wage of the newly hired workers will exceed the €2,500-threshold if the mini-van becomes profit-making. Although a 35-hour week has been stipulated, in the case of production defects the workers have to repair the cars and deliver perfect quality through unpaid extra work. The agreement was widely considered as a contribution to combating unemployment and safeguarding Germany as a production location.

But far more important are the attempts by employers and unions to find a new balance with the works councils system. Multi-employer agreements tend to be framework agreements providing general rules and selective options, defining the margin of pay increases and offering patterns for the regulation of new issues, with the transposing of company specific "fine-tuning" of sectoral provisions by local management and works councils. The prerequisite for this newly emerging change in procedural mechanisms is the empowerment of company actors via so-called "opening clauses." These clauses allow the delegation of collective bargaining authority to the company level but insist that works agreements have to remain within their framework. Some examples illustrate this new practice. First, hardship clauses. In the event of a financial crisis at an individual enterprise, hardship clauses aimed at safeguarding jobs by avoiding bankruptcy through worker concessions will come into effect. They allow exemptions from pay rises, reductions in wage levels, cutbacks and annulments of bonuses, and reductions in working time without compensation in exchange for employment security. Second, flexibilization. The standard 35-hour week has been made more flexible in most industries through allowing its extension or reduction throughout the year, albeit balanced out overall. Annualized hours schemes have also been introduced. Some collective agreements provide options transferring to the actors at company level the discretion to decide whether the collectively stipulated pay rises should be fully or partially implemented through wages or reduced working time. Third, differentiation. Deviations from uniform standards wage rates with regard to special requirements of certain categories of employees are increasing. In many industries, employers are permitted to pay 10–20 percent less if they employ young or unemployed workers.

This decentralization process is thus combined with a substantial increase in the status of works councils where their collective bargaining role has been enhanced. In some industries, works agreements settled within the margins of multi-employer agreements require the approval of both unions and employers. In other industries, unions and employers' associations have to be informed or consulted and often the company actors have the right to resolve "fine-tuning" issues independently. This development towards a new balance between the collective bargaining and works councils systems is favored by employer associations because on the one hand, decentralization favors tailor-made agreements and on the other hand, the fact that supplementary works agreements are negotiated by works councils, who do not have the right to call a strike, protects employers covered by sectoral collective agreements from worker "militancy." Employer associations fear that a collective bargaining system based on single-employer contracts would increase the vulnerability of those companies where unions are strong enough to pursue a militant strategy, pushing through pace-setting agreements and engaging in leapfrogging. Therefore, employer associations are wary of the emergence of the "British disease" (of the 1960s and 1970s), jeopardizing the social peace and undermining employer solidarity. In the view of most employers, the new kind of interaction strengthens the high trust/low conflict employment relationship. The unions have eventually also become proponents of this new interplay, having come to recognize the opportunities of recruiting workers from within a more heterogeneous workforce through less uniform conditions. In their view, the new divisions of labor safeguard their strategic leadership in the collective bargaining arena.

New issues in collective bargaining

A number of new issues are gaining ground as subjects for collective bargaining. Although traditional "bread-and-butter" issues still play a major role, new issues have arisen as a result of significant economic and social changes, these being pensions, the informal labor market, immigrant labor, and liberalization. Given the aging population and the consequent pressure on the statutory pension scheme, the government in 2002 cut by 4 percent the value of statutory pensions. The unions recognized the opportunity to establish pensions as a new field of collective bargaining where private, non-work related pension schemes are relatively uncommon. Thus unions and employers' associations have signed collective agreements which seek to make optimal usage of the existing pension law provision. The growing informal and unregulated economy has produced a "twilight" labor market, estimated by the government to be around 4 million workers. Most of these are female part-timers, unemployed workers, or non-EU foreigners without legal permission to look for jobs. For different reasons, the main actors are determined to combat this; the government gains less revenue (taxes, contributions) while employers abiding by the rules of the regular labor market feel threatened by unfair competition by those who do not, and unions fear the erosion of collectively settled standards. However, there are deep-seated divisions between the social partners on how to tackle this problem.

In view of the eastern enlargement of the EU and the expected influx workers from these countries into the German labor market, a growing number of unions are demanding the introduction of industry-specific minimum wages. With enormous wage differentials (10:1), the incentives for Eastern European workers to emigrate or in border regions commute daily are huge. The unions hope a minimum wage structure will prevent a downward wage spiral. Until now, an overall minimum wage has not been introduced. The only industry where such pressures could be brought under control is the construction industry, as a result of the EU Directive on posted workers, and the social partners in this industry agreeing a minimum wage of around €9 per hour which has been made binding for all domestic and foreign companies on German construction sites. Finally, the social repercussions of EU liberalization policy, which covers the public sector and state industry, have become major concerns of the unions. Although privatization is not required *per se*, the obligations are to put contracts out to competitive tender and to dismantle state-owned enterprise monopolies. The repercussions of liberalization on industrial relations are not simply German problems but affect all unions in EU member states. A transnational macro-economic framework has been established and the markets have been Europeanized with multinationals as the major players (Dolvik 2000, Jacobi 1998). The more national industries are being replaced by European industries, the less sustainable are the national systems of industrial relations. Cross-border union co-operation, co-ordination of collective bargaining, harmonization of union structures including cross-border partnerships and mergers, and the creation of EU-wide collective bargaining and participation models are now urgently necessary. Whether these will help contribute to the overcoming of recognition problems remains to be seen.

Conclusion

This chapter has explained why, for unions in Germany, union recognition *per se* is a marginal issue for them. This contrasts heavily with the situations which trade unions experience in both Britain and the US. Thus legal recognition problems with employers and the rare cases of new craft or professional unions are not major topics on the agenda of the established workers organizations. That said, the real challenge is the trend towards union-free zones in the private service sector and to works councils-free

SMEs. Combating the perils of erosion, the unions have gradually started to develop new strategies and create new organizational structures. The recently changed political climate, business scandals, and economic instability have revealed the risks of unregulated markets and weakened the appeal of neo-liberalism, thus providing the unions with a new chance for a reduction of social uncertainty via orderly labor relations. In contrast to neo-liberal hopes that the decentralization and individualization of labor relations will continue, thus weakening the collective bargaining system and participation model, the analysis presented here suggests that the modernization of industrial relations will make collectively regulated labor relations more attractive and revitalize the unions' profile and appeal amongst the heterogeneous workforce. The unions have the chance to create a new balance of social cohesion through a mixture of egalitarian and differentiated strategies in conjunction with the Europeanization of union structures and policies in order to respond to the problems caused by structural ruptures and the internationalization of the economy.

13 Conclusion
Drawing up a balance sheet

Gregor Gall

Introduction

The spread of the "organizing culture" in the late 1990s/early 2000s provides the clearest evidence so far that unions in Britain have in thought, if not also in deed, begun to come to terms with their post-1979 decline and to map out ways for rebuilding their influence. Cries of "too little, too late" from workers and sympathetic critics may be justified, given the reassertion of managerial prerogative, as partial cause and consequence of unions' decline, the associated deleterious outcomes for workers, and the fact that unions are not merely "acted upon" but can act themselves. Nonetheless, the main purposes of this volume have been to examine and analyze the manifestations, outcomes, and consequences of the processes of rebuilding. Collectively, the material (historical and contemporary case studies, overviews of union activity and employer hostility, and studies of different industrial relations systems with comparative dimensions) straddle two concerns. On the one hand, that of union recognition, employment law, and industrial relations systems and, on the other, union organizing, union organization, and operating environment. Considering whether unions are, for example, taking advantage of the ERA necessitates examining union organizing activities with regard to gaining recognition (as opposed to union organizing *per se*). This chapter, thus, seeks to synthesize the volume's findings, and then relate these to some of the macro-issues and debates which were laid out in the Introduction. Unlike a number of edited volumes that lack concluding chapters, it, therefore, attempts to provide a coherent end point to the volume.

Union action and environment

Unions are not passive bystanders in the processes that determine their fates. Given the debate over union capacity to influence membership growth (see, for example, Bain and Price 1983), the following may be accepted as a truism: without remedial organizing action by unions, current union membership and recognition levels in Britain and Canada, Germany and the US would be lower. But given falling unemployment in Britain and throughout many of these countries, it might have been expected that degrees of stabilization and growth in union membership and union recognition would have been higher. This expectation is further accentuated in Britain, with a relatively more favorable political environment as a result of a Labour government and the social dimension of the EU. The EU agenda and much of its transference into domestic law (e.g. rights for part-time and temporary workers) does not appear to have undermined unions by providing rights for workers regardless of union status. Indeed, unions have been central both to influencing the particular forms these rights have taken and to securing their effective implementation. Nevertheless, unions do not appear to be particularly benefiting from this role by virtue of positive demonstration effects on recruiting and retaining members. This brief discussion indicates the salience of recognizing the complex interaction between union action and external environment which determines movement in union membership and recognition, rather than analyses that counterpose the two in a mutually exclusive way. The following sections attempt to examine the processes underlying these issues.

Employer power

Employer consent, of whatever form, is the basis for the existence of union recognition, though not union membership or organization. Even where unions can compel employers to grant recognition, some degree of employer permission is required, particularly for the subsequent operation of recognition. Given that unions are "secondary organizations" (Offe and Wiesenthal 1980: 72) where unions seek to organize workers who are already employed and organized into certain groups, that employers generally have access to superior resources, and that part of the business of management is the control of workers in a generally unquestioned manner, workers and their collective organs of representation are more often than not the weaker party in the employment relationship. Employers, in general, can rely on support from the state in the maintenance of their property relations and attendant powers. Moreover, workers cannot "merge" like capital but must "associate" (ibid.: 74) and then mobilize together through the construction of collective consciousness and organization to exercise power. The strength of constructing collective organization is the dialogical method by which unions operate, but the weakness is how this is ranged against the monological process by which employers function. Summarizing these points, and speaking generally, workers have to construct their powers in conditions not of their own making and in their own time, over and above their employment as wage-laborers. Ample evidence can be found in this volume to demonstrate that this configuration gives employers superior power resources and authority, allowing them to frequently mount successful resistance to recognition campaigns.

However, cases also exist where recognition has been granted, either because employer resistance did not exist, was not significant, or was overcome. The salient question here is then: what are the variables that help explain the different employer position outcomes? These are likely to include the general state of the economy, the condition of relevant product and labor markets, state support, regulatory regimes, fellow employer aid (through associations), and union organization. From these the degree of resource available to employer (and union) can be gauged, alongside the likely costs of certain actions. Clearly, some employers will have more resources than others and, thus, more room for maneuver (as is also the case with unions). To this we can add management strategy and tactics to help explain how these resources are deployed. These may be guided by employer and management beliefs ranging on a spectrum from unitarism to pluralism. Where employers tend towards agnosticism with regard to recognition, union strength, union credibility, and union product are important. Union credibility concerns union reputation, based on employers' experience of bargaining activity, while union product relates to union bargaining agendas and the approximation to the "business case" for recognition. Where employers tend towards resistance, union strength becomes more important but, in some circumstances, employer choice of other more "appropriate" unions as "lesser evils" nullifies this potential leverage.

One of the most useful ways to conceptualize how unions respond to resistant employers is to see their task as building a coalition or alliance of sufficient support for a sufficient period of time to overcome management opposition. The coalition can be conceived in terms of qualitative and quantitative dimensions where components comprise personnel and institutions within and without the employing organization. The internal dimensions pertain to the numerical breadth and depth of support from workers, union members, works councilors/staff forum reps, and union activists. The external dimensions pertain to the numerical breadth and depth of support from workers, members of relevant unions and, more generally, families, consumers, community groups, union organizations (local, regional, and national relevant union, trades council, regional, and national TUCs), local and national politicians, opinion formers and celebrities and the local and national media. The breadth and depth of support can be gauged, for example, in terms of union density, membership commitment in mobilizations, external numbers involved in demonstrations, and consumer boycotts and the intervention of local MPs. The aim of such coalitions is to *de facto* impose, or threaten to impose, costs of various kinds on the employer such that the price of granting recognition is lowered relative to the price of not granting recognition. Amongst these might be interference with the following: customers and suppliers, organizational image and influence in local and national business and political communities, and organizational productivity and production. The import of recognition law, public policy, and public opinion here are regarded as contextual factors in influencing the scale of costs.

Union recognition and labor laws

Differing configurations and complexions of union recognition legislation have been shown to be of importance in both acting in favor of and against the interests of workers and their unions. The social, political, and economic environments in which these laws operated were also demonstrated to be of significance in influencing their utility to workers and unions. This is because recognition laws are enabling laws, providing the opportunity for unions, should they wish, to attempt to gain recognition using state agencies. They are not universal laws, operating in a blanket fashion where employers are subject to punitive measures for not recognizing unions. Nor do they automatically entitle unions to recognition as a result of merely applying to the state agency. Unions are cast in the position of always having to take the initiative and demonstrate their support. The onus is on them and the laws in themselves guarantee nothing, however supportive they are viewed to be. Unions must fall back on their own resources for they receive no state support, as businesses do (tax breaks, grants, and other assorted financial incentives) and political parties sometimes do. Moreover, in most countries, unions are not free to aggregate their power and resources to target certain employers in order to gain recognition. Thus, restrictions on industrial action (strikes, secondary or sympathy action, mass and secondary picketing, refusing to work with non-union members and non-union produced materials and so on) are commonplace. This further restricts unions' ability to take advantage of recognition laws.

At a higher level of historical analysis, the experience of Britain, Canada, Germany, and the US suggests recognition laws, operating within established relations of political economy, predominately perpetuate the power imbalance between capital and labor in the workplace and in society. Little evidence can be found of recognition laws constituting, or providing opportunities for, substantial challenges to managerial prerogative. But the decisive variable here, excepting periods of war and occupation (as in Germany), concerns "long waves," namely whether a society is experiencing an upswing or downswing in working-class struggle in political and industrial terrains. Recognition laws, framed and/or operating in periods of upswing will tend to provide better results for unions than those framed and/or operating in periods of downswing. Of course, the reasons for the creation of recognition laws are more complex than just whether unions are in strong enough positions, by virtue of an upswing, to compel their creation. That said, workers and unions, currently confronted by challenges from employers and their own weaknesses, find it hard not to discriminate between recognition laws (and industrial relations systems) of various countries, such as Britain, Canada, Germany, and the US, with the result that those in Canada and Germany are found to look more appetizing.

This does not, of course, detract from the continuing historical dilemma for unions, namely, the extent to which they should seek to be self-sufficient and independent of other parties in the employment relationship, or dependent upon the state for support in their relationship with employers. Independence implies being better able to withstand periods of reduced state support or, indeed, state interference, but the independence should not be equated with strength in a straightforward manner. Without some dependence, unions, facing more powerful employers, may not be able to develop the strength from which a degree of independence is possible. This is another "Catch 22" situation (see Introduction). Moreover, no matter how supportive recognition laws are, as in Germany, there is a limit to the reach of the law, particularly where TNCs are concerned. Consequently, it may be suggested that it is the particular match (degrees, types with regard to issues) of independence and reliance that is salient.

Union form and practice

Although none of the chapters directly engaged with Fairbrother's thesis of "union renewal" and the preferred attendant union "form" of "active, engaged and participative workplace unionism" (see Introduction), they touched upon issues raised by the thesis. While "union renewal," as put forward by Fairbrother, is largely concerned with already unionized work-places with recognized unions, it has a wider resonance to unions as national organizations and to where, why, and how unionization and union organization originally emerge and develop. Generally, the chapters indicate that the conditions for union renewal exist and that union renewal has taken place, albeit with a number of important qualifications and contexts. Thus, not all the prerequisites for renewal were present (cf. Fairbrother 1989), membership participation and control were far from always dominant, and renewal is taken to comprise more than just the component of workplace unionism, giving it a wider meaning than Fairbrother does. The evidence in this volume also suggests that renewal emerges not simply or even solely from workplace activity by workers and union members. Rather this activity is sometimes stimulated, but more often developed from isolated and fragile beginnings (see also Gall and McKay 2002), by organs of national unions, often those deemed by Fairbrother to be centralized, hierarchical, and reformist.

One salient point to emerge from this is that FTOs can, and often do, play a positive organizing and mobilizing role. For all the usage of the rhetoric of "organizing" (particularly when counterposed to "servicing") and what this implies for self-organization by grassroots members, FTOs remain important personnel in the creation, prosecution, and successful outcomes of unionization and recognition campaigns. In the absence of a wider milieu of local lay activists in each union and throughout the union movement to assist workers, alongside workers' lack of self-confidence and self-belief relative to previous periods, the skills, experience, and resources of FTOs are increasingly important. Moreover, they often have a greater ability to be independent from employers, which newly unionized workers employed by an organization whose management regard a union as an irritant or worse are less likely to possess (as a result of fear of reprisal). Such independence of voice and resource is valuable to campaigns. This is not, however, to suggest that FTOs, as a particular representation of national unions, are not prone to tendencies towards demobilization, centralization, and accommodation in terms of their members and employers (as some chapters have indicated). But it is to say that, in the present context of grassroots union activism not yet being as vibrant as it was the late 1960s/early 1970s, decentralized systems of employment relations, and widespread employer antipathy towards unions, "top-down" organizing by the FTOs of centralized unions is generally productive.[1] Were grassroots activism to be stronger, this inference may then become incorrect – the inference is a contingent one. Therefore, the models or approaches of "managerial" and "professional" unionism put forward by Heery and Kelly (1994), as opposed to their "participative" unionism, have a utility in certain periods. Similarly, the need for "servicing" (largely by FTOs) is still apparent given the weakness of much new workplace unionism and that some servicing is optimal by virtue of economies of scale (e.g. legal advice and representation on employment issues).

Another salient issue to emerge from Fairbrother's thesis (and found also in the work of Hyman 2001) concerns which union "form" has most appeal to existing and potential union members, in terms of union rebuilding, and which is the most durable and effective in delivering co-determination of the employment relationship. Union form concerns union structure, internal processes, and ethos. Often an adjunct to, or part of, organizing approaches is a social movement perspective, with its wider definition of trade union activity, process, and aspirations as the "tribune" of the oppressed and disadvantaged. There is a degree of congruence between Fairbrother's sponsored union form and the latter. However, the social movement perspective implies both a greater reliance on, and involvement with, forces outside the workplace, these being national unions, pressure groups, and progressive milieus, and a wider focus than immediate workplace concerns. As yet, the implementation of this perspective is sufficiently slight as to make analysis of its impact and utility difficult.

Union organizing: the emergence of a new paradigm?

The evidence in this volume does not suggest either that there is one best method or approach to union organizing, judged by efficacy, or that union "organizing" is superior to its assumed opposite, "servicing" in terms of union recruitment and participation – the dichotomy being fallacious. Neither does it suggest that all of the methods of organizing that were used were particularly new or innovative. To assess the efficacy of particular organizing approaches and tactics (or bundles of them) would not only require that a much larger number of recognition campaigns were examined alongside studies of national unions, where differing environmental conditions could be controled for to make for rigorous comparative analysis, but that there were sufficiently conceptually distinctive approaches to organizing which unions then deployed. Conceptual distinctiveness is not aplenty – indeed, organizing has come to encompass many different meanings. In any case, and given that "mix and match" hybrids are adopted within and across individual unions and unions respond to prevailing circumstances, to conduct research of issues on efficacy is difficult.

Thus, for example, a number of major unions in Britain have chosen not to participate in the Organising Academy while others have varying degrees of participation in it. If the Organising Academy could be taken, for argument's sake, as one example of a potentially distinctive approach, then it does not necessarily have universal appeal. The non-participating unions do not eschew organizing but they do not endorse the Organising Academy either. Over and above this, the graduates of the Organising Academy have differing views of what organizing is and should be. Moreover, they are subsequently then employed by unions who again have differing views. At every turn, models and approaches begin to sound a little more hollow. Of course, this does not preclude analysis and generalization. Rather, it suggests union actions and environments need to be recognized as particularly complex and inter-related.

Following from this, it is does not seem particularly appropriate to talk of a new paradigm in union activity, if by paradigm we mean not only a new turn in the pattern of union orientation towards members and potential members but also a widespread and permanent one. Neither can we talk in terms of a transformation in the nature and degree of member participation in, and control over, lower level structures of trade unionism. We can, however, talk of not insignificant shifts in national union strategies for worker and membership mobilization which are connected to union rebuilding and revitalization.

Mobilization theory

Mobilization theory, following Kelly (1998), has been shown to be a generally helpful framework for understanding the generation, processes, and outcomes of recognition campaigns. Grievances and injustices are known to be relatively widespread throughout workplaces in Britain and other western economies, so the possibility of collective action and organization exist. Whether possibility becomes probability or actuality depends on the key role of individuals – activists of different types such as shadow stewards or politically motivated individuals. Their role was reaffirmed as being crucial to identifying, formulating, and articulating grievances as well as organizing for redress. In particular, these individuals have demonstrated an understanding of the necessity of collectivism (action, consciousness, organization) to advance workers' interests. In doing so, they have often engaged in forms of self-organization prior to approaching a union to secure the various resources necessary to mount a campaign for recognition. In approaching a union, these activists have been required to present a credible proposal centered on levels of union membership, worker support, and likely employer response. A number of chapters have suggested that certain refinements of how mobilization theory is currently received may be necessary, while others have pointed towards ways in which mobilization theory may be developed and extended through elaboration and specification to further its utility. One aspect that appears to need particular attention is the use of mobilization theory in terms of unions as organizations, where their internal dynamics and relationships between different constituent parts, authority structures, and political processes are often influential in determining union values and behavior, especially with regard to the deployment of union resources and, thus, organizing approaches and tactics. The complexity of unions, as the key mobilizing vehicle, suggests that they are required to be analyzed as a specific sub-set within the framework.

Statutory union recognition and demonstration effects

For those concerned with the balance of power within workplaces and society, and for advocates of the civilizing and democratizing influences of unions, one of the critical questions arising from the research is whether the scale and efficacy of the collective union effort in recruiting and organizing new members and in new areas in Britain is commensurate to the task of rebuilding the union movement into a powerful actor *vis-à-vis* employers and the state. To gain some idea of what this might mean, we can look back to the presence, organization, and influence of unions in the 1970s as a reference point. During this decade, and without viewing it in an overly romanticized way, unions and their members had a high level of self-confidence and displayed a significant degree of vibrancy, based on extensive organization and influence within workplaces and society. The most important question that then arises for the purposes of this volume from this line of inquiry is whether the ERA's statutory recognition provisions, in tandem with the union organizing, are capable of resulting in such an outcome.

It has become clear from past experience in Britain that the most useful impacts of statutory recognition provisions for unions are their demonstration and shadow effects, rather than the quantity of their usage *per se*.

Consequently, the most important measure is not the total number of cases where statutory recognition has been granted and how many workers are covered by these awards. As Metcalf (2001: 18) points out, the volume of cases and union wins needed to make a substantial and positive *direct* impact on the existing coverage of recognition would far exceed what the CAC is capable of dealing with. As before, and with Britain's voluntarist industrial relations traditions, the presence of statutory mechanisms and the "messages" sent out by its case outcomes are more important. Thus, Millward *et al.* (2000: 235) essentially miss the point of how statutory recognition can have its biggest impact, when they write that it is "inconceivable that the procedures, however widely and vigorously used, will lead to the restoration of collective bargaining to the extent that existed in 1980." Simply put, a large volume of cases with a majority of unambiguous union wins in the various determinations (i.e. not just final awards) will be needed to demonstrate to employers that there is little to be gained from refusing voluntary recognition where a statutory application will then be forthcoming. Thus, when approached by unions with a credible presence, most employers will conclude for reasons (see Gall and McKay 1999: 610–11) that signing a voluntary agreement is the most appropriate action to take. In such a context, unions will be stimulated to mount widespread campaigns, leading to a bandwagon effect: more employers signing agreements will lead to the creation of a normalization effect on the attitudes and behaviors of other non-union employers. A virtuous upward spiral is then created. Not only does recognition feed further recognition, but recruitment stimulates recognition and vice versa (Bain and Price 1983). This is to envisage the kind of continuous growth that unions experienced from 1960 to 1979 in Britain.

Of course, there are many obstacles to realizing this scenario. These relate to the outcome of CAC determinations, whether unions have the resources to move into new areas where organizing costs are higher, whether employers without union recognition are simply "non-union" or "anti-union" and whether the process of a virtuous upward spiral can extend for long enough to reverse the years of decline in union recognition. Examining the CAC determinations, by the end of June 2002, the 188 applications had resulted in 39 voluntary agreements, 19 automatic awards and 25 awards through ballots, with 12 results failing to meet the thresholds. This represents a positive outcome, given that 61 applications have been withdrawn before a decision on admissibility was taken (of which 31 were resubmitted), 94 were accepted with only 13 being rejected, and 23 were subsequently withdrawn before the determination of the bargaining unit. In the determination of the bargaining unit, 26 were in favor of that chosen by the union, 6 in favor of that proposed by the employer, and 9 were not contentious. Only 2 applications failed the thresholds of support after new and non-union proposed bargaining units were determined. Amongst the "scalps" are well-known companies like Honda, MTV, Virgin and Easyjet airways, and the *Bristol Evening Post*, owned by the "non-union friendly" *Daily Mail* and General Trust.

"So far, so good" would not be an inaccurate assessment of how the unions have fared. Notwithstanding union criticisms of the procedures, how they have been operated (see TUC 2001c) and how these have influenced the relatively low number of applications, the messages to employers contemplating resistance are not ones that will bring them much succor (see Younson 2002). Furthermore, the CAC's decisions have been reaffirmed in the two cases of judicial review so far and automatic awards have been made in the face of employer demands for ballots and with the 40 percent threshold only just being met. One part of the equation, fairly unambiguous overall pro-union outcomes, may thus be present but the relatively low volume of cases does not meet the other required part. The focus of attention now turns to whether unions have the resources to take advantage of this relatively favorable outcome to gain more voluntary deals and add to them by increasing the number of applications with successful outcomes. If they do, then the shadow and demonstration effects of the ERA are likely to be stronger than under the periods of the previous statutory mechanisms. This is essential to make a significant difference to current levels of recognition.

Presently, hundreds of campaigns, covering nearly 500,000 workers, are underway, in which around 50,000 workers are in workplaces with in excess of 50 percent density. This indicates unions are expending not inconsiderable resources. There is clearly also scope for further campaigns that do not have to start from scratch. WERS98 (Cully *et al.* 1999: 93) found 8 percent of workplaces had a union presence but no recognition. In these, the average density is 23 percent with "only" 44 percent being below 10 percent (one of the thresholds for acceptance of an application to the CAC). Some 85 percent of these are in the private sector. CBI (1998: 23) data shows a similar picture. One interpretation could be "the future looks bright," but another might be that doubts arise over the limited extent of campaigning and the location of these campaigns compared to the task at hand. Unions have further financial, organizational, personnel resources available but it seems unlikely that they will, like their US counterparts, substantially increase the proportion (e.g. to 30 percent of expenditure) of these devoted to organizing new workers and new areas. Another might concern efficacy. With 50,000 workers ostensibly eligible for automatic recognition, this could be seen as both a strength (getting to that point) and a weakness (employers refusing to grant recognition). Furthermore, 90 percent of workers covered by campaigns have yet to reach the 50 percent threshold.

This relates to the next sequential issue, namely, whether employers without recognition are "non-union" or "anti-union," the former seemingly being an easier target. Large swathes of unorganized workers are within organizations with very little or no previous contact with, or experience of,

238   *Gregor Gall*

unions. They are consequently more costly to organize, in regard of time and resources. Those in non-union organizations may be said to have no or little demand for trade unionism, any latent demand being satisfied or dissipated through deliberate or unconscious union substitution. By contrast, those in anti-union organizations may be said to have their demand suppressed (see Gall and McKay 2001). "Anti-union" can also refer to employers who respond to an actual, potential, or hypothetical union threats and non-union to those employing organizations which have merely never been "troubled" by workforce propensity to unionize. Although employing organizations may display both elements of such dichotomous phenomena and practices across space and time, the simon-pure versions have significant implications for the costs of organizing for national unions in the context of resource limitation whereby organizing approaches in non-union organizations will meet polite workforce indifference rather than workforce and employer hostility, while organizing approaches in anti-union organizations will be met with fear and apprehension on the part of the workforce as a result of management actions.

It may, therefore, be the case that non-union companies are the most cost-effective targets if workers there can be cognitively liberated so that they realize they have grievances (assuming they do) and these are best resolved through unionization and union recognition. Cost-effectiveness is judged not just to involve union outlay (financial and personnel resources) measured against returns, assessed by union density and achievement of recognition, over time (volume by return over time), but also additional costs imposed upon union personnel and campaigns by employers. Greater relative cost-effectiveness is envisaged under non-unionism because this type of employer style is predicated neither upon union suppression, where additional costs are imposed on union membership/internal activity, nor upon the price of entry to the workplace/access to the workforce being raised. The difficulty is, however, in finding workers in non-union organizations that can act as "proselytizers" and to overcome the apparent contentment. By contrast, workers in anti-union organizations are more likely to have grievances but lack the capability and willingness to resolve these through unionization/recognition for fear of punitive measures. "Mobilization theory" informs this scenario assessment. In anti-union organizations, high costs to both organizing and opportunities to act can quell forward momentum. In non-union organizations, costs are lower but difficulties just as great, albeit of a different form. Personal sacrifice by activists is needed in both. In the former, it may involve activists' jobs. In the latter, it may involve just activists' time.

However, an important assumption in these assessments is that a non-union employer does not become an anti-union employer, and this may be erroneous. An employer prepared to spend resources on one method to avoid trade unionism may be prepared to do so on another involving suppression. Unions will only find the answers to these conundrums by testing the water in each particular case. With this information to hand, decisions on the utility of beginning or continuing recognition campaigns can be made. However, this may not produce positive union public relations material – "Union X refused to help us organize as they said it was too expensive!" – and may bring about internal union controversy.

Such calculations, given limitations in union resources, are important components in helping to assess whether a virtuous upward spiral of recognition feeding recruitment and recruitment feeding recognition can be created to reverse the years of decline in both. For how long would such a spiral have to last in order to wipe out the losses since 1979? A rough answer would be forty years of gradual, unspectacular, and continuous growth, averaging, by proxy for both, a higher aggregate annual increase (of 150,000 members) in union membership than has been the case in recent years (85,000 members). Setting aside the inability of any commentator to predict so far ahead, we can, nonetheless, discuss likely conditions under which this could take place. These concern union resources, employer response, the legal and public policy context, and the balance and interaction between them. The following discussion highlights the salient considerations within these three areas for the purposes of "informed futurology."

Unions are generally under-resourced relative to the task of substantially increasing their membership and reach (i.e. recognition and influence with employers). Unable to fund, by whatever means and for whatever reasons, further dedicated full-time organizers or recruiters or other FTOs, the absence of a large milieu of lay activists who are predisposed, often through left-wing ideologies, to make the personal sacrifices necessary to unionize workplaces from within or without is marked. Whether these activists are union members, community or student activists matters much less than their absence and willingness to expend their time and effort. It remains unclear whether the financial return from recent growth in members will outweigh the costs of recruiting and servicing them to allow further resources to be put into recognition campaigns. Even if it is, the amounts may not be substantial.

With regard to employer response, the issues revolve around the following. First, whether the unions have used up their pool of easy recognition "victories" and will now face "harder nuts to crack" in terms of starting from lower membership presence. Second, whether the increase in recognition agreements creates a normalizing effect on those employers presently without recognition and those who are non- or anti-union, such that both willingness to resist declines and willingness to endorse increases. Third, as before, whether employers without recognition are "anti-union" or "non-union."

The outcomes of applications to the CAC so far have been shown to be relatively favorable toward the unions and not a haven for resistant anti-union employers. This trend would be required to continue but on a larger scale. Just as importantly, is whether the government's review of the ERA creates a more favorable environment for gaining recognition and whether the relative renaissance of unions as social partners in public life of the last few years continues. The unions' agenda for reforming the ERA's recognition provisions (see Towers, this volume) seems unlikely to bear fruit given the government's belief that the provisions are working well and are delivering their intended outcome of low usage of the CAC and the predominance of voluntary agreements. Moreover, the unions are not presently in a bargaining position of sufficient strength to impose their will and show few signs of attempting mobilizations to create this leverage. The Blair Labour government, based on its rhetoric of "governing for all" and "fairness not favors," which belies an endorsement and practice of neoliberalism, is unlikely to encourage the resuscitation of the union movement to the point where it exercises greater influence in society. Its support for an "enterprise economy" undermines any moves towards extending or upholding workers' rights. This makes the question of whether this relatively more friendly government will continue in power for as long as the Conservatives (1979–97) not unimportant but, arguably, less critical than the other factors.

The assessment of the scenario outlined earlier suggests that either unions should seek more ambitious growth within the array of the known contemporary conditions, i.e. grow over ten years to return to 1979 levels, or have a much more modest target of a million members over the next 5–10 years. The former would require an upswing in successful industrial struggle and worker mobilization of the scale of type witnessed in 1910–20 or 1968–74 (see Kelly 1998). The latter would require a more gradual upswing of the order of 1949–67. But skeptics of union revitalization (e.g. Machin 2000a, 2000b) may rightly ask whether the growth in membership and new agreements constitutes anything significant and whether unions in Britain are running very fast merely to stand still. Further, critics may reasonably suggest there will be small ups and downs along the road of continuing deunionization. This perspective clearly doubts the possibility of either route to growth.

Partnership

"Partnership" and its various guises ("partnership working," "partnership agreements," "partnership deals") at company and workplace levels have widely been recognized by many commentators to elude easy definition, save to say they revolve around the notion of mutual cooperation and mutual gain (e.g. integrative bargaining). To what extent to do the overviews and case studies support the "outcomes thesis" of advancing union–management company or workplace-level partnerships in Britain (see, e.g., Brown 2000) and what light do they shed on the processes and consequences of partnership? From the material itself, it cannot be concluded that this thesis of advancement is unwarranted or can be contradicted. This is because of the slim evidential basis that the material provides in terms of number of studies and their particular locations, where union recognition has not been long-standing or is absent. However, the evidence does provide a basis for suggesting that the move towards partnership is not the only substantial trend within contemporary industrial relations in Britain (or elsewhere). "Traditional" union behavior, in terms of aspiration and practice and based less on mutual gains and more on counterposing interests and their pursuit through mobilization and distributive bargaining, is evident.

More substantially, we can infer from the preceding chapters that where recognition does not exist, is being campaigned for, or has been recently granted albeit reluctantly, the prospects for partnership are generally poor. This situation arises because of the combination of employer resistance to any genuine forms of co-determination of the employment relationship, particularly through union mediums, and the inability of the unions to present themselves as strong bargaining partners often as a result of employer hostility. Thus, employer unwillingness to act jointly and union incapacity to enforce joint working under and through recognition explain the paucity. Where unions are capable of securing recognition from a reluctant employer, partnership may not ensue, for the act of organizing and mobilizing the workforce may lead to substantial and long-term polarization of attitudes (and consequent practices) around conflict and opposition amongst management, union activists and FTOs, and union members. Organizing in this context is likely to lay more stress on zero-sum or distributive bargaining, particularly through the union recruitment pitches and demonstrations of worker support and willingness to act.

But partnership may ensue from some recognition campaigns using extensive organizing and mobilization where changes in management and/or ownership within the time of the campaign bring different perspectives and styles to bear such that the employer now becomes favorable to some types of recognition. This process signifies a recalculation of costs and benefits, producing a different outcome. The calculation may be that the union "won't go away," necessitating a way to contain, and benefit from, its presence through recognition. But partnership may also ensue in situations of extensive mobilization because of national unions' promotion of a partnership agenda. Unions which explicitly endorse partnership will seek to impose this agenda, where necessary, on an unwilling section of their membership (local or workplace unionism) in circumstances of either large high-profile, "blue-chip" companies and/or where they are seeking to gain recognition from multi-site employers. Even unions that do not explicitly or enthusiastically endorse partnership are also likely to adopt this approach when campaigning for recognition from multi-site employers. The utility of the partnership approach here is that it more easily allows a union with relatively low but hard-gained membership presence throughout the employing organization to make a successful pitch for recognition. Thus "organizing for partnership" involves attempting to make the leap from weak union presence to recognition, not through relying on union strength (with density serving as a proxy) but by offering to "add value" to the employer's organization. More explicitly than is normally the case, the national union promotes and offers the "business case" for trade unionism (see Gall and McKay 1999: 610), seeking to become a credible and valued partner in the eyes of the employer. This holds out the prospect of a relatively quicker, less difficult, less expensive, and more controllable process by which the national union can gain recognition, compared to the alternative – the long, hard, and sometimes unsuccessful slog of building up membership across sites or within large organizations where workforce turnover, limited resources, and employer hostility frustrate efforts. The dynamics of the latter, being more akin to the "organizing approach," are generally different, involving workplace activism contesting managerial prerogative. So too are the implications of this approach for union resources and loci of control within the union. Activists may view the means and ends of "organizing for partnership" as ranging from substitutionism to micro-class collaboration.

If the "partnership"/"organizing for partnership" approach bears fruit, the union will perhaps seek to build up its membership to higher levels, akin to those of the more conventional organizing approach. The partnership here is an exchange of employer support for, or neutrality on, union membership and organization in return for securing union cooperation with, and the generation of legitimation for, various changes in the organization of work. The approach seeks recognition not through imposing costs on the employer but by providing benefits to the employer. Employer and union interests may coincide with high union membership to deliver and enforce this exchange. If the organizing for partnership approach fails, then more robust union campaigning may be undertaken, with implications for the probability of subsequently adopting partnership working, or the union may decide to walk away. Little can be said about the material outcomes of the partnership approach, assuming that these can be directly related to the consequent "partnership working," for the material is not primarily concerned with bargaining outcomes. But it is likely that, because union independence of agenda and ideas and strength of mobilizing members are consequently constrained in these circumstances, bargaining outcomes, controlling for labor, and product market influences, will be less substantial than normally anticipated under traditional bargaining arrangements.

Abstracted from the contributors' material and then articulated in such a way as to starkly counterpoise the issues, there is, nonetheless, ample opportunity for greater diversity and complexity in actual process and outcomes, albeit based on the above tensions and trajectories. As Heery (2002) demonstrates, there is considerable room for commonality and overlap between partnership and organizing approaches in practice. Contextualization of the specific configurations of union leverage, union motives, management power and policy, and so on at company/workplace level provide the surest way of understanding and explaining individual case process and outcomes. That said, it is worth noting that the dynamics and forces operating on, and within, partnership in existing and long-standing unionized environments are likely to substantially differ from new recognition agreements. One aspect of this is that partnership agreements are often found in areas of economic activity which are experiencing retrenchment and continuing market volatility, helping occasion union behavior that is more cooperative and integrative.

Concluding remark

All the authors in this volume hold it to be a nostrum that strong trade unions are essential to counterbalance employer power, in order to generate democratic and civilized societies. They are, thus, concerned with the activities of unions to reconstruct their influence and power by reasserting themselves through self-activity. In this, their assessments and analyses have subsequently considered a plethora of issues and debates. What is the overall message to emerge from their studies? It is one of relative hope, where unions are attempting, in spite of many unfavorable conditions, to create collective influence for groups of workers who have previously been unorganized. It is hoped that the many facets of this process, recounted and analyzed in this volume, will be of use to union activists and officials in taking this struggle forward. One of the next steps for the milieu of such minded academics is to document, analyze, and explain the bargaining outcomes of the tranche of new recognition agreements.

Acknowledgment

As editor, I would like to record my thanks to Ed Heery and Phil Taylor for providing comments on the chapters written by me.

Note

1 This does not confound the attested wisdom that there is no substitute to well-respected activists within the workplace (see later in chapter).

Bibliography

Abbot, B. (1993) "Small firms and unions in services in the 1990s" *Industrial Relations Journal* 24/4: 308–17.

ACAS (1977) *IBM: Report No. 44*, London: ACAS.

ACAS (1981, 1991, 1995–9, 2001) *Annual Report*, London: ACAS.

Adams, R. (1995) *Industrial Relations under Liberal Democracy: North America in Comparative Perspective*, Columbia: University of South Carolina Press.

AFL-CIO Committee on the Evolution of Work (1985) *The Changing Situation of Workers and Their Unions*, Washington, DC: AFL-CIO.

AFL-CIO Committee on the Evolution of Work (1994) *The New American Workplace: A Labor Perspective*, Washington, DC: AFL-CIO.

AFL-CIO (1999) *Americans' Attitudes toward Unions*. (Posted online at http://www.aflcio.org/labor99/am_attitude.htm).

AFL-CIO (2001) *Worker Rights in America*, Washington, DC: AFL-CIO. (Posted at www.aflcio.org/rightsinamerica/report.pdf).

AFL-CIO (2002) *Work in Progress,* Washington, DC: AFL-CIO, 7 January.

Armstrong, P., Carter, B. Smith, C. and Nichols, T. (1986) *White Collar Workers, Trade Unionism and Class*, London: Croom Helm.

Aronowitz, S. (1998) *From the Ashes of the Old*, Boston and New York: Houghton Mifflin Company.

Ashcroft, B. and Love, J. (1993) *Takeovers, Mergers and the Regional Economy*, Edinburgh: Edinburgh University Press.

Bain, G. and Price, R. (1983) "Union growth: dimensions, determinants and destiny" in Bain, G. (ed.) *Industrial Relations in Britain*, Oxford: Basil Blackwell, pp. 3–34.

Bain, P. and Taylor, P. (2000) "Entrapped by the 'electronic panopticon'? Worker resistance in the call center" *New Technology, Work and Employment* 15/1: 2–18.

Bain, P. and Taylor, P. (2001a) "Seizing the time? Union recruitment potential in Scottish call centers" *Scottish Affairs* 37: 104–28.

Bain, P. and Taylor, P. (2001b) "Taylorism, targets and the quantity-quality dichotomy in call centers" Paper presented to 19th Annual International Labour Process Conference, University of London.

Bain, P. and Taylor, P. (2002) "Ringing the changes: trade union organization in call centers in the financial sector" *Industrial Relations Journal* 33/3: 246–61.

Barling, J., Fullagar, C. and Kelloway, E. (1992) *The Union and its Members: A Psychological Approach*, New York: Oxford University Press.

Batstone, E., Boraston, I. and Frenkel, S. (1977) *Shop Stewards in Action: The Organization of Workplace Conflict and Accommodation*, Oxford: Basil Blackwell.

Batt, R. (2000) "Strategic segmentation in front-line services: matching customers, employees and human resource systems" *International Journal of Human Resource Management* 11/3: 540–61.

Beaumont, P. (1981) "Trade union recognition: the British experience 1976–1980" *Employee Relations* 3/6: 1–39.

Beaumont, P. (1987) *The Decline of Trade Union Organization*, London: Croom Helm.

Beaumont, P. and Harris, R. (1990) "Union recruitment and organizing attempts in Britain in the 1980s" *Industrial Relations Journal* 21/4: 274–85.

Benn, T. (1989) *Diaries 1973–76: Against the Tide*, London: Hutchinson.

Bernstein, A. (1999) "All's not fair in labor wars" *Business Week* 19 July, p. 43.

Bertelsmann Stiftung and Hans-Böckler-Stiftung (eds) (1998) *Mitbestimmung und neue Unternehmenskulturen – Bilanz und Perspektiven*, Gütersloh: Verlag Bertelsmann Stiftung. (For the summary and the recommendations of the Co-determination Commission see http://www.boeckler.de or http://www.mpi-fg-koeln.mpg.de.)

Bispinck, R. (2001) "Germany" in Fajertag, G. (ed.) *Collective Bargaining in Europe 2000*, Brussels: European Trade Union Institute, pp. 147–72.

Black, S. (1983) "Numerically controlled machine tools in a heavy engineering manufacturing and assembly plant: Caterpillar Tractor Company" in Buchanan, D. and Boddy, D. (eds) *Organizations in the Computer Age: Technological Imperatives and Strategic Choice*, Aldershot: Gower.

Blyton, P. and Turnbull, P. (1998) *The Dynamics of Employee Relations*, second edition, Basingstoke: Macmillan.

BNA (1998) *NLRB Representation and Decertification Elections Statistics*, Washington, DC: Bureau of National Affairs, May.

Bowers, T. (2000) *Branson*, London: Fourth Estate.

Brecher, J. and Costello, T. (eds) (1990) *Building Bridges: The Emerging Grassroots Coalition of Labor and Community*, New York: Monthly Review Press.

Bronfenbrenner, K. (1997) "The role of union strategies in NLRB certification elections" *Industrial and Labor Relations Review* 50/2: 195–212.

Bronfenbrenner, K. (2001) "Changing to organize" *The Nation* 3 September, pp. 16–20.

Bronfenbrenner, K., Friedman, S., Hurd, R., Oswald, R. and Seeber, R. (eds) (1998) *Organising to Win: New Research on Union Strategies*, Ithaca: ILR Press.

Bronfenbrenner, K. and Juravich, T. (1995) *Union Organizing in the Public Sector: An Analysis of State and Local Elections*, Ithaca: ILR Press.

Bronfenbrenner, K., and Juravich, T. (1998) "It takes more than house calls: organising to win with a comprehensive union-building strategy" in Bronfenbrenner *et al.*, *Organising to Win*, pp. 19–36.

Brown, W. (2000) "Putting partnership into practice in Britain" *British Journal of Industrial Relations* 38/2: 299–306.

Bruce, P. (1989) "Political parties and labor legislation in Canada and the United States" *Industrial Relations* 28/2: 115–41.

Bryson, A. (1999) "Are unions good for industrial relations?" in Jowell, R., Curtice, J., Park, A., and Thomson, K. (eds) *British Social Attitudes – the 16th Report: Who Shares New Labour Values?*, Aldershot: Ashgate, pp. 65–96.

Bryson, A. and McKay, S. (1997) "What about the workers?" in Jowell, R., Curtice, J., Park, A., Brook, L., Thomson, K. and Bryson C. (eds) *British Social Attitudes – the 14th Report: The End of Conservative Values?*, Ashgate, Aldershot, pp. 23–48.

Burawoy, M. (1998) "The extended case method" *Sociological Theory* 16/1: 4–33.

CAC (2001) *Annual Report*, London: Central Arbitration Committee.

Callaghan, G. and Thompson, P. (2001) "Edwards revisited: technical control and call centers" *Economic and Industrial Democracy* 22/1: 13–39.

Carter, B. (2000) "Adoption of the organizing model in British trade unions: some evidence from Manufacturing, Science and Finance (MSF)" *Work, Employment & Society* 14/1: 117–36.

Chaison, G. and Dhavale, D. (1990) "A note on the severity of the decline in union organizing" *Industrial and Labor Relations Review* 43: 366–73.

Charlwood, A. (2000) "Influences on trade union organizing effectiveness in Great Britain" Working Paper, *The Future of Unions in Modern Britain*, London: Center for Economic Performance, London School of Economics.

Cohen, L. and Hurd, R. (1998) "Fear, conflict and union organizing" in Bronfenbrenner *et al.*, *Organizing to Win*, pp. 181–96.

Cohn, J. (1997) "Hard Labor" *The New Republic* 6 October, pp. 21–6.

Colgan, F. (1999) "Recognizing the lesbian and gay constituency in UK trade unions: moving forward in UNISON" *Industrial Relations Journal* 30/ 5: 444–63.

Commission on Industrial Relations (1971) *Standard Telephone & Cables Limited*, Cmnd. 4598, London, HMSO.

Commons, J. (1909) "American shoemakers, 1648–1895: a sketch of industrial evolution" *Quarterly Journal of Economics*, 24: 39–98.

Compa, L. (2000) *Unfair Advantage: Workers' Freedom of Association in the United States under International Human Rights Standards*, New York: Human Rights Watch.

Confederation of British Industry (1998, 1999a, 2000, 2001) *Employment Trends Survey*, London: CBI.

Confederation of British Industry (1999b) *CBI Employment Legislation Impact Survey*, September, London: CBI.

Craft, J. (1991) "Unions, bureaucracy, and change: old dogs learn new tricks very slowly" *Journal of Labor Research* 12/4: 393–405.

Cranfield School of Management (1999) *Labour Market Developments in the Travel and Tourism Sectors of the British Economy: Implications for the Transport Salaried Staffs Association*, Cranfield: Cranfield University.

Cully, M., Woodland S., O"Reilly, A. and Dix, G. (1999) *Britain at Work: As Depicted by the 1998 Workplace Industrial Relations Survey*, London: Routledge.

Cunningham, I. (2000) "Prospects for union growth in the UK voluntary sector: the impact of the Employment Relations Act 1999" *Industrial Relations Journal* 31/3: 192–205.

CWU (2000) *Voice*, March, London: Communication Workers Union.

Dabscheck, B. (1999) "Review of Rethinking Industrial Relations" *Labour and Industry* 10/1: 134–6.

Darlington, R. (1994) *The Dynamics of Workplace Unionism: Shop Stewards' Organization in Three Merseyside Plants*, London: Mansell.

Darlington, R. (1998) "Workplace union resilience in the Merseyside Fire Brigade" *Industrial Relations Journal* 29/1: 58–73.

Darlington, R. (2001) "Union militancy and left-wing leadership on London Underground" *Industrial Relations Journal* 32/1: 2–21.

Delaney, J., Fiorito, J. and Jarley, P. (1991) *Union Innovation and Effectiveness: Results from the National Union Survey*, Iowa City, IA: University of Iowa College of Business, Industrial Relations Research Institute.

Delaney, J., Jarley, P., and Fiorito, J. (1996) "Planning for change: determinants of innovation in U.S. national unions" *Industrial and Labor Relations Review* 49/4: 597–614.

Deshpande, S. and Fiorito, J. (1989) "Specific and general beliefs in union voting models" *Academy of Management Journal* 32/4: 883–97.

Diamond, V.R. (1992) *Organizing Guide for Local Unions*, Silver Spring, MD: George Meany Center for Labor Studies.

Dibb Lupton Allsop (1995–2001) *The Industrial Relations Survey*, London: Gee.

Dicken, P. and Lloyd, P. (1976) "Geographical perspectives on United States Investment in the United Kingdom" *Environment and Planning A/8*: 685–705.

Dickens, L. (1978) "ACAS and the union recognition procedure" *Industrial Law Journal* 7/3: 160–77.

Dickens, L. and Bain, G. (1986) "A duty to bargain? Recognition and information disclosure" in Lewis, R. (ed.) *Labour Law in Britain*, Oxford: Blackwell, pp. 80–108.

Dickson, M. (1984) *To Break a Union – the Messenger, the State and the NGA*, Manchester: Booklist.

Dickson, T., McLachlan, H., Prior, P. and Swales, K. (1988), "Big Blue and the unions: IBM, individualism and trade union strategies" *Work, Employment and Society* 2/4: 506–20.

Dolvik, J. (2000) "Building Regional Structures: ETUC and the European industry federations" *Transfer* 6/1: 58–77.

Donovan, Lord (1968) *Royal Commission on Trade Unions and Employers' Associations*, *Report*, Cmnd. 3623, London: HMSO.

Doran, F. (1989) "Industrial action in the North Sea: lessons for the future" *Blowout* 2, September, OILC, Aberdeen.

DTI (1998) *Fairness at Work*, Department of Trade and Industry, London: The Stationery Office, CM 3968.

Dubinsky, L. (2000) *Resisting Union-Busting Techniques: Lessons from Quebec*, London: Institute of Employment Rights.

Dunning, J. (1958), *American Investment in British Manufacturing Industry*, London: George Allen & Unwin.

Dunning, J. (1998) "US-owned manufacturing affiliates and the transfer of managerial techniques: the British case" in Kipping, M. and Bjarnar, O. (eds) *The American-ization of European Business: The Marshall Plan and the Transfer of US Management Models*, London: Routledge.

Eaton, A. and Kriesky, J. (2001) "Union organizing under neutrality and card check agreements" *Industrial and Labor Relations Review* 55/1: 42–59

Emmott, M. (1999) "Collectively cool" *People Management*, 28 January, pp. 54–5.

Fairbrother, P. (1989) *Workplace Unionism in the 1908s: A Process of Renewal*, London: Workers' Educational Association.

Fairbrother, P. (2000) *Unions at the Crossroads*, London: Mansell.

Fantasia, R. (1988) *Cultures of Solidarity: Consciousness, Action and Contemporary American Workers,* Berkeley: University of California Press.

Federal Ministry of Labour and Social Affairs (1998) *Co-determination in the Federal Republic of Germany*, Bonn (contains Works Constitution Act and the German Act on European Works Councils texts in English – see http://www.bma.bund.de).

Findlay, P. (1992) "Electronics: A 'Culture' of Participation?" in Beirne, M. and Ramsay, R. (eds) *Information Technology and Workplace Democracy*, London: Routledge, pp. 56–91.

Findlay, P. (1993) "Union recognition and non-unionism: shifting patterns in the electronics industry in Scotland" *Industrial Relations Journal* 23/3: 28–43.

Fine, J. (2000/1) "Community unionism in Baltimore and Stamford" *Working USA* 4: 59–85.

Finlayson, J. and McEwan, T. (1998) "Whither the trade unions?" *Policy Perspectives* 5: 6.

Fiorito, J. (2001) "Human resource management practices and worker desires for union representation" *Journal of Labor Research* 22/2: 335–54.

Fiorito, J. and Bozeman, D.P. (1996–7) "Fear and loathing (and bribery) in the workplace: worker perceptions of employer responses to union organizing" *Journal of Individual Employment Rights* 5: 137–52.

Fiorito, J. and Young, A. (1998) "Union voting intentions: the role of HR policies and organizational structure" in Bronfenbrenner *et al. Organizing to Win,* pp. 232–46.

Fiorito, J., Hendricks, W. and Gramm, C.(1991) "Union structural choices" in Strauss, G., Gallagher, D. and J. Fiorito (eds) *The State of the Unions,* Madison, WI: Industrial Relations Research Association, pp. 103–37.

Fiorito, J., Jarley, P. and Delaney, J. (1995) "National union effectiveness in organizing: measures and influences" *Industrial and Labor Relations Review* 48/4: 613–35.

Fiorito, J., Jarley, P., and Delaney, J. (1998) *Luddites, IT, and Cyberunions: Information Technology and National Unions,* Tallahassee: College of Business, Florida State University.

Fiorito, J., Jarley, P. and Delaney, J.T. (2001a) *Information Technology, Union Organizing, and Union Effectiveness,* Working paper, Tallahassee: Florida State University.

Fiorito, J., Jarley, P. and Delaney, J. (2001b) "National unions as organizations" in Ferris, G. (ed.) *Research in Personnel and Human Resources Management* 20: 231–68.

Fiorito, J., Jarley, P., Delaney, J. and Kolodinsky, R. (2000) "Unions and information technology: from Luddites to cyberunions?" *Labor Studies Journal* 24: 3–34.

Firn, J. (1975) "External control and regional development: the case of Scotland" *Environment and Planning A/*7: 393–414.

Fisk, C., Mitchell, D. and Erickson, C. (2000) "Union representation of immigrant janitors in southern California: economic and legal challenges" in Milkman, R. (ed.) *Organizing Immigrants: The Challenge for Unions in Contemporary California,* Ithaca: ILR Press.

Fletcher, B. and Hurd, R. (1998) "Beyond the organizing model: the transformation process in local unions" in Bronfenbrenner *et al. Organizing to Win,* pp. 37–53.

Fletcher, B. and Hurd, R. (2001) "Overcoming obstacles to transformation: challenges on the way to a new unionism" in Turner *et al. Rekindling the Movement,* pp. 182–208.

Forbath, W. (1992) "Law and shaping of labour politics" in Tomlins, C. and King, A. (eds) *Labor Law in America: Historical and Critical Essays,* Baltimore: Johns Hopkins University Press, pp. 201–30.

Forsyth, D. (1972) *US Investment in Scotland,* New York: Praeger.

Forte, C. (1986) *Forte: The Autobiography of Charles Forte,* London: Sidgwick and Jackson.

Fossum, J. (1999) *Labor Relations,* seventh edition, Boston: Irwin McGraw-Hill.

Freedman, A. (1985) *The New Look in Wage Policy and Employee Relations* (Report 865), New York: The Conference Board.

Freeman, R. and Kleiner, M. (1990) "Employer behavior in the face of union organizing drives" *Industrial and Labor Relations Review* 4/3: 351–65.

Freeman, R. and Medoff, J. (1984) *What Do Unions Do?* New York: Basic Books.

Freeman, R. and Rogers, J. (1999) *What Workers Want,* Ithaca: ILR Press.

Freeman, R. and Rogers, J. (2002) "Open source unionism: beyond exclusive collective bargaining," *Working USA* 5: 8–40.

Frenkel, S., Korczynski, M., Shire, K. and Tam, M (1999) *On the Front Line: Organization of Work in the Information Society,* Ithaca: Cornell University Press

Friedman, S., Hurd, R., Oswald, R. and Seeber, R. (eds) (1994) *Restoring the Promise of American Labor Law,* Ithaca: ILR Press.

Fusfeld, D.R. (1985) *The Rize and Repression of Radical Labor in the United States, 1877–1918,* Chicago: Charles H. Kerr.

Gagala, K. (1983) *Union Organizing and Staying Organized,* Reston, VA: Reston.

Galenson, Walter (1986) "The historical role of American trade unionism" in Lipset, S. (ed.) *Unions in Transition: Entering the Second Century,* San Francisco: ICS Press, pp. 39–73.

Gall, G. (1993) "What happened to single union deals?" *Industrial Relations Journal* 24/1: 71–5.

Gall, G. (1994) "Trade union recognition strikes" Unpublished paper, Stirling: University of Stirling.

Gall, G. (1998) "The prospects for workplace unionism today: evaluating Fairbrother's union renewal thesis" *Capital and Class* 66: 149–57.

Gall, G. (1999) "What is to be done with organized labor?" *Historical Materialism* 5: 327–43.

Gall, G. (2000a) "Debating mobilization, class struggle and the left: a response to a reply by Kelly" *Historical Materialism* 7: 175–80.

Gall, G. (2000b) "New technology, the labor process and employment relations in the provincial newspaper industry" *New Technology, Work and Employment* 15/2: 94–107.

Gall, G. (2000c) "In place of strife?" *People Management,* 14 September, pp. 26–30.

Gall, G. (2001) "A review of *Unions at the Crossroads* by P. Fairbrother" *Capital and Class* (in accompanying *Head and Hand*) 75: 60–2.

Gall, G. (2002) "The employer strikes back" *Unions Today,* January, pp. 22–3.

Gall, G. and McKay, S. (1999) "Developments in recognition and derecognition in Britain 1994–1998" *British Journal of Industrial Relations* 37/4: 601–14.

Gall, G. and McKay, S. (2000) "Union recognition in Britain: the dawn of a new era?" Paper presented to British Universities Industrial Relations Association conference, Warwick, Britain.

Gall, G. and McKay, S. (2001) "Facing 'fairness at work': union perceptions of employer opposition and response to union recognition" *Industrial Relations Journal* 32/2: 94–113.

Gall, G. and McKay, S. (2002) "Trade union recognition in Britain, 1995–2001: turning a corner?" Unpublished paper, Stirling: University of Stirling.

Gall, G., Bain, P., Gilbert, K., Mulvey, G. and Taylor, P. (2001) "Worker mobilization, collectivism and trade unionism in call centers in Britain" Paper presented to *Employment Research Unit 16th Annual Conference,* Cardiff University.

Gallie, D. and White, M. (1993) *Employee Commitment and the Skills Revolution,* London: Policy Studies Institute.

Gallie, D. (1996) "Trade union allegiance and decline in British urban labor markets" in Gallie, D., Penn, R. and Rose, M. (eds) *Trade Unionism in Recession,* Oxford: Oxford University Press, pp. 140–74.

Gamson, W. (1992) *Talking Politics,* Cambridge: Cambridge University Press.

Gennard, J. and Steuer, M. (1971) "The industrial relations of foreign owned subsidiaries in the United Kingdom" *British Journal of Industrial Relations* 9/2: 143–59.

Getman, J., Goldberg, S. and Herman, J. (1976) *Union Representation Elections: Law and Reality*, New York: Russell Sage.

Gifford, C. (ed.) (2001) *Directory of US Labor Organizations, 2001 Edition*, Washington, DC: Bureau of National Affairs.

Gordon, E. (1991) *Women and the Labour Movement in Scotland*, Oxford: Oxford University Press.

Gould, W., IV (1994) *Agenda for Reform: The Future of Employment Relationships and the Law*, Cambridge, MA: MIT Press.

Gould, W., IV (2000) *Labored Relations: Law, Politics and the NLRB – A Memoir*, Cambridge, MA: MIT Press.

Greene, A., Black, J. and Ackers, P. (2000) "The union makes us strong? A study of the dynamics of workplace union leadership at two UK manufacturing plants" *British Journal of Industrial Relations* 38/1: 75–93.

Guest, D. (1992) "Employee Commitment and Control," in Hartley, J. and Stephenson, G. (eds) *Employment Relations: The Psychology of Influence and Control at Work*, Oxford: Blackwell, pp. 111–35.

Guest, D. and Conway, N. (1999) "Peering into the black hole: the downside of new employment relations in the UK" *British Journal of Industrial Relations* 37/3: 367–89.

Guest, D. and Hoque, K. (1994) "The good, the bad and the ugly: employment relations in new non-union workplaces" *Human Resource Management Journal* 5/1: 1–14.

Hakim, D. (2001) "Big loss at Nissan seems to undercut UAW objectives" *New York Times on the Web*, 10 May (Posted at http: //www.nytimes.com/2001/10/05).

Hawes, W. (2000) "Setting the pace or running alongside? ACAS and the changing employment relationship," in Towers, B. and Brown. W. (eds) *Employment Relations in Britain: 25 Years of the Advisory, Conciliation and Arbitration Service*, Oxford: Blackwell.

Heckscher, C. (2001) "Living with flexibility" in Turner *et al. Rekindling the Movement*, pp. 59–81.

Heery, E. (1998) "The re-launch of the Trades Union Congress" *British Journal of Industrial Relations* 36/3: 339–50.

Heery, E. (2000a) "Trade unions and the management of reward," in White, G. and Drucker, J. (eds) *Reward Management: A Critical Text*, London: Routledge, pp. 54–83.

Heery, E. (2000b) "New Unionism Research Project" Bulletin No. 8, Cardiff: Cardiff University.

Heery, E. (2002) "Partnership versus organizing: alternative futures for British trade unionism" *Industrial Relations Journal* 33/1: 20–35.

Heery, E. (2003) "Evolution, renewal, agency: developments in the theory of trade unions" in Ackers, P. and Wilkinson, A. (eds) *Reworking Industrial Relations: New Perspectives on Employment and Society*, Oxford: Oxford University Press.

Heery, E. and Kelly, J. (1994) "Professional, participative and managerial unionism: an interpretation of change in trade unions" *Work, Employment and Society* 8/1: 1–22.

Heery, E., Delbridge, R., Salmon, J., Simms, M. and Simpson, D. (2001) "Global labor? The transfer of the organizing model to the United Kingdom" in Debrah, Y. and Smith, I. (eds) *Globalization, Employment and the Workplace: Diverse Impacts*, London: Routledge.

Heery, E., Simms, M., Simpson, D., Delbridge, R. and Salmon, J. (2000a) "Organising unionism comes to the UK" *Employee Relations* 22/1: 38–57.

Heery, E., Simms, M., Delbridge, R., Salmon, J. and Simpson, D. (2000b) "The TUC's Organising Academy: an assessment" *Industrial Relations Journal* 31/5: 400–15.

Heery, E., Simms, M., Delbridge, R., Salmon, J. and Simpson, D. (2000c) "Union organizing in Britain: a survey of policy and practice" *International Journal of Human Resource Management* 11/5: 986–1007.

Hewett, J. (2000) "Staff have their say at Pizza Express" *IPA Bulletin*, 1, November.

Hoffmann, J. (2000) "Industrial relations and trade unions in Germany: the pressure of modernization and globalization" in Waddington, J. and Hoffmann, R. (eds) *Trade Unions in Europe – Facing Challenges and Searching for Solutions*, Brussels: European Trade Union Institute, pp. 249–75.

Hoffmann, R., Jacobi, O., Keller, B. and Weiss, M. (1998) *The German Model of Industrial Relations between Adaptation and Erosion*, Düsseldorf: Hans-Böckler-Stiftung.

Howell, C. (1996) "Women as the paradigmatic trade unionists? New work, new workers and new trade union strategies in Conservative Britain" *Economic and Industrial Democracy* 17/4: 511–43.

Hurd, R. (1994) *Assault on Workers' Rights*, Washington, DC: AFL-CIO.

Hurd, R. (1998) "Contesting the dinosaur image: the labor movement's search for a future" *Labor Studies Journal* 22: 5–30.

Hyman, R. (1975) *Industrial Relations: A Marxist Introduction*, London: Macmillan.

Hyman, R. (1992) "Unions and the disaggregation of the working class" in Regini, M. (ed.) *The Future of Labor Movements*, London: Sage.

Hyman, R. (1999) "Imagined solidarities: can trade unions resist globalization?" in Leisink, P. (ed.) *Globalization and Labour Relations*, Cheltenham: Edward Elgar.

Hyman, R. (2001) *Understanding European Trade Unionism – Between Market, Class and Society*, London: Sage.

Incomes Data Services (2000) *Report* 817, September.

IRS (2000) "Due recognition" *IRS Employment Trends* 712, September, pp. 4–11.

Jacobi, O. (1998) "Contours of a European collective bargaining system" in Kauppinen, T. (ed.) *The Impact of EMU on Industrial Relations in European Union*, Helsinki: Finnish Labour Relations Association, pp. 289–97.

Jacobi, O. and Mueller-Jentsch, W. (1990) "West Germany – continuity and structural Change" in Baglioni, G. and Crouch, C. (eds) *European Industrial Relations*, London: Sage, pp. 127–53.

Jacobi, O., Keller, B. and Mueller-Jentsch, W. (1998) "Germany – facing new challenges" in Ferner, A. and Hyman, R. (eds) *Changing Industrial Relations in Europe*, Oxford: Blackwell, pp. 190–238.

Jacoby, S. (1985) *Employing Bureaucracy: Managers, Unions and the Transformation of Work in American Industry, 1900–1945,* New York: Princeton University Press.

Katz, H. (2001) "Afterword: whither the labor movement?" in Turner *et al. Rekindling the Movement*, pp. 339–49.

Katz, H. and Kochan, T. (2000) *An Introduction to Collective Bargaining and Industrial Relations*, second edition, New York: Irwin McGraw-Hill.

Kelly, J. (1996) "Union militancy and social partnership" in Ackers, P., Smith, C. and Smith, P. (eds) *The New Workplace and Trade Unionism*, London: Routledge, pp. 77–109.

Kelly, J. (1997) "The future of unionism: injustice, identity and attribution" *Employee Relations* 19/5: 400–14.

Kelly, J. (1998) *Rethinking Industrial Relations: Mobilization, Collectivism and Long Waves*, London: Routledge.

Kelly, J. (2000) "Mobilization and class struggle: a reply to Gall" *Historical Materialism* 7: 167–74.

Kelly, J. (2001) "Review of Fairbrother *Unions at the Crossroads*" *International Journal of Human Resource Management* 12/1: 146–9.

Kelly, J. and Heery, E. (1989) "Full-time officers and trade union recruitment" *British Journal of Industrial Relations* 27/2: 196–213.

Kelly, J. and Heery, E. (1994) *Working for the Union: British Trade Union Officers*, Cambridge: Cambridge University Press.

Kessler, S. (1995) "Recognition: CIR and ACAS experience" *Employee Relations* 17/6: 52–66.

Kessler, S. and Palmer, G. (1996) "The Commission on Industrial Relations in Britain 1969–74: a retrospective and prospective evaluation" *Employee Relations* 18/4: 6–96.

Klandermans, B. (1989) "Introduction: social movement organizations and the study of social movements" *International Social Movement Research* 2: 1–17.

Knox, W. and McKinlay, A. (1999) "Working for the Yankee Dollar: American inward investment and Scottish Labour, 1945–70" *Historical Studies in Industrial Relations* 7: 1–26.

Knox. W. and McKinlay, A. (2002), "Bargained Americanization: workplace militancy and union exclusion *c*.1945–74" in Kipping, M. and Tiratsoo, N. (eds), *Americanization in 20th Century Europe: Business, Culture, Politics*, Volume 2, Lille: University of Lille Press.

Kochan, T., Katz, H. and McKerzie, R. (1991) "Strategic choice and industrial relations theory: an elaboration" in Katz, H. (ed.) *Proceedings of the Second Bargaining Group Conference*, Ithaca: ILR Press, pp. 90–113.

Köhnen, H. (2001) *"Das System WalMart,"* Düsseldorf: Hans-Böckler-Stiftung.

Kumar, P. (1993) *From Uniformity to Divergence: Industrial Relations in Canada and the United States*, Kingston, Ontario: IRC Press.

Labor Notes (2002) "AFL-CIO Convention Stays the Course" *Labor Notes* 274, p. 14.

Labour Research Department (1997) *Travel Industry Staff Survey*, London: LRD.

Labour Research Department (2001) "Building unions in call centers" *Labour Research* 90/7: 9–12.

Labour Research Department/Trade Union Congress (1996–2002) *Trade Union Trends/Trade Union Trends; Focus on Union Recognition*, London: TUC.

Lazarovici, L. (2001) "Bigger, faster, better organizing" *America@Work* 6/1: 8–11.

Leisink, P. (1997) "New union constituencies call for differentiated agendas and democratic participation" *Transfer* 3: 534–77.

Leminsky, G. (2000) "Managers of co-operative change – tested in conflict" in Hoffmann, R., Jacobi, O., Keller, B. and Weiss, M. (eds) *Transnational Industrial Relations in Europe*, Düsseldorf: Hans-Böckler-Stiftung, pp. 139–48.

Lester, W. (2001) "Unions gain sympathy this Labor Day" *Tallahassee Democrat*, 30 August.

Levitt, M. with Conrow, T. (1993) *Confessions of a Union Buster*, New York: Crown.

Lipset, S. (1986) "North American labor movements: a comparative perspective" in Lipset, S. (ed.) *Unions in Transition*, San Francisco: Institute for Contemporary Studies, pp. 421–52.

Lipset, S. (1990) *Continental Divide: The Values and Institutions of the United States and Canada*, New York: Routledge.

Lipset, S. and Marks, G. (2000) *It Didn't Happen Here: Why Socialism Failed in the United States*, New York: W.W. Norton and Co.

Lloyd, C. (2001), "What do employee councils do? The impact of non-union forms of representation on union organization" *Industrial Relations Journal* 32/4: 313–27.

Logan, J. (2001) "Is statutory recognition bad news for British Unions? Evidence from the history of North American industrial relations" *Historical Studies in Industrial Relations* 11: 63–108.

Logan, J. (2002) "Consultants, lawyers and the 'union free' movement in the USA since the 1970s" *Industrial Relations Journal* 33/3: 197–214.

Lubell, S. (1941) "Post-mortem: who elected Roosevelt?" *Saturday Evening Post*, 25 January.

Machin, S. (2000a) "How are the mighty fallen" *Center Piece* 5/2: 28–30.

Machin, S. (2000b) "Union decline in Britain" *British Journal of Industrial Relations* 38/4: 631–46.

MacInnes, P. and Sproull, A. (1989) "Union recognition and employment change in Scottish Electronics" *Industrial Relations Journal* 20/1: 32–46.

Mahon, A. (2000) "Rocking the chocolate machine" in *Scotland into the New Era*, Edinburgh: Canongate.

Maranto, C. and Fiorito, J. (1987) "The effect of union characteristics on NLRB certification election outcomes" *Industrial and Labor Relations Review* 40/2: 225–40.

Martin, R. (1999) "Mobilization theory: a new paradigm for industrial relations?" *Human Relations* 52/9: 1205–16.

Mason, B. and Bain, P. (1991) "Trade union recruitment strategies: facing the 1990s" *Industrial Relations Journal* 22/1: 36–45.

Mason, B. and Bain, P. (1993) "The determinants of trade union membership in Britain: a survey of the literature" *Industrial and Labor Relations Review* 46/2: 332–51.

Masters, M. (1997) *Unions at the Crossroads: Strategic Membership, Financial and Political Perspectives*, Westport, CT: Quorum.

Masters, M. and Atkin, R. (1999) "Union strategies for revival: a conceptual framework and literature review," in Ferris, G. (ed.) *Research in Personnel and Human Resources Management* 17: 283–314.

McAdam, D. (1988) "Micromobilization contexts and recruitment to activism" *International Social Movement Research* 1: 125–34.

McAdam, D., McCarthy, J. and Zald, M. (1996) "Introduction: opportunities, mobilising structures and framing processes – towards a synthetic, comparative perspective on social movements" in McAdam, D., McCarthy, J. and Zald, M. (eds) *Comparative Perspectives on Social Movements*, Cambridge: Cambridge University Press.

McBride, A. (2000) "Promoting representation of women within Unison" in Terry, M. (ed.) *Redefining Public Sector Unionism: Unison and the Future of Unions*, London: Routledge.

McGrath, M. (2000) *Interview with President of CWA Local 7026*, Tucson, Arizona, 8 June.

McIlroy, J. (1979) *Trade Union Recognition – The Limitations of Law*, Studies for Trade Unionists, London: WEA.

McIlroy, J. and Campbell, A. (1999) "Organising the militants: The Liaison Committee for the Defence of Trade Unions: 1966–1979" *British Journal of Industrial Relations* 37/1: 1–31.

McKinlay, A. and McNulty, D. (1992) "At the cutting edge of new realism: the engineers' 35 hour week campaign" *Industrial Relations Journal* 23/3: 205–213.

McKinlay, A. and Melling, J. (1999) "The shop floor politics of productivity: work, power and authority relations in British engineering, *c*. 1945–57," in Campbell, A., Fishman, N. and McIlroy, J. (eds) *British Trade Unions and Industrial Politics: The Post-War Compromize, 1945–64*, Aldershot: Ashgate, pp. 222–41.

McLoughlin, I. (1996) "Inside the non-union firm" in Ackers, P., Smith, C. and Smith, P. (eds) *The New Workplace and Trade Unionism: critical perspectives on work and organization*, London: Routledge, pp. 301–23.

McLoughlin, I. and Gourlay, S. (1992) "Enterprise without unions; the management of employee relations in non-union firms" *Journal of Management Studies* 29/5: 669–91.

McLoughlin, I. and Gourlay, S. (1994) *Enterprise Without Unions; Industrial Relations in the Non-union Firm*, Buckingham: Open University Press.

Metcalf, D. (1991) "British unions: dissolution or resurgence" *Oxford Review of Economic Policy* 7/1: 18–32.

Metcalf, D. (2001) "British unions: dissolution or resurgence revisited" Discussion Paper 493, London: Center for Economic Performance, London School of Economics.

Milkman, R. and Wong, K. (2000) "Organizing the wicked city: 1992 South Californian drywallers' strike" in Milkman, R. (ed.) *Organizing Immigrants: The Challenge for Unions in Contemporary California*, Ithaca: Cornell University Press.

Millward, N. (1994) *The New Industrial Relations?* London: PSI.

Millward, N., Bryson, A. and Forth, J. (2000) *All Change at Work? British Employment Relations 1980–1998, as Portrayed by the Workplace Industrial Relations Survey Series*, London: Routledge.

Millward, N., Stevens, M., Smart, D. and Hawes, W. (1992) *Workplace Industrial Relations in Transition*, Aldershot: Dartmouth.

Minkin, L. (1992) *The Contentious Alliance: Trade Unions and the Labour Party*, Edinburgh: Edinburgh University Press.

Mountjoy, B. (1997) Telephone communication with author, November.

Nissen, B. (ed.) (1999) *Which Direction for Organized Labor?*, Detroit: Wayne State University Press.

Nolan, P. (1999) "Review of *Rethinking Industrial Relations*" *Work Employment & Society* 17/3: 575–6.

Offe, C. and Wiesenthal, H. (1980) "Two logics of collective action: theoretical notes on social class and organizational form" *Political Power and Social Theory* 1: 67–115.

OILC (1989) *Discussion Document*, Pembroke Hotel, 5 September, Aberdeen: OILC.

OILC (1990) *Blowout*, 7, September, OILC, Aberdeen.

OILC (1991a) *The Crisis in Offshore Trade Unionism*, Aberdeen: OILC.

OILC (1991b) *Striking Out! New Directions for Offshore Workers and Their Unions*, Aberdeen: Offshore Information Center.

OILC (1992) *Blowout*, 26 August, OILC, Aberdeen.

Osterman, P., Kochan, T., Locke, R. and Piore, M. (2001) *Working in America: A Blueprint for the New Labor Market*, Cambridge, MA: MIT Press.

Oxenbridge, S., Brown, W., Deakin, S. and Pratten, C. (2001) "Collective employee representation and the impact of law: initial responses to the Employment Relations Act 1999" Working Paper No. 206, Cambridge: ESRC Center for Business Research, University of Cambridge.

Passey, A. Helms, L. and Jas, P. (2000) *The Voluntary Sector Almanac 2000*, London: National Council of Voluntary Organizations.

Pitt, D., Huntley, J. and Levine, N. "Laboratories of de-regulation? Sub-national telecommunications policy – American implications for Europe" *Journal of Information Law and Technology* 1.

Price, R. (1991) "The comparative analysis of union growth" in Adams, R. (ed.) *Comparative Industrial Relations: Contemporary Research and Theory*, London: HarperCollins Academic.

Rainnie, A. (1989) *Industrial Relations in Small Firms: Small Isn't Beautiful*, London: Routledge.

Reed, T. (1989) "Do union organizers matter? Individual differences, campaign practices and representation election outcomes" *Industrial and Labor Relations Review* 43/1: 103–19.

Richardson, F. and Walker, C. (1948) *Human Relations in an Expanding Company: A Study of the Manufacturing Departments in the Endicott Plant of the International Business Machines Corporation*, New Haven, CT: Yale University Press.

Riddell, C. (1993) "Unionization in Canada and the United States: a tale of two countries" in Card, D. and Freeman, R. (eds) *Small Differences that Matter: Labour Markets & Income Maintenance in Canada and the USA*, Chicago: University of Chicago Press, pp. 109–48

Robinson, I. (1994) "Organizing labour: the moral economy of Canadian–American union divergence 1963–1986" *Queen's Papers in Industrial Relations,* Kingston, Ontario: Queen's University.

Rose, J. and Chaison, G. (1996) "Linking union density and union efficiencies" *Industrial Relations* 35/1: 78–105.

Rose, J. and Chaison, G. (2001) "Unionism in Canada and the United States in the 21st century" *Relations Industrielles* 56/1: 34–62.

Roy, D. (1980) "Repression and incorporation – fear stuff, sweet stuff and evil stuff: management's defenses against unionization in the South" in Nicols, T. (ed.) *Capital and Labour: Studies in the Capitalist Labor Process*, London: Athlone Press.

Royle, T. (2000) *Working for McDonald's in Europe – the Unequal Struggle*, London: Routledge.

Sciacchitano, K. (1998) "Finding the community in the union and the union in the community: the first-contract campaign at Steeltech" in Bronfenbrenner *et al. Organising to Win*, pp. 150–63.

Scott, A. (1994) *Willing Slaves? British Workers under Human Resource Management*, Cambridge: Cambridge University Press.

Scott, M., Roberts, I., Holroyd, G. and Sawbridge, D. (1989) *Management and Industrial Relations in Small Firms*, London: Department of Employment.

Sewel, J. and Penn, R. (1996) "Trade unionism in a hostile environment: an account of attempts to organize the North Sea Off-shore oil industry between 1970 and 1990" in Gallie, D. Penn, R. and Rose, M. (eds) *Trade Unionism in Recession*, Oxford: Oxford University Press, pp. 286–318.

Shostak, A. (1999) *CyberUnion: Empowering Labor through Computer Technology.* Armonk, NY: M.E. Sharpe.

Silvia, S. (1999) "Every which way but loose: German industrial relations since 1980" in Martin, A. and Ross, G. (eds) *The Brave New World of European Labor – European Trade Unions at the Millennium.* New York: Berghahn Books, pp. 75–124.

Simms, M., Heery, E., Delbridge, R., Salmon, J. and Simpson, D. (2001) "The diffusion of the organising model: evidence from 1998 and 2001 national surveys" Paper presented to the TUC New Unionism Task Group, London.

Simms, M., Stewart, P., Delbridge, R., Heery, E., Salmon, J. and Simpson, D. (1999) "Unionising call center workers – the Communication Workers' Union campaign at TypeTalk" Paper presented to 17th International Labour Process Conference, University of London.

Sloane, P. (1967), "Wage drift: with reference to case studies in the engineering industry of central Scotland – Part II" *Journal of Economic Studies* 2/2: 61–73.

Smith, P. and Morton, G. (1993) "Union exclusion and the decollectivization of industrial relations in contemporary Britain" *British Journal of Industrial Relations* 31/1: 97–114.

Sneade, A. (2001) "Trade union membership since 1999–2000: an analysis of data from the Certification Officer and the Labour Force Survey" *Labour Market Trends*, September: 433–44.

Steuer, M. and Gennard, J. (1971) "Industrial relations, labour disputes and labour utilization in foreign-owned firms in the United Kingdom" in Dunning. J. (ed.) *The Multinational Enterprise*, London: Allen & Unwin, pp. 89–144.

Strathclyde Business School (1986), *East Kilbride: A Labour Study*, East Kilbride: East Kilbride Development Corporation.

Taylor, P. and Bain, P. (1999) "'An assembly line in the head': work and employee relations in the call center" *Industrial Relations Journal* 30/2: 101–17.

Taylor, P. and Bain, P. (2001a) "Trade unions, workers' rights and the frontier of control in UK call centers" *Economic and Industrial Democracy* 22/1: 39–67.

Taylor, P. and Bain, P. (2001b) "Subterranean worksick blues: humour as subversion in two call centers" Paper presented to Critical Management Studies Conference, UMIST, Manchester.

Taylor, P., Mulvey, G., Hyman, G. and Bain, P. (2002) "Work organization, control and the experience of work in call centers" *Work, Employment & Society* 16/1: 133–50

Terry, M. (1991) "Annual Review Article 1990" *British Journal of Industrial Relations* 29/1: 97–112.

Terry, M. (1999) "Systems of collective employee representation in non-union firms in the UK" *Industrial Relations Journal* 30/1: 16–30.

Tilly, C. (1978) *From Mobilization to Revolution*, New York: McGraw-Hill.

Towers, B. (1997) *The Representation Gap: Change and Reform in the British and American Workplace*, Oxford: Oxford University Press.

Towers, B. (1999a) ". . . the most lightly regulated labor market . . . The UK's third statutory recognition procedure" *Industrial Relations Journal* 30/2: 82–95.

Towers, B. (1999b) *Developing Recognition and Representation in the UK: How Useful is the US Model?* London: Institute of Employment Rights.

Troy, L. (2000) "US and Canadian industrial relations: convergent or divergent? *Industrial Relations* 39/4: 695–713

TUC (1997) *Organising First*, July, London: TUC.

TUC (2000) "US style union busting will not work in UK" Press Release 6 June, London: TUC.

TUC (2001a) *Calls for Change, 2nd TUC report of Calls to the "It's Your Call" Hotline*, London: TUC.

TUC (2001b) *Today's Trade Unionists*, London: TUC.

TUC (2001c) "TUC submission to the Government Review of the Employment Relations Act 1999" October, London: TUC.

Turner, L (1999) "Review of rethinking industrial relations" *British Journal of Industrial Relations* 37/3: 507–9.

Turner, L., Katz, H., and Hurd, R. (eds) (2001) *Rekindling the Movement: Labor's Quest for relevance in the 21st Century*, Ithaca, NY: ILR Press.

Undy, R., Ellis, V., McCarthy, W. and Halmos, A. (1981) *Change in Unions: The Development of UK Unions since the 1960s*, London: Hutchinson.

Upchurch, M. and Danford, A. (2001) "Industrial restructuring, 'globalization,' and the trade union response: a study of MSF in the South West of England" *New Technology, Work & Employment* 16/2: 100–17.

US Bureau of Labor Statistics (2002) *Union Members in 2001*, Washington, DC (posted online at http: //www.bls.gov/cps/).

Visser, J. (1988) "Trade unionism in Europe: present situation and prospects" *Labour and Society* 13/1: 125–82

Voos, P. (1984) "Trends in union organizing expenditures: 1953–1977" *Industrial and Labor Relations Review* 38/1: 52–63.

Voos, P. (1987) "Union organizing expenditures: determinants and their implications for union growth" *Journal of Labor Research* 8/1: 19–30.

Voss, K. and Sherman, R. (2000) "Breaking the iron law of oligarchy: union revitalization in the American labor movement" *American Journal of Sociology* 106/2: 303–49.

Waddington, J. (2000) "The German union movement in structural transition: defensive adjustment or setting a new agenda?" in Hoffmann, R., Jacobi, O., Keller, B. and Weiss, M. (eds) *Transnational Industrial Relations in Europe*, Düsseldorf: Hans-Bückler-Stiftung, pp. 113–37.

Waddington, J. and Whitston, C. (1997) "Why do people join trade unions in a period of membership decline?" *British Journal of Industrial Relations* 35/4: 515–46.

Wallace, M. (1996) *Single or Return? The History of the Transport Salaried Staffs Association*, London: TSSA.

Walsh, J. (1998) "A force to be recognized," *People Management*, 17 September, pp. 31–5.

Weekes, B., Mellish, M., Dickens, L. and Lloyd, J. (1975) *Industrial Relations and the Limits of the Law: The Industrial Effects of the Industrial Relations Act 1971*, Oxford: Blackwell.

Weiss, M. (1987) *Labour Law and Industrial Relations in the Federal Republic of Germany*, Frankfurt: Kluwer.

Wever, K. (1998) "International labor revitalization: enlarging the playing field" *Industrial Relations* 37/3: 388–407.

Wills, J. (2001a) "Trade union organizing in twenty-first century Britain" Working Paper 3, *Geographies of Organized Labour: The Reinvention of Trade Unionism in Millennial Britain*, London: Queen Mary College, University of London.

Wills, J. (2001b) "Community unionism and trade union renewal in the UK: Moving beyond the fragments at last?" *Transactions of the Institute of British Geographers* 26: 465–83.

Wills, J. and Simms, M. (2001) "Building reciprocal community unionism in the UK" Working Paper 4, *Geographies of Organized Labour: The Reinvention of Trade Unionism in Millennial Britain*, London: Queen Mary College, University of London.

Wood, S. (2000) "Learning through ACAS: the case of recognition" in Towers, B. and Brown, W. (eds) *Employment Relations in Britain: 25 years of the Advisory, Conciliation and Arbitration Service*, Oxford: Blackwell, pp. 123–52.

Wood, S. and Goddard, J. (1999) "The statutory union recognition procedure in the Employment Relations Bill: a comparative analysis" *British Journal of Industrial Relations* 37/2: 203–45.

Wood, S. Moore, S. and Willman, P. (2002) "Third time lucky for statutory recognition procedure in the UK?" *Industrial Relations Journal* 33/3: 215–33.

Woolfson, C., Foster, J. and Beck, M. (1996) *Paying for the Piper – Capital and Labor in Britain's Offshore Oil Industry*, London: Mansell.

Wright, M. (1998) "Collective bargaining institutions in highly unionized British companies: erosion or collapse?" *International Journal of Employment Relations* 6/2: 19–42.

Wright, M. (2000) "Management industrial relations policy in highly unionized companies in Britain" *Personnel Review* 29/5: 543–64.

Wright, M. and Dunn, S. (1994) "Maintaining the status quo? An analysis of the contents of British collective agreements, 1979–1990" *British Journal of Industrial Relations* 32/1: 23–46.

Yates, C. (2000) "Staying the decline in union membership: union organizing in Ontario, 1985–1999" *Relations Industrielles* 55/4: 640–71.

Younson, F. (2002) "Employers facing own goal" *People Management*, 7 March, p. 19.

Zabin, C. (2000) "Organizing Latino workers in the Los Angeles manufacturing sector: the case of American Racing Equipment" in Milkman, R. (ed.) *Organizing Immigrants: The Challenge for Unions in Contemporary California*, Ithaca, NY: Cornell University Press.

Zeitlin, J. (1985) "Shopfloor bargaining and the state: a contradictory relationship," in Tolliday, S. and Zeitlin, J. (eds) *Shopfloor Bargaining and the State*, Cambridge: Cambridge University Press, pp. 1–45.

Index

For Product Safety Concerns and Information please contact our EU
representative GPSR@taylorandfrancis.com
Taylor & Francis Verlag GmbH, Kaufingerstraße 24, 80331 München, Germany